THE ECLIPSE OF **EQUALITY**

THE ECLIPSE OF **EQUALITY**

Arguing America on **MEET THE PRESS**

SOLON SIMMONS

Stanford University Press

Stanford, California

Stanford University Press
Stanford, California

Printed in the United States of America on acid-free, archival-quality paper

Library of Congress Cataloging-in-Publication Data

Simmons, Solon, author.
    The eclipse of equality : arguing America on Meet the press / Solon Simmons.
        pages cm
    Includes bibliographical references and index.
    ISBN 978-0-8047-7798-8 (alk. paper)
        1. Equality—United States. 2. Social conflict—United States. 3. Rhetoric—
Political aspects—United States. 4. Meet the press (Television program)
5. Political culture—United States. 6. Public opinion—United States. 7. United
States—Politics and government—1945–1989. 8. United States—Politics and
government—1989– I. Title.
HN90.S6S56   2013
305.5—dc23
                                                                    2012041611

    ISBN 978-0-8047-8646-1 (electronic)

To Larry Spivak,
without whom none of this would have been possible

But there is only one thing which gathers people into seditious commotions, and that is oppression.

—John Locke, *A Letter Concerning Toleration*, 1689

The happiness of America is intimately connected with the happiness of all mankind; she is destined to become the safe and worthy asylum of virtue, integrity, tolerance, equality, and peaceful liberty.

—Letter from Gilbert du Motier, the Marquis de Lafayette,
to his wife, Adrienne, en route to the revolution, April 1777

The things a man believes most profoundly are rarely on the surface of his mind. . . . Somewhere along the line, of course, these things have been tested and justified, in his personal experience and in the cumulative experience of his country. Each of the truths he lives by has a history.

—Eric Johnston, president, US Chamber of Commerce,
America Unlimited, 1944

CONTENTS

PREFACE

THIS BOOK HAS TAKEN A LONG TIME TO CONCEIVE, research, and write, and the difficulties I encountered in producing it say as much about our intellectual context as they do about the nature of the subject matter. I am an academician formally trained in the discipline of sociology, but this is not merely a sociological book. It was influenced as much by political science, history, anthropology, philosophy, psychology, conflict resolution, and a variety of other truncated approaches to knowledge that fall under the broad label of humanities and social science. I hope it draws on the craftsmanship of sociological thinking, while appealing to the broad community of engaged thinkers who have much more to say to one another than they are comfortable to admit or demonstrate. I wrote the book as I thought a good book ought to be written, with rigorous, reliable, and reproducible attachment to the data while maintaining only loose affiliation with any of the many discursive communities in which I have traveled (and there have been quite a few). Therefore, if this book seems to speak to your subspecialty or disciplinary niche, it does. Read and run with it. As many have tried to convince me along the way, I think there is something of a methodology revealed in the project, but I will make no fetish of it other than to say that good history, like good television and good conversation, makes for good sociology.

Among the findings of the book are the silences of concerns not covered in it. So many of the issues that matter to you do not matter enough to our national elites for them to spend much time debating them on *Meet the Press*—which means they are marginalized in our democratic debate.

If you don't find your interests reflected in these pages, do something about it! Our national leaders all had a hand in writing this book by providing its subject matter in regular intervals. If you wish that right now you were reading a book about other, more pressing subjects, I suggest you take it up with your congressperson.

1

NOTHING IS MORE IMPORTANT
Arguing America

A lot of things are important, but in the context of this week, nothing is more important than getting that done, this week.

—Edwin Meese, March 16, 1986[1]

ALMOST SEVENTY YEARS AGO, on a Sunday evening between the surrenders of the Germans and the Japanese in World War II, two visionaries of the public spirit named Martha Rountree and Lawrence Spivak launched a radio program in the basement of a Washington, D.C. hotel that would change the world. Like so many inventions that emerged from the chaos of that great conflict, *Meet the Press* was something genuinely new. Their idea was to argue America, to subject national decision makers at the peak of their influence to critical and probing questions in front of the mass public, thereby bringing the representative and the represented into closer discursive contact. Every week, Spivak and Rountree assembled a panel of ace reporters to fire pointed questions at the week's most salient decision maker in order to get "the story behind the story"—the strategic focus of the policy discussion without the technical dross. It is not that this was the first political talk show—other public affairs programming had been on the radio years before *Meet the Press*—but Spivak and Rountree had found the magic formula: they would use elite print reporters to stage a mass broadcast of a press conference in a conversational style. They would bridge the democratic divide by asking what was described as "the questions you would ask if you were here" and dream big, as it was only possible to do in that pregnant moment after World War II. Martha Rountree imagined that she might one day interview figures like Winston Churchill, Joseph Stalin, and Henry Wallace, thereby transforming the way democracy was lived and performed. As we look back over the astonishing record of the program, which critiqued every major news event from the establishment of the United Nations, hosted every president after Eisenhower, and showcased the more memorable efforts of the world's popes, philosophers, poets, and kings, Rountree's dream has become our reality.

Center Stage of the National Conversation

In a book celebrating the fifty-year anniversary of *Meet the Press*, the official chronicler of the program, Rick Ball, made a claim about the show's first driving presence, Lawrence E. Spivak, that sounds hyperbolic but is really only descriptive: "Larry Spivak dared to ask the direct question on behalf of the American people. He made *Meet the Press* part of the democratic process."[2] It is fascinating to imagine that there was a time when one could not expect the secretary of state or the winner of the Iowa straw poll to appear before an attentive and suspicious audience of more than three million people to justify her views and actions. Through a clever combination of insider intrigue and mass appeal, *Meet the Press* muscled its way onto center stage of the national conversation. Now, not only is it possible to use the intimacy of the camera lens to facilitate character assessments of our national leaders but leaders are also expected to reveal themselves to this kind of interrogation in order to reach the pinnacle of American politics. Through diligent commitment to its original format, *Meet the Press* has become the mark of legitimacy in American politics. To avoid a *Meet the Press* appearance is to admit defeat.

On June 15, 2008, in a tribute program to the show's most famous host, Tim Russert, Doris Kearns Goodwin, a celebrated historian and one of the most ebullient and devoted of the program's guests and commentators, responded to a question about Russert's legacy that holds for the program as a whole.

Tom Brokaw (NBC News): And it seems to me, Doris, that in the future, historians will have a rich archive in the *Meet the Press* recordings of the people who have passed through these studios—who they were, how they evolved, and what they became.

Doris Kearns Goodwin: No question about that. I mean, think about the nineteenth century. We had diaries; we had letters. That's what allows historians to re-create those people who lived then. In this broadcast world, what these recordings will show people years from now is not just the questions he asked, not even just the answers he got, but which people were able to acknowledge errors, which people ruffled under his questions, which ones could share a laugh. You'll get the temperament of these people. They're going to come alive.

As Goodwin recognized, these old shows are important records through which to satisfy our idle curiosities and are also social science data that promise to reveal how American elites narrated history as it happened, revealing how they thought, felt, and spoke about their country, the values on which they based their decisions and policies, and the historical examples and guiding images they used to make their cases come to life. If *Meet the Press* is the mark of legitimacy in American politics, the analysis of its archive is the study of legitimate American arguments. For those who did not live through these events, the *Meet the Press* archive reveals deep channels of political thought and culture, time out of mind of man. For those who did live through them, *Meet the Press* is a systematic record of the state of the elite core of national conversation as it was lived rather than as it is remembered.

Meet the Press is the longest-running television series; there have been more than thirty-five hundred episodes of the program over sixty-seven years of regular operation, and they continue each week. Apart from innovations like adding a roundtable and reducing the number of questioners from four to one, the interview format has remained largely consistent over time, as has the nature of the questioning. The array of guests is of consistently high quality and from the full spectrum of national and global elites. Pick your favorite influential person, and you will probably find him or her at some key moment in his or her career answering questions before a national audience with questions that you might have liked to ask.[3] Put another way, *Meet the Press* is a longitudinal collection of consistently prepared and high-quality focus groups and interviews that have been conducted with national leaders in steady intervals and with consistent management for nearly seven decades from the end of World War II to the present time. If in 1945 one had set out to produce a prospective study of the evolution of the national policy conversation over the course of the coming "American Century," it would have been difficult to devise a better plan than this.

Before we wax elegiac about the accomplishments of this organ of the National Broadcasting Company, it will be helpful to remember that there are reasons to be suspicious about the program itself and of the role it plays in politics and society. Not everyone gets to appear on *Meet the Press*, nor are all of the issues vital to the republic discussed there. *Meet the Press* does reflect the central tendencies of elite opinion, but the performers represent a rarefied slice of the public whose concerns are close to those who have provided them with the opportunities they enjoy. The tension involved in characterizing this kind of program reflects the tension of representative democracy; even as the program represents the vital center of the political classes, many people are left out and many points of view are ignored. In a 1991 interview on C-SPAN about *Meet the Press's* sister program, *This Week with David Brinkley*, Brinkley was asked about this tricky problem of elitism in shepherding the national debate.

Interviewer: Some critics charge that the Sunday-morning programs appeal only to an intellectual elite.

David Brinkley: What's wrong with that?

Interviewer: Do you have a sense of who your audience is?

Brinkley: Uh, I'm not sure it would be an intellectual elite, but there is very little of a popular, gossipy nature in it, and I think that is a somewhat loaded term, intellectual elite, but I think it is designed for people who really care about public affairs in this country and the world, and would like to maybe bounce their own opinions off ours and see how they compare. Um, not intellectual elite, but those who care about what's happening in the world.[4]

Brinkley's awkward response reveals the tension at the heart not only of public affairs programming but also democracy itself. Not all voices are heard, and not all ideas get equal play. Those that do are often restricted by their appeal to those who have power. The liberal economist John Kenneth Galbraith, a frequent guest on *Meet the Press*, coined a phrase to capture the kinds of arguments that one finds on the program: the "conventional wisdom"—"ideas which are esteemed at any time for their acceptability"—an ironic phrase that summarizes the challenge of governing a polity in which, despite our best efforts, some people are more equal than others. Most of us are doomed to parrot the ideas of some defunct opinion leader, producing unavoidable interpretive disparities. The historian Eric Goldman's description of our plight remains one of the best.

The dominant groups in America had simply done what dominant groups usually do. They had, quite unconsciously, picked from among available theories the ones that best protected their position and had impressed these ideas on the national mind as Truth.[5]

What about political bias? It has become a national pastime to criticize the mainstream media for their gatekeeping function and implicit political biases, but bias is not a problem on *Meet the Press* unless by that you mean bias against the issues for which there is no effective and organized interest or against the more volatile extremes of the political spectrum. The issues that people care most about may never be discussed at length or in a balanced way on the program, but not because the producers and journalists are biased against them. Issues like immigration, gender equality, and abusive powers of corporations may find little play on Sunday morning, but this only reflects the dominant ideology of the country, not that of the staff of *Meet the Press*. Inadvertently, the show's producers do act as gatekeepers of a kind, but what they protect is the integrity of their take on the conventional wisdom as they go about protecting the company brand. One of the reasons that *Meet the Press* has survived what must be seen as several lifetimes in the television news business is that a natural system of feedback in a competitive marketplace ensures that it keeps its focus on what it has set out to do. It is a barometer of the conventional wisdom. It is an index of arguments that succeed, and those arguments that fail to convince will simply precipitate out of this level of the conversation.[6]

The interpretations that make it across the *Meet the Press* threshold have something more important than novelty; they have the robust aura of legitimacy about them. In this harsh glare of public scrutiny, most arguments wither, as do many guests. Those that survive may be little more than dressed-up clichés, but these are clichés with currency. They are the arguments that move America and, in so doing, channel American civic identity just as Jefferson's words in the Declaration did in the beginning. This is what it means to argue America—to bring the country into existence through an act of cooperative imagination. In this sense, many of us can be founders of the republic anew by introducing arguments that stick, thereby delineating the cultural repertoire.

Few things are as important as knowing where this conventional wisdom is headed at any point in time. In the vernacular of our time we speak about this as "the story," "the narrative," or the "theory of the case." What we are getting at is the gist of the policy debate and general direction in which our leaders plan to take the country. We often think of the history of political philosophy as an enduring debate between ideas and interests between Plato and Machiavelli. We might better think of it as a debate between Plato and Homer, that is, between reason and myth: the strategic and literary dimensions of political experience. It is along this literary dimension where analysis meets imagery, and one doesn't find it in the Gallup Poll or the General Social Survey.

Less sophisticated than a conference at the Brookings Institution or a Yale seminar, what you see on *Meet the Press* is what you get—the leading plotlines of the American political storybook. Love them or hate them, these are the ideas that will work, and they work because they have already worked in the past. This idea—known in some circles as "performativity"—is the inescapable circularity of symbolic politics, and it remains the magic formula of Sunday-morning politics as it was in Spivak's day.

In a sour mood, a critic might justly say of *Meet the Press* that it is a platform for what Antonio Gramsci called hegemony: a process of moral and intellectual leadership through which people consent to and reproduce the structures of power that operate in their own society.[7] Even in the absence of coercive power, by changing the categories of thought itself, leaders find it possible to direct the people toward ends that they never anticipated and to which they would never have consented. The forum was well exploited by Joseph McCarthy, George Wallace, and others for this purpose. But it is also one where critical voices can think aloud in creative ways. Radical thinkers like Ralph Nader, Ross Perot, Henry Wallace, Grover Norquist, and Ron Paul have all made use of the show in that way.

I think of *Meet the Press* as a regular forum for the American influential, where the most pertinent arguments for the most pressing social issues are shared before a relevant audience. It's the place where the rhetorical rubber hits the road of governance. Its archive should interest you because it is a unique record of peak-level American discursive history, and it is one that still exists in largely uncorrupted form. Because of Larry Spivak's grit and determination, almost the entire record of the program—transcripts, radio broadcasts, television film canisters, letters, and other related material—is sitting in the Library of Congress waiting to be rediscovered. It is like an ice core of the political climate from which one can sample fresh snowpack each week. Thousands of articles have been written using Michigan's National Election Studies data or Chicago's General Social Survey, but the *Meet the Press* archive is a data set that has as yet been largely unexamined. Just as we look back to the old Gallup Polls to investigate the tidal forces in American mass opinion, so, too, we can use the *Meet the Press* archive to time the rhythms of the tides of the conventional wisdom. Both sources are indicators of strategic possibilities.

The Players

It would be impossible to review all of the outsized personalities who appeared on this stage, but to orient and prepare the reader for the selections presented, it will help to have a sense of the most important players on the programs over the years.[8]

Hosts and Moderators

Lawrence (Larry) Spivak—The font of this novel experiment in democracy, who not only bankrolled the program and shepherded it through its first thirty years but also preserved the records of the program at a time when such things were not done. A neocon before neoconservatism was cool, Spivak was a true public intellectual who lives on in this, his greatest product.

Martha Rountree—The visionary saleswoman of the *Meet the Press* idea who carried the program from an idea to full function. Her folksy accent and deferential tendencies belie her powerful ambition, which was ever on display for those on the lookout for it. As is likely true of many pioneering women of this era, Rountree's experience on *Meet the Press* serves as a kind of placeholder for women in the public sphere more generally. It is not an exaggeration to say that Rountree was responsible for selling *Meet the Press* at the outset to the Mutual Broadcasting System, and she was a constant presence in the founding epoch. Yet she was always overshadowed by Larry Spivak and the other larger-than-life men who appeared, and she made her exit in 1954 when she sold her ownership stake.

Albert Warner—The first regular moderator of *Meet the Press*, providing a kind of star power for the fledgling show. Warner was a true showman, with a lilting and engaging voice, capable of turning even the most fraught discussions into an entertainment spectacle.

Ned Brooks—The straight-shooting moderator of the program from 1953 to 1965. Brooks had been around the program from its early days. He was moderator through some of the most volatile moments of the period, including the civil rights movement and the Kennedy assassination.

Bill Monroe—One of the program's most familiar faces and producer and moderator of the program from 1975 to 1984. As moderator, Monroe carried the show through its transition period after Spivak's departure. His reign was marked by his stentorian voice and tough style of questioning, as well as his decision to sit with the panel of questioners.

Marvin Kalb—A notable transitional figure who in concert with NBC's Roger Mudd carried the program from Monroe's era until the late 1980s. Kalb had a tough delivery and academic style that was matched to a richly textured voice that colored much of the program's journey through the Reagan presidency.

Tim Russert—The most famous of the program's hosts, who oversaw the expansion of the show in its post-panel format. Russert was a larger-than-life figure who managed the impossible task of overshadowing Larry Spivak in the show's history. He was the host of the show from 1991 until his untimely death in 2008.

David Gregory—The first permanent host after the tragic death of Tim Russert. Gregory's style has brought the program firmly into the twenty-first century. The tone of the show is now less combative and chummy than was characteristic under Russert's leadership.

Notable Questioners

If you haven't been watching the program for more than twenty years, you might be unaware that there has been one foundational format revision for *Meet the Press* that changes the basic feel of the show. From its debut on radio, *Meet the Press* had a structure in which newspaper reporters came to the show with their own newsmaking questions, while the host or moderator kept the discussion lively and balanced. Larry Spivak then played the role of permanent panel member and in that way had more independent influence on the tone than he would as the moderator. The format evolved after Bill Monroe left the show in the 1980s and has slowly gravitated toward the version we know today on all the Sunday shows, where a single star questioner confronts the newsmaker and the roundtable.

May Craig (*Portland, Maine, Press Herald*)—One of the most colorful panelists, famous for her garish hats and no-nonsense style of questioning. Craig was among the most frequent of the show's questioners and was notable for her pithy and moralistic style that cut to the heart of an issue. I think of her as the skeptical voice of middle America.

Ernest K. Lindley (*Newsweek*)—One of Spivak's early ace reporters. Lindley had become famous as part of Franklin Delano Roosevelt's press corps. Lindley's incisive yet folksy style of delivery was endearing and characteristic of the early episodes.

Marquis Childs (*St. Louis Post-Dispatch*)—A unique American product, with a midwestern pedigree and a vaguely aristocratic accent that made him hard to place while providing him a certain gravitas that the typical member of the press corps lacked. A regular performer on the program through much of its early life, Childs was distinguished there for his insights into the challenges of comparative capitalisms that were a natural outgrowth of his interest in the Swedish compromise between capitalism and Socialism.

David Broder (Washington Post)—Often well described by Tim Russert as the dean of the Washington press corps. Broder became a regular panelist on *Meet the Press* and survived as questioner after the demise of the panel format. Broder's early presence was intense and impassive, but he slowly matured into a more playful and balanced professional role in his own league.

Robert Novak (Wall Street Journal)—The self-described prince of darkness. Novak played the role of the tough conservative in an era when that was not always the popular thing to do. Novak was well known through the famous Evans and Novak column but was one of the most frequent and incisive panelists on *Meet the Press*, who like Broder, survived as a questioner until near the end of his life.

Irving R. Levine (NBC News)—Came onto the program as an economic correspondent and had the opportunity to handle many of the most exalted economists. Levine was known for his ever-present bowtie and deadpan delivery. Levine's role in the national conversation was pronounced both on *Meet the Press* and on NBC more generally in that he was its expert on economics in a time of great transformation.

Gwen Ifill (NBC News)—The only African American reporter to appear in this list. Ifill has played almost as important a role on *Meet the Press* as she has done in her more recently familiar roles at the *Jim Lehrer News Hour* and *Washington Week*. Although her contributions to *Meet the Press* were broad, Ifill stands out in this volume in those scenes where race was most poignantly discussed, where her questions were as penetrating and timely as were those of May Craig before her.

David Brooks (New York Times)—Perhaps the most versatile and widely sourced opinion writer and political columnist in the country. Brooks has made *Meet the Press* one of his regular stops and is known for his eye for popular culture and his balanced, right-of-center perspective that cuts through rhetoric with analytical precision.

The list of questioners is only a small sample of the long list of Washington insiders who plied their trade on NBC's Sunday-morning show. Only the most memorable questioners who also appear in the examples I cite in this book have been introduced here. Other pillars of the program like Andrea Mitchell, E.J. Dionne, Chuck Todd, and Elizabeth Drew do not appear in the transcript sample material despite their powerful influence.

The Performances

This book takes you through a series of four passes through American discursive history as revealed through the unique perspective of the *Meet the Press* archive, each time focused on a distinctive and central issue. Because the program has documented every political skirmish in national politics since World War II, I am forced to skip over a lot, but I try to focus on the issues that represent the major conversations and most important moral debates that confronted the nation under its gaze.

One consideration in focusing my attention is the volume of conversation on a given topic. On this criterion two topic areas stand out: first, war and foreign affairs, and second, economics, debt, and taxation. These two areas represent the major premise of over half of all the episodes that have aired since 1945. A short answer to the question, What is the American national argument about? is foreign policy with a heavy dose of economics. While we lately find ourselves intrigued by struggles over sexuality, gender relations, immigration, abortion, gun control, and religious conservatism, war and recession, the projection of American power abroad, and its use to foster shared economic prosperity at home are the things that appear of most interest to national policy elites. Presumably the reason is that they are the most central and salient questions of political governance.

Another consideration is quality. I have chosen to write longer explorations of the debates about race and class struggle even though these topics account for far fewer episodes in terms of the raw number of weekly conversations devoted to the topic. But even when these more divisive considerations were not explicitly placed on the table, they were often in the cards, lurking in more innocent-looking hands. In the case of race, it is only a mild overstatement to echo W. E. B. Du Bois's assertion that the problem of the twentieth century was the problem of the color line. Race and racial stereotypes are almost impossible to avoid in the national conversation after World War II, and racial conflict produced some of the country's most inspiring leaders in that period along with some of the most divisive confrontations. As represented in the *Meet the Press* record, when the national conversation opens, it is dominated by the southern segregationist and, through a passionate series of feints and reversals over time, ends with a popular African American president.

The same is true with respect to the issue of class struggle and labor relations, but with an inverted image of the conversation on race. A good case could be made that *Meet the Press* began as a forum for substantive debate about the issues of class and class struggle in an age when superpowers confronted one another across an ideological divide that was defined by this problem, but it ended with the topic serving almost as taboo for those of good political taste. Of the first twenty regularly scheduled radio programs of *Meet the Press*, eleven were devoted to the problem of class struggle and union power, this at a time when the Far East was on fire and Europe was in shambles. By today's standards this seems almost unbelievable. Not only has the general topic of proactive labor power (strikes, collective bargaining, living wage campaigns) been consigned to the dustbin of American history but the sense that class conflict is a serious problem facing the country feels almost un-American to bring up in serious conversation. No great icon of the class struggle has emerged in American politics to match the likes of Martin Luther King or Roy Wilkins or even Jesse Jackson. Instead, we see a record of antiheroes best represented by Jimmy Hoffa or fallen stars like Ralph Nader in the ranks of those who have visibly promoted a foundational critique of economic power on either the workers' or consumers' rights fronts.

For each of the topical conversations I explore in this book, foreign and economic policy, race and class, I see a common theme; the American debate has developed in the direction of an image that I have chosen for the title of the book, the eclipse of equality. What we see after the close of World War II is a fundamental shift in the way that political causes are consecrated in the ennobling rhetoric of our democratic tradition. Just as Americans are committed to the values of national security, personal freedom, and tolerance of out-groups, so, too, they have traditionally thought of themselves as a people committed to ensuring economic opportunity to individuals irrespective of their background. But, as the record of elite conversations in the *Meet the Press* archive reveals, successive cohorts of opinion leaders and newsmakers have simply forgotten how to care about the threat to civil peace that might arise from those who command concentrations of economic power—what Aristotle would have called the Few. Accordingly, once-potent narratives of class struggle, occupational stratification, and even comparative social mobility have been consigned to merely symbolic status, having lost their substantive focus and analytic concision; as a result, we are passing through an "eclipse" of one of the driving principles of the liberal, or small-*d*, democratic imagination.

As it has always been, popular politics is a game in which one civil threat is played off against another to the advantage of established interests, but we have lived through something extraordinary; along a circuitous and tangled path, one of the canonical civil virtues, equality, has been effectively removed from serious consideration. Therefore, ours is a public sphere in which we fight for freedom, inveigh against intolerance, and struggle for security, while we have little of substance to say about surging economic inequality in terms either of outcome or opportunity. Even the word has changed in meaning. When someone speaks today of equality in politics, we immediately think of groups rather than individuals, in terms of diversity more than equality itself. Unsurprisingly, in fits and starts, economic inequality has become a problem of sufficient salience to beget the kinds of novel social movements we see everywhere percolating as global justice movements pivot in their emphasis from tolerance to equality.

American politics is organized around a seeming paradox. On the one hand, it functions concretely through an ineffectual system of checked powers that demand compromise, and on the other, it can move forward only when concerned groups of partisans organize around polarizing, Manichean political ideologies that define their causes as the essence of liberty and their opponents' as synonymous with oppression. More than in any other country, American politicians must govern together yet campaign apart. Without a message drenched in the binary and polluting oppositions of the American creed, no coalition can expect to govern for long. To argue America is to channel the energies of civil power, and this demands the artful deployment of riveting civil drama. Friends and colleagues in the American elite must learn to cooperate while they, at the same time, denounce each other in the language and idioms of the rhetoric of liberty. They have to govern at the center, while extemporizing from their base. How it is they have done this, and to what effect, is the story I explore in the remainder of the book.

2

BASICALLY TOTALLY DYSFUNCTIONAL
The Rhetorical Roots of Protracted Social Conflict

But it's fair to say what we have is—we have these profound ideological and philosophical differences that make Washington basically totally dysfunctional.

—David Gregory, July 15, 2012

ONE ADVANTAGE OF HAVING READ, HEARD, OR SEEN nearly every episode of *Meet the Press* is that I have developed a nose for honing in on its interesting moments when they arise. One of those came in the hot summer of 2012 after much of my research for this book was complete. David Gregory responded to the antitax activist Grover Norquist with the uncharacteristic exasperation represented in the previous quotation, describing American political culture as "basically totally dysfunctional." It is an interesting moment not only because the mild and unflappable David Gregory momentarily lost his characteristic poise but also for what it says about the state of American politics. Putting aside well-worn debates about whether any institution or practice can be thought of as functional for the whole of society, note how powerful it is to hear a Washington insider of Gregory's caliber admit what everyone already knows: Beltway politics have hit a point in which good people seem no longer able to work with one another toward common and mutually beneficial goals. Washington appears broken. Reality itself appears riven by hostilities that produce a kind of social autism, much like that described long ago by the social psychologist Theodore Newcomb: inconsolable rivals peddle incompatible versions of the world to a frustrated public that oscillates, in turn, between moral panic and numb exhaustion.[1]

But not all is lost. Political dysfunction, what others like the conflict analyst Edward Azar have described as protracted social conflict, simply indicates that political division has entered a phase in which it becomes necessary to look past merely rational alternatives toward the deeper levels of symbolic politics.[2] Whereas in periods of relative normative consensus, conflicts of interest may lead to troubling and nettlesome disputes, when conflicts cross the divide into deeply symbolic territory, appeals to rational interests and common sense are no longer sufficient means toward resolution. When moral visions are enlisted in a cause, they take control and dictate outcomes to well-meaning actors. Wherever and whenever this happens, participants in the spectacle find themselves befuddled and frustrated, and in our era of permanent campaign the spectacle never stops. The discursive atmosphere feels toxic, and things no longer seem to make sense. Anyone too deeply involved appears from the outside to be less than fully rational. Even seemingly innocent language becomes freighted with cryptic and polluting references, supported by a rich symbolic history. Each successive discursive sortie in the larger struggle seems to conform to some generative code with literary dimensions that remains obscured beneath the surface like semiotic landmines from some forgotten escalation.

Things seem this way because this is how they are. People are people from Tallahassee to Timbuktu, and when things turn hot, they berate one another with coded histories of their collective trauma to the point of abject confusion. Satisfying as this can be, it tends to distract from productive policy discussion. So what Washington needs is a cadre of code breakers who can help us make sense of what this dysfunctional confrontation is all about, and although there are plenty of ingenious experimental psychologists running for code breaker–in–chief, to this point the leading intellectual lights are half blind; they see only that part of the solution that their disciplinary training has prepared them to see. We have known since the days of the French sociologist Émile Durkheim that psychology alone is woefully inadequate for explaining society-level phenomena, and since much of what we believe as individuals is the product of idiosyncratic and half-remembered institutional struggles over the interpretation of the past, we need a framework suitable for decoding sociocultural phenomena, not merely neuropsychological ones. To crack the conflict code, we need to have a clear picture of the evolved structure of our biological hardwiring, our neuro-anatomy, but we also have to have a clear picture of our political culture; we need to learn to mine the contingent history of our symbolic politics.

As much as the invariant aspects of our moral psychology matter in political process, so, too, do the idiosyncratic and plastic features of our political culture. Intuitions rule in processes of moral judgment, but they do not present themselves directly and unmediated by our dreams and delusions. The answer to the question, Why can't Americans talk to one another, is not primarily that Republicans and Democrats vary in the way they have linked their innate biological dispositions to what they see, but rather that they vary in the way what they see conforms to stylized pictures of the world presented to them by elite actors with strategic agendas. We will find the answer both in the metaphors we live by and in the myths we manufacture on the fly.[3]

Before our animal instincts can be put to strategic use, they have to be linked to public policy by symbolic means. Our moral infrastructure may have been systematically transmitted from our ancient hominid ancestors, but it has been idiosyncratically attached to the empirical world through the symbols that we have inherited from our very human grandparents. If we want to understand what divides a conservative from a liberal, we will benefit more by understanding how propagandists and moral entrepreneurs used the grand narratives of Thomas Hobbes, John Locke, Karl Marx, and W. E. B. Du Bois to consecrate their causes and desecrate their opponents than we will from documenting how bonobos resemble Occupy Wall Street protestors.[4] The political psychologists and neuro-anatomists will do much in advancing our understanding of the mechanics and form of our moral intuitions, but they will accomplish little in moving forward our understanding of the meaning and content of the same.

The interpretation of symbolic politics has to work simultaneously on what the psychologists Richard Petty and John Cacioppo called the central and peripheral routes to attitude formation.[5] In a competitive public sphere, the morality-inducing modules that derive from our evolutionary past must be attached to the symbolic vehicles of our historical present to produce compelling interpretations of who is a friend and who is an enemy, what is a sensible plan and what is utter folly. Lived experience cannot present itself to our unconscious unmediated by ideology—and ideologies, like families, have a genealogy that we can trace. Where we find this story is in the history of public performances of political division.

Decoding Dysfunction: Three Preliminary Principles

In the 1960s, when the political scientist Murray Edelman published his seminal work on the centrality of symbolism, ritual, and emotion for politics, his view was commonly seen as an intriguing anomaly along the driving path toward an objective science of politics.[6] Today leading and highly visible experts have broken down the barriers between emotion and reason, rational interest and identity, and are selling their work in large runs to both practical politicians and cloistered academics alike. At the cutting edges of both the "hard" sciences of symbolism and democracy and the "creative" centers of interpretive social science, we can see convergences that point the way toward sensible ways to plan our lives. Not long ago, the evolutionary biologist E. O. Wilson imagined that the divide between modes of knowing, between science and literature, logic and culture, would slowly be narrowed as we learn more about the world.[7] In a sense, recent work in psychology and sociology does suggest that the seemingly permanent gap between the hard and historical sciences may be narrowing.

The reason for this happy state of affairs is what always drives epochal change in science, the invention of a better mousetrap. Like latter-day Galileos, with the development of telescopes of the brain in the form of EEG and fMRI technologies, creative and sensitive neuro- and cognitive scientists have made dizzying progress in breeching the walls of one of the last refuges of mystery, what Charles Darwin once called "the citadel itself"—the human mind.[8] This new breed of brain scanners has been busily discovering new Americas one after another, from Antonio Damasio's deconstruction of Cartesian dualism to Richie Davidson's investigation of the benefits of meditation for well-being, to Drew Westen's demonstrations of our propensities to polarize through rationalization.[9] We can now speak with a confidence born of empirical experience about how important emotions are for rational thought and how symbols, metaphor, and ritual are irreducible elements of what it means to be human.[10]

But as is the case in all protracted conflicts, if the two cultures described by C. P. Snow are beginning to come together again, the E. O. Wilsons of the world have not yet fully recognized the deeper motivations of the interpretive camp: the profoundly disorienting impact of antifoundational thinkers like William James, the later Ludwig Wittgenstein, Clifford Geertz, Richard Rorty, Jacques Derrida, and even Émile Durkheim and the early Karl Marx, to merely draw a list. Although it is impossible to summarize this literature in a sentence, suffice it to say that these thinkers have taught us how fragile and fungible our knowledge about the world (especially the social world) necessarily is. The piece missing from this puzzle is a thoroughgoing contribution from this interpretive side of this intellectual struggle that recognizes the extent of the contingency in our reflective commitments regarding the links between our deepest convictions and our institutional evaluations.

The First Principle: Intuitive Primacy, or Reason Is the Slave of the Passions

But let's begin with the hard science that teaches us that emotions often matter more for moral judgment than does thoughtful reflection. In the hands of virtuoso performers like the psychologist Jonathan Haidt, we have learned how our moral judgments can be rendered as products of multilevel processes of natural selection without falling into the racist traps of the social Darwinists of the last century. In Haidt's recent book *Our Righteous Minds* and in his larger oeuvre, he convincingly demonstrates how a Darwinian perspective on group selection can be married with a theory of moral sentiments consistent with the philosopher David Hume's views on emotional primacy, which he blends with a turn to sociology in the work of Émile Durkheim. From Durkheim, Haidt borrows the view that human beings are tribal beings who are not only selfish but also groupish. They fight not only for their own survival but also for the survival of the tribe, and the glue that binds them is the notion of the sacred, and sacredness, like faith, is a matter of intuition more than reason.

At the heart of Haidt's political project for his moral psychology is the concept of *intuitive primacy*. When people make routine moral judgments, Dionysus rules and Apollo is his servant.[11] The biological mechanism for this evolutionary adaptation is what Haidt describes as moral foundations, which can be thought of as "taste buds of the righteous mind." Borrowing from David Hume and classical Chinese philosopher Mencius, he argues that morality is an innate human characteristic that has evolved as humans have evolved. It can be divided into a small set of "universal cognitive modules upon which cultures construct moral matrices." It is upon these universal foundations, whose original triggers can be identified in theory, that advanced moral systems are erected.[12]

Novel situations put the old taste receptors to new uses, but the endless varieties of moral cuisine that we encounter around the world are all soundly postulated to share the same faculties of moral taste, just as the varieties of food are designed to appeal to our innate capacity to sense sweet, sour, salt, bitter, and savory. So, our moral lives, while influenced by our capacity to rationalize our innate intuitions, are structured by these five innate capacities: to care for the weak, to be fair to other members of the group, to be unified in opposition to those who would threaten the group, to submit to those who command respect, and to recognize the purity of those things that have been marked off from the secular world. In this way, our righteous minds are organized in advance of experience, but there is not a fixed range of triggers that might stimulate a moral intuition of attraction or repulsion, wherever our reason might incline us.

The Second Principle: The Opinion Industry, or Your Beliefs Are a Battlefield

But there is something important missing from this social intuitionist school of moral psychology and its doctrine of intuitive primacy, and that is the role played by strategic ideologues in real civil societies, whose energetic efforts might be described as an *opinion industry*. The moral judgments of individuals in isolation may be dominated by emotions, but open societies are subject to an industry run by opinion leaders whose product is your inner life, and these opinion leaders are often quite rational in their approach. It might be little surprise that a sociologist would criticize a psychological school of thought with the claim that it pays too much attention to the isolated individual and not enough to the social context in which the individual finds herself, but that is exactly the problem the social intuitionist model faces. Although subjects in a psych lab may favor their instinctive impulses over the analytical capacities when making moral judgments, mass publics—individuals aggregated in interdependent groups—face a different challenge. Here moral quandaries take the form of public issues that have somehow been translated into a form that is distinct from that of the personal troubles faced by the isolated individual. As Jürgen Habermas argued, these things are decided in the public sphere, not the private mind.[13] When moral challenges are presented in public, they are intensely mediated through newspapers, magazines, television shows, and social media pings.[14]

The power of the public sphere only becomes more important to recognize as it becomes a crucial feature of democratic self-concept in advanced democracies like the United States. Although different societies vary in their tastes for demagoguery, ours is one in which rational debate is supposed to take priority over manipulative emotional appeal. When policy makers adopt a perspective, they want to appear as if they have a sound rational justification for what they are doing. When lawmakers or opinion leaders make an argument in a celebrated public setting like *Meet the Press*, they do so with the benefit of legacies of powerful analytical arguments that link policies with desirable outcomes and desirable outcomes with deeply held principles. In other words, public sphere debate is supposed to take place through Petty and Cacioppo's peripheral, rational route, which trades in theories and values, not the central route that deals in emotions and symbols. When it does not, community leaders find themselves vulnerable to charges of demagoguery and innuendo peddling.

In real civil societies, in contrast to the idealized ones that theorists like Habermas imagine, there is a specialized role for the strategic ideologue, who is not there merely to rationalize what has already been decided by intuitive process. Instead, the ideologue's job is to provide rational justifications that sober and clever people could support in the quiet of their study for a given course of action. In public deliberation, arguments that cannot pass a minimal bar of logical cogency will simply fail to convince, whereas they might past muster in private deliberation. Moreover, vast sums are spent and entire careers are dedicated to providing the raw material for mass justification.

The Third Principle: The Consecration of Causes, or Even Secular Ideas Are Sacred

The principle of intuitive primacy ensures that most moral judgments will follow emotional cues rather than rational considerations. The widespread presence of well-trained and richly remunerated strategic ideologues ensures that in public debate, there is a kind of medium-term balance struck between what Jonathan Haidt described as the emotional dog (intuition) and its rational tail (reason). This leads to a third principle drawn from cutting-edge sociological scholarship that gets us most of the way down the path toward decoding political dysfunction, *the consecration of causes.*

The key to cracking moral code is to recognize that we like or are compelled to reduce complex problems to simple distinctions between good and evil, sacred and profane. The moral code has a binary structure of opposing themes that sorts the raw from the cooked, from which polluting and ennobling associations can be drawn.[15] This is the contribution of the sociologist Jeffrey Alexander.[16] For Alexander, solidarity—the basis of moral feeling—is generated through coded civil discourse, which is itself structured by sets of oppositional binaries. These mark off the good from evil and tell us what it means to be "us" and what it means to be "them."[17]

Implicit in Alexander's interpretation of codes and narratives in civil discourse is the way that political storytelling by strategic ideologues works on both of Petty and Cacioppo's routes, the intuitive and the rational, at the same time. In public storytelling we have a balanced dialogue maintained through narrative processes that "encode" analytical and empirical claims with deeper meanings. Through the use of symbolic devices and past associations, narrative attempts to align convictions developed through processes of conscious reasoning, what we might call streamlined stories or theories of change, with the intuitive imagery of the unconscious.[18] This matching of story and telling produces a sense of deeper meaning, which when attached to matters of public moment, gives meaning a sacred character. Social issues become imbued with the kind of sacred meaning that can be derived only from the image of the moral community. What results is a kind of religious interpretation of all political events, even when these events are treated in purely secular terms. In this sense, ideology is the heir to religion. Since the era of Enlightenment, references to the civil sacred have been shrouded in an intricate secular code that employs our religious instincts for modern ends.

Alexander's coded, contingent binaries provide us with a new way of seeing protracted social conflict.[19] When interpretations of some salient social issue differ, rival groups attempt to "represent others in negative and polluted categories and to re-present [themselves] in terms of the sacred."[20] When the coded meaning of events comes into contest, each side sees the other through the lens of its own sacralized narratives: Muslims were thought to hate our freedoms after 9/11; "welfare queens" are imagined to siphon off the fruits of the labors of hardworking people; capitalists are imagined to plot world domination; racists are imagined to dress up their bigotry in phony neoliberal economic theories. All contests risk devolving into a kind of crusade in which democracy and civilization themselves hang in the balance.

Sensing this theoretical context with animal cunning, effective opinion leaders tell stories that contain defensible analytical components (theoretical propositions backed by data and values consistent with their principled worldview) as well as intuitive triggers that enhance solidarity—"in your heart, you know he's right." We who consume popular social science have become so riveted by the concept of narrative because we have discovered that leaders appear authentic when they use narrative process, literary politics, as a way to align reason and intuition toward their chosen goal. Good leaders know without being told that it is in narrative that heart and mind come together, leaving a trace of its passing that can be used at some later date. What is left over when the telling is done are stories with independent power. This presents us with the last piece of the puzzle.

The Power of the Political Storybook: Of Barbarians, Bureaucrats, Bigwigs, and Bigots

Taken together, the three preceding principles of moral reasoning in real civil societies can be thought of as pieces of the puzzle of dysfunctional discourse and protracted conflict. Intuitive primacy demands that we give due respect to the wild side. The widespread presence of strategic ideologues and the opinion industry demands that we treat the *polis* as distinct from the person. States are like souls in certain respects, but they differ in the way that they can institutionalize the balance between emotions and rational thinking.[21] The third principle worked out in Jeffrey Alexander's cultural sociology, the consecration of causes, implies that the kinds of stories opinion leaders will tell are constrained to conform to both the prevailing analytical standards and the archetypal imagery of primitive conditioning. Every mass campaign in civil society is forced to appeal in a fundamental way to coded binary distinctions that distinguish "us" from "them" in epic terms.

A fourth principle, *the power of the political storybook*, presents us with the final piece of this puzzle.[22] The idea here is simple: Once stories have been dramatically presented to mass publics in a way that both mobilizes the masses and transforms foundational institutional arrangements, they are seared into mass consciousness and thereafter become readily available to future ideologues. These are some examples: George Washington crossing the Delaware River on Christmas Day in 1776 to displace the Hessian garrison in Trenton; Thomas Jefferson penning the Declaration of Independence and galvanizing the revolution against monarchical authority; Franklin Roosevelt declaring that happy days were here again in the height of the Great Depression; and Martin Luther King Jr. rallying the public on the steps of the Lincoln Memorial to decry racial exclusion.

These collective resources have been written into the American political storybook and enjoy relative autonomy from the objective conditions and problems the public faces.

The moral psychologists have convincingly demonstrated that emotions rather than rational thinking often drive individuals, but reason is present in public debate—the stories we tell about abusive power, which distinctive abuses inflect the civil code, often have their roots in the history of objective oppression, as John Locke famously suggested.[23] To finally crack the code, we turn back to questions about the nature and forms of power and what makes them distinctive.

A productive place to start is Max Weber's essays on power, authority, and legitimacy, where we will discover the forensic tools we need to examine political nature and explicate the rhetorical root causes of protracted conflict. Weber recognized that in order to make sense of social order, one needed a theory of the distribution of power within the community. In his classic essay "Class, Status and Party," he wrote, "We understand by 'power' the chance of a man or of a number of men to realize their own will in a communal action even against the resistance of others who are participating in the same action."[24] This definition is still workable if we add to it another idea developed in his essay "Politics as a Vocation" to address the principle of security: "A state is a human community that (successfully) claims the monopoly of the legitimate use of physical force within a given territory."[25] Combining the three forms of power, delineated by the class, status, and party trio, with the implicit category of the state itself, we can see a four-category typology emerge, each category reflecting a distinctive kind of threat to civil society. Along with these four threats are four kinds of villains to populate our political storybooks.[26] I call these barbarians, bureaucrats, bigwigs, and bigots. The barbarian is an external or internal other who uses lawlessness as a threat to the whole of the community, which the state guards against. The bureaucrat is a threat to the community who emerges through partisan forces in government once a state is established. A bigwig is a threat to the community who emerges from the private power of small and powerful groups who command resources. A bigot is a threat to the community who uses popular stereotypes, connections, and derisive images to hector and discriminate against minorities.

In a political story, heroes are essential but the villain matters the most. Villains are those who abuse one of the canonical forms of power,[27] and once a story has been played out in dramatic form in history, there is no other symbolic residue of the story that can compete with it.[28] The villain marks the kind of power to speak truth to. One should never underestimate the political value of a Genghis Khan, a King George, a John D. Rockefeller, or an Adolf Hitler.[29] Once you have scarred people with stories stocked with clear and identifiable villains, every political actor in the future is vulnerable to being cast in that role.[30]

These categories help explain why Franklin Roosevelt, Martin Luther King Jr., Thomas Jefferson, and George Washington serve as our archetypal American heroes. They are heroes worth commemorating in marble as one would have the gods of the ancients because their adversaries can be categorized abstractly into the canonical categories of villainy. Roosevelt was that rare figure in American politics who led a mass movement to constrain the abuses of concentrated economic power and the corporate bigwigs who wielded it. King was a larger-than-life defender of the range of core principles of American democracy, but one who dramatized more than anything else the evils of racial bigotry and the abuses endemic to an ethnic caste system. Jefferson was the hero of liberty who opposed the power of the government and its executives and bureaucrats to control people's lives. Washington was the unique representative of the American political community, who stood against the forces that opposed the American political community at its core. Washington then came to represent order itself against the forces of barbarism that threatened to disrupt it. In these four figures, in the stories derived from their lives and struggles, and in the variations on the themes that their stories present to previous generations of Americans, we discover the rhetorical and cultural roots of political conflict in contemporary America.

Although these rhetorical categories are useful in decoding polarized political talk in the United States, they are of general use in any setting. As there are four distinctive forms of organized power that are relevant for political life, there is a weak tendency for leaders around the world and throughout history to consecrate their causes with reference to this set of usual suspects of canonical abusers. Moreover, each of these categories has been the subject of extensive philosophical debate. The great theorist of class politics was Karl Marx in his landmark book, *Das Kapital*. The most cogent theorist of cultural alienation and "double consciousness" was the African American scholar W. E. B. Du Bois, and his most famous book on the topic is *The Souls of Black Folk*. John Locke was the seminal

Table 1. The four rhetorics of civility

Imagery of abusive power	Civil virtue	Structural constituency of abusive power	Weber's power categories	Virtuoso theorist	Stylized ism
barbarians	security	the Other	state	Thomas Hobbes	conservatism
bureaucrats	freedom	the One	party	John Locke	liberalism
bigwigs	equality	the Few	class	Karl Marx	socialism
bigots	tolerance	the Many	status	W. E. B. Du Bois	multiculturalism

philosopher of liberalism and human rights who formulated the critique of government overreach in his *Second Treatise* on government. Finally, Thomas Hobbes was the original theorist of civil society, who developed a perspective on sovereign power and state authority that undergirds most political thought that came after his, even when it was developed in opposition to his thinking.[31]

The categories dovetail as well with Aristotle's typology of regimes.[32] The bureaucrat is the villain of the story when abusive power is held by the One; the king or the dictator requires an apparatus of power, a government, through which he can oppress. The bigwig is the villain of the story when power is held by the Few; aristocracies and oligarchies abuse their exalted status to prey on the little guy.[33] The bigot is the story's villain when power is held by the Many; polities and democracies can abuse their majority status to subject minorities to injustice. This is what we mean by the disparaging sense of the word "populism." Missing from Aristotle's typology is what lies outside the regime, a universal category that we might simply call the Other. Whether in the form of foreign tyrants or domestic criminals, the Other is the basis of the barbarian's villainy and the polity is defined at the border between that Other and the people.

Together these categories describe four rhetorics of civility,[34] anchored in civil virtues that provide citizens and subjects with ways of thinking, feeling, and speaking about political matters with cogency and conviction. They demonstrate the power and relative autonomy of the political storybook.[35] They also sketch out four canonical themes that describe what any given conflict is all about. There is advantage to be had in classifying conflicts in terms of the extent to which their participants see the stakes of their struggles in terms of the civil virtues: security, freedom, equality, and tolerance.

Every Sunday morning, we can see these rhetorics put to work as rival figureheads slug it out with one another as they argue America. The dynamism of political debate and the impasses of principled disagreement cannot be understood without resort to them. Using these categories, we can explain the descent of American politics into seeming dysfunction. Each side sees the policies, leaders, and values of the other through the lens of their own well-worn stories, images, and interpretations. Democrats present the Republicans as war-crazed white men who are unwilling to share the fruits of their ill-gotten booty with women and the rising peoples of the global south. Republicans present Democrats as deluded do-gooders, who in their zeal to promote diversity and equality threaten to throw the world into chaos and to destroy the productive economic engine that gave birth to the first new nation. Democrats tell alarming stories about bigots and bigwigs, while Republicans tell stories about the threats of bureaucrats and barbarians.

3

SPREADING DEMOCRACY AROUND THE WORLD
A World Made Safe for Private Enterprise

Well, I'm in favor of spreading democracy in every part of the world.
But there are many ways to spread democracy. You can't cram
democracy down the throats of people.

—Senator Claude Pepper, November 27, 1947

THE CONTINUING FOREIGN POLICY CONVERSATION about war and security, force and freedom on *Meet the Press* is remarkable in its span and depth. We see outstanding personalities in the news grappling with Winston Churchill's "Iron Curtain" speech; Douglas MacArthur being relieved of command in Korea; events in Somalia that led, among other things, to the movie *Black Hawk Down*; or those surrounding ethnic cleansing in Bosnia or the Rwandan genocide. Newsmakers have discussed the Cuban missile crisis and the custody battle for a hapless Cuban boy–made–icon Elián Gonzáles. We see American icons cozying up to Joseph McCarthy and subsequently distancing themselves from him. We see the drama of the Berlin crisis along with later calls to "tear down this wall."

No area of national concern has taken up more time and energy or has produced greater excitement or more bitter disappointment than that about war and peace and the proper use of American power in the world. We can conservatively estimate from the *Meet the Press* record that more than twelve hundred episodes have covered the broader themes of international relations—over a third of all episodes. This sheer volume dwarfs that on any other topic and probably reflects both how crucial the theme is for the vitality of American life and how fraught it is in a country always eager to see better angles in the workings of history. George Washington had warned his young republic to avoid entangling alliances with European powers. However, after World War II, with America now in the international driver's seat, these sentiments would not long survive.

Less than two years after VE Day, Congress accepted Truman's demand that aid be given to Greece and Turkey, and the Cold War was on. The Marshall Plan and the establishment of the Atlantic alliance that would become NATO intensified conflict with the Soviet Union, along with the somewhat alien civil rhetoric of security through a balance of power. Even so, the American liberal ethos proved flexible enough to adapt itself in occasionally perverse ways to the nearly impossible challenges that quickly arose as American foreign entanglements proliferated.

The central irony of the foreign policy debate is that it is probably the area of most importance to national policy elites, but it is the area in which most Americans have invested the least substantive attention. We talk a lot about liberty and repression around the world, but we have little sense of what that means in practical terms. There is no issue area in which the "pictures in our heads" that Walter Lippmann described are more important than in matters of peace and war, and consequently there is no issue in which pitching a plausible story to one's domestic audience is more important.[1]

Because of the volume of material on foreign policy discussed on *Meet the Press*, it is not possible to provide an exhaustive representation of the conversations that have taken place over the span of the American Century, but here I will provide a representative sense of the flavor and focus of those conversations with an emphasis on how distant events were placed in the narrative context of the American political storybook. This simplified story demonstrates that there has been no rhetorical approach through which to consistently justify American foreign policy interventions apart from the unerring focus of the Republican Party (and of most Democrats) on the cause of individual rights as they apply to the pioneers of global private enterprise. American elites were not comfortable spilling blood for oil, but they would defend the American way of life—by which they meant a system of loosely regulated private enterprise—to the bitter end. The result was no cynical security game, but the link between liberal principle and realist policy became ever more implicit as time wore on.

This aggressive liberal ethic was embodied clearly in Eric Johnston, the midcentury president of the US Chamber of Commerce, a visionary businessman who led the Motion Picture Association through the second Red Scare. Johnston correctly predicted that it would be necessary for the country to fight a number of foreign wars in order to fashion a world made safe for private enterprise. In Johnston's view, confrontation was inevitable; the United States was committed to a system of business orga-nization in which there was little room for the kinds of social protections from the disruptions of the market that struck citizens of the develop-ing world as matters of obvious common sense. From Latin America, to Southeast Asia, to the Middle East and Africa, the United States would find itself bogged down in violent confrontations, visible and covert. In most cases, the imagined enemy was international Communism, but as often the true adversary was the emergent, ad hoc host of critics of lais-sez-faire, laissez-passer capitalism, and these ragtag resisters found ever new "weapons of the weak," to borrow a phrase from the political scientist John Scott,[2] through which to challenge the coming liberal world order.

Like a boorish lover, the Americans never seemed to correctly inter-pret the brush-off. Lacking a developed ethic of equality, the American political classes were unable to understand, even when they had the incli-nation to be curious, why it was that so much of the world seemed to reject the American plan for a democratic and liberal capitalism in favor of the obvious oppressions of petty and backward rivals. George W. Bush crystallized this confusion when he claimed that the United States was attacked on September 11 because its enemies "hate our freedom." To the world's desperate poor and those with an alternative conception of a moral economy, the rugged, corporate individualism on the model put forth by the US Chamber of Commerce seemed more like a fantasy vision than a reflective commitment to a prominent branch of Enlightenment philoso-phy; they did hate it, along with its champions.[3]

Because American foreign policy has been so harsh and aggressive, it is tempting to suggest that it is in the area of national security that an unabashedly conservative strain of the political tradition reveals itself, which gives the lie to Louis Hartz's famous liberal tradition thesis,[4] but this would be off the mark. Critics of American foreign policy sense hypocrisy at its core and dismiss most arguments about global democ-racy as cynical, clumsy efforts to rationalize global empire. But Ameri-cans from Washington to Wilson to George W. Bush saw themselves as promoting what Jefferson had described as the "empire of liberty," which was based on a sacralized vision of Enlightenment-era political economy. Even when it revealed a conservative temperament, the American Cen-tury abroad would be one in which the principles of Anglo-American business liberalism would play out its violent script in defense of the sacred principles of the rights of private property while others looked on in confusion and disbelief. This chapter focuses on how the American creed evolved as it confronted the chaos and brutal realities of the post–World War II period.

The Maximum of Freedom

Now what the answer is, frankly, . . . I do not know. All I can say is that in my opinion, we ought to encourage the promotion of private enterprise abroad because I think that you cannot—in my personal opinion—you cannot secure the maximum of freedom of the individual without private enterprise.

—Eric Johnston, February 13, 1949

If their public performances on *Meet the Press* are any guide, American leaders managed that part of the world that was left to them after World War II with a sense of desperate uncertainty. For more than a decade, power was held securely by the Democratic Party and its larger-than-life savior Franklin Roosevelt; by 1945, Roosevelt was dead, and his successor, the unknown and untested Harry Truman, was faced with widespread concerns about his capacity to govern that would culminate in a pivotal, scolding congressional election in the fall of 1946. These were uncertain times. Humankind had invented the capacity for its own destruction with the nuclear bomb. The world had lived through two world wars accompanied by atrocity on a scale previously undreamed of, and a new threat was emerging in occupied Germany in the form of Soviet Communism. In this atmosphere, every event had an air of crisis about it, leaving room enough for opportunistic entrepreneurs of the public spirit to peddle their wares in nationally televised debates that would be astoundingly consequential. After persistent effort, the newly ascendant conservatives of the Republican Party first stymied and then humbled the remaining class-conscious New Dealers to promote a vigorous and pioneering liberal project to safeguard private property around the world.

The context for postwar reform was set by that transformative election of 1946, an election that provokes interest from a number of angles. The Democratic Party was split between its racist southern wing and its northern liberals. The Republican Party under the image of Lincoln the Emancipator had superior multicultural credentials, but it was also complicated on the social justice front, split between its newer laissez-faire liberals and the remaining followers of great Republican Progressives like Robert Lafollette, Hiram Johnson, and even Teddy Roosevelt. These cross-cutting cleavages led to subtle distinctions in the uses of ideological labels like liberal, radical, conservative, reactionary, and reformer. The unsettling solidarities born of war and the complexity of party coalitions at the time made it difficult to know left from right. FDR had cleverly appropriated the term "liberal" to apply to his social rights agenda, and keen wits from Lionel Trilling to Louis Hartz were busy writing conservatism out of the American political tradition. Confusion reigned at the level of ideas.

Uncertainty about social categories produced fascinating tensions that led to massive political realignment. For purposes of contrast with what is to come, it is good to reflect on just how "liberal" were the most respected members of the Republican Party in this era, as the following exchange from February 1, 1946, with the Progressive Republican senator Wayne Morse of Oregon demonstrates.

Larry Spivak: But Senator, the word "liberal" has been given a terrific beating; would you give some idea of what you mean by it?

Wayne Morse: Well, as I refer to liberalism in the Republican Party, I mean that the Republican Party must make very clear to American farmers, American consumers, American workers, that it stands to seeing to it that all groups in this country are given equal protection in what I consider to be the guarantees of a representative government. Now let me be more specific. It happens to be my view that there are strong, powerful business groups in America that seem to think that the Republican Party ought to be the party of business. I say to them, if you want a businessman's party, start one and see how many votes you get. . . . The real danger to the party as I see it is that there are those who seek to make it a class party instead of an American party.

Not all liberal Republicans were so squeamish about fighting for the traditional rights of business. Foremost among these was "Mr. Republican," Senator Robert Taft of Ohio, who was one of the most entertaining and charming guests to appear with regularity on *Meet the Press*. Taft was the son of the counterprogressive Republican president and Supreme Court justice William Howard Taft, and he brought with him a kind of nostalgia for the days of stalwart Republicanism prior to the insurgent campaigns earlier in the century. A darling of *Meet the Press* right up to his death in 1953, Taft was the very model of what we would now describe as a conservative with libertarian tendencies, but he seems to have thought of himself as an Anglo-American classical liberal more in the mold of John Stuart Mill than Leonard Trelawny Hobhouse.[5] He was no war hawk and was notably progressive in promoting the cultural rights of African Americans, especially when contrasted with his southern opponents from the Democratic Party like the senator from the Ku Klux Klan, Theodore Bilbo.

Taft was also the sort of fan of industrial capitalism that Karl Marx would have derided for his belief in *le doux commerce*—the gentleness of commerce. In Taft's vision of liberal society, the goal was to outcompete the Russians, proving to the world the superior virtues of free-market capitalism. He had opposed entry into the war and was among the leading figures opposing a new one with the Russians if such confrontation could be avoided. It is this dovish character of neoliberalism that most distinguishes its early forms from those we now know. The following exchange from January 31, 1947, with Taft, the new Senate leader, demonstrates how pacific was the corporate-friendly classical liberalism of the Republican Party as it planned for a transition from the war footing developed under Democratic rule.

Jay Franklin (Consolidated News Features): Senator, while we're on the subject of foreign affairs, I wonder what your point of view is of the defense of this country against Communism. Do you think we are better defended by fortifying the Arctic Circle or by having elaborate police measures to test the loyalty of our citizens or by having a really productive economic system?

Robert Taft: Well, do you mean protection against Russia or against Communism, Mr. Franklin?

Franklin: Aren't they pretty well wedded to each other, Senator?

Taft: No, I think the two are entirely different. Uh, Russia's a military force, is a military threat, and has to be met by military defense or military offense. Uh, the Communism is best met, I think, by an aggressive development of our present system and the—both our governmental and business system, to such a point that the people are clearly better off, as they are—I think they're better off today—clearly better off than anyone can think they would be under Communism.

Franklin: Well then, you think, Senator, that we can combine a policy of official friendship with the Russian state and equally official hostility to the—what you might describe as the official religion of the Russian people.

Taft: Yes, I certainly do. I don't think peace in this world depends on everybody having the same form of ideology for their own government. If they'll confine their ideology to their own country, I don't think [*lilting voice*] there's any danger of, uh, serious danger of that being a cause of war.

This savvy student of political identification knew how to separate the Russian from the Communist. Taft Republicans could, for a time, still accept coexistence with a Communist alternative, so long as it kept out of their business. The last thing they wanted to do was to encircle the Russian bear with a democratic alliance, thereby provoking it to lash out unnecessarily. Their job was simply to outcompete the alternative. This tendency temporarily placed neoliberalism on an intersecting path with the more radical of the remaining New Dealers of the opposing party, like Claude "Red" Pepper. Pepper, who claimed on November 27, 1947, "Unless we're willing to be blown to some other world to get away from a world where Communism exists, we've got to live in a world with Communism." But this irenic bipartisan convergence would not outlast a Communist bomb and a Communist China.

The "free Europe" ideal that would animate Democratic Party policy with the containment doctrine of Harry Truman and the then-contentious and aggressive anticommunist initiatives embodied in the Marshall Plan and Atlantic Pact (NATO) were only slowly developing. The Democratic Party was vulnerable to opportunistic positioning of its role in the "big three" war conferences in Tehran, Yalta, and Potsdam, which would feed into a narrative of Democratic corruption and betrayal nourished by foreign policy setbacks in China and Korea along with evidence of domestic treason. All of it was kindling for the fire that consumed the country in the McCarthy era.

Right after the war, the founder of *Meet the Press*, Larry Spivak, was critical of Republican insinuations of "secret commitments" to Communist regimes by leaders of the Democratic Party that "cost millions of lives and billions of dollars," but as the narrative of red-baiters like Richard Nixon found anchors in unfolding current events, *Meet the Press* joined the vanguard of the Red Scare.[6] In fact, understanding the early rise of *Meet the Press* requires understanding the Red Scare of which it became a part. The program played a powerful and provocative role in exploring the early social dramas of Communist infiltration that turned the country against the state-sponsored egalitarianism that the Democratic Party had only recently embraced. Anticommunism was a story that could sell, and Larry Spivak was eager to heighten the drama when stories in this genre emerged.[7]

The secretary general of the Communist Party in America, Earl Browder, appeared on the program four times before it became illegal to be a member of that organization in 1954, and the program was also an important stop for crusading ex-Communists who were eager to do in their old cause.

Among the major explosive performances on the program were the accusations of Whittaker Chambers against the State Department official Alger Hiss, suggesting he was a Communist agent. Undoubtedly, this anticommunist drama would have played out in a similar way without the benefit of *Meet the Press*, but it was on this program that Chambers, the ex-Communist and once editor of *Time* magazine, made his public accusation against Hiss that would lead to his downfall. The fear and moral outrage directed at the US government that resulted from the Hiss trial and his conviction for espionage was central to the rise of Joseph McCarthy and a narrative of widespread Communist infiltration of American society. As an amplification device for the public mood, *Meet the Press* was there to help along the process that resulted in McCarthyism.

Like the more moderate Robert Taft, Joseph McCarthy was a frequent guest on *Meet the Press*, where he was received with warmth and a spirit of hope. Here is the introduction he received in his freshman appearance on February 28, 1947, which is colorful and filled with ironic prescience.

Albert Warner (moderator): Facing the press table is Senator Joseph R. McCarthy, Republican of Wisconsin. He is the youngest member of the Senate, a bachelor. He's a veteran of the war, an enlisted man, who earned a commission and was promoted to captain, a rear seat gunner on a Marine Corps dive bomber who participated in seventeen missions against the Japanese in the Solomon Islands. The senator was born on a Wisconsin farm, went from grade school to earn his living, decided at nineteen he wanted an education, took his high school curriculum in one year, became a lawyer, and was elected to a circuit judgeship from which he took a leave of absence to go to war. And then he created a political upset in the Republican primary by overturning the fifty-year Lafollette dynasty and defeating Robert M. Lafollette Jr., who had served twenty-one years in the Senate. Senator McCarthy makes news when his gunner's eye sights the line of fire in battles over budget, labor legislation, and rent control. For the senator represents a new era in the Senate: youth and change, a prophecy of things ahead.

Note how this young politico was lionized as a conservative midwestern hero, positioned to replace the "dynasty" of the Progressive Wisconsin

Lafollette clan. We know now what they did not, that the ambition of the younger Lafollette was derailed by a postwar Red Scare even more destructive than the one that stymied his father in the wake of World War I and that *Meet the Press* was going to play along in one of the least admirable episodes in American history.

The story of how the pursuit of Communist infiltration became general in the period is well enough known not to spend much time on it here, but what makes the McCarthy experience on *Meet the Press* so interesting is how McCarthy changed as did the opportunities for demagoguery. When the major struggles against collectivism were domestic in nature, McCarthy came off as a bit player in the neoliberal social drama. It is only after the Russians tested the bomb and Communists took over China in 1949 that we see a qualitative change in Joseph McCarthy and in the *Meet the Press* record on Communism more generally.

McCarthy was no fire breather in his early days as a television star. His first three appearances on the show reflect a fairly mild and concerned conservative politician who promoted balanced views on labor issues, military strategy, and civil liberties. But on February 24, 1950, McCarthy appeared on the program with a gun in his lap, promoting the kinds of outlandish charges that would make him iconic.

McCarthy is the figure best remembered in this security-saturated civil discourse of the Red Scare, but other figures capitalized on the new mood to consecrate more practical policy goals like debt reduction and undermining support for foreign aid. One of these fellow-traveling fire breathers for freedom was William Jenner, the conservative senator from Indiana. In his performance of May 4, 1949, in the tipping point of the anti-Red flake out, he demonstrated how one could blend polarizing civil binaries to make a composite enemy of the bureaucrat and the barbarian to promote a domestic agenda that foreshadows arguments current in our own time.

William Jenner: The only hope for the peace of the world is a strong militarily
and economic America. And with this pact, plus our other foreign commitments, plus our federal cost of government, our local cost of government, and the projected Fair Deal that is to come, I come back to the simple economic question: Can America afford to do all of these things for ourselves and all over the world at the same time? [*striking emphasis on the last statement*] . . . Can the American taxpayer go on and pay for the socialization of Great Britain's industry? Do you expect the American taxpayer to pay

for free medicine in England? Buying toupees, fifty-dollar toupees for bald-headed Englishmen and rubber girdles for the fat women of England?

Larry Spivak: Are those the same girdles—

Jenner: And free false teeth, free babies, everything from the cradle to the grave? Is America expected to do that forever? After all, the Marshall Plan was a plan of peace. It was to help them get back on their feet economically, and they're back on their feet. Now must we go on forever?

Spivak: Well, Senator, we're not talking about the Marshall Plan; we're talking about the North Atlantic Pact.

Jenner: Well, the North Atlantic Pact is just another step in the spending program of Europe.

Just as Jenner conflated the security goals of what would become NATO with support for beleaguered Europe, so he demonstrated their danger through the effects of stimulus programs being promoted here at home. Through a process of sympathetic magic, he could boil down into a single image all of the subversive Progressive ideas into an anti-image of a free republic much like the television personality Glenn Beck would describe decades later. The enemy for Jenner, McCarthy, and their reluctant allies like Robert Taft and Everett Dirksen of Illinois, was the Progressive state—the egalitarian welfare state that sought to promote its ideals abroad in causes like the fight for Korea and at home in examples like the farm policy called the Brannan Plan. Jenner attacked that plan with more force than he did the European initiatives. For Jenner and McCarthy, Progressive social policy, both here and abroad, reeked of the taint of Karl Marx. Communism was the cudgel through which they fought the midcentury social rights activist to a stalemate and introduced a taint on any critique of concentrated economic power. But colorful as they were, Jenner and McCarthy were little more than shock troops of the anticommunist faction of the American establishment. What the prominent leaders of this establishment wanted in 1949 was a world safe for industrial property rights, and if these bad cops could keep Truman's Fair Dealers on the defensive, the good cops could propose a positive alternative for the use of American power in the cause of world freedom from the inside and in more palatable terms.

On *Meet the Press*, the good cop for global capitalism after World War II was Eric Johnston, a close associate of Larry Spivak from *American Mercury* days.[8] Johnston was a guest on *Meet the Press* three times, first in his position as president of the US Chamber of Commerce, second as the president of the Motion Picture Association of America (famous for the blacklist), and finally as Harry Truman's reluctant economic stabilization administrator in the price-control regime instituted during the Korean War. In his second appearance, on February 13, 1949, Johnston laid out his world philosophy in a disarmingly honest way that shows us the main thread of the private-enterprise philosophy that runs from the Truman administration through Reagan and on to Obama.

The logic of Johnston's worldview was derived from John Locke's *Second Treatise* and the Fifth Amendment of the US Constitution; it focused on the old British idea that had birthed the law of the seas and secure global trade. Americans hated war and wanted no empire, but they did feel a responsibility to promote secure markets in which individuals could trade without fear of the highwayman or warlord. They would fight for the rights of private property and the freedom to trade as a way of life. Since property had aggregated into vast agglomerations, this meant that to promote private property, it would be necessary to use American firepower to advance and secure the corporate rights of citizens engaged in large-scale and bureaucratically dense entrepreneurial activities. War would serve peace by combating the enemies of the private-enterprise system, and for an American foreign policy establishment facing a deeply entangled world, Hobbes and Locke had joined hands.

Arthur Sylvester (*Newark Evening News*): What do you think is going to be the impact on our country if, as you point out in your article, that short of Communism, most of the democratic countries are going toward a permanent Socialism?

Eric Johnston: Well, I think abroad we have two conflicts—two aims and they are rather in conflict. One is a political aim and that is to perpetuate democracy in all the countries of the world: the freedom of man, his sanctity and his freedom—individuality, his dignity. The second is an economic motive. And that economic motive is to, to perpetuate or to encourage private enterprise in the countries abroad. And frequently those two motives are in conflict—the economic and the political.

It seemed that private enterprise required a fair amount of public power behind it. One of Johnston's questioners was perplexed by this overt appeal to the visible hand of the US government on behalf of the interests of business.

Tom Reynolds (*Chicago Sun-Times*): What you are actually advocating is the use of American private dollars as a political weapon in the economic struggle that is going on around the world then.

Eric Johnston: If you want to call it that. I think that is some part of an analysis of it.

Arthur Sylvester: Aren't you in effect, though, taking the risk out of risk capital?

Johnston: No, because business would have all of the other ordinary business risks.

Sylvester: What are they?

Johnston: The only thing I would want to ensure them against is the extraordinary business risks of nationalization, confiscation, or destruction by war. The ordinary business risks are the same risks you run in this country.

As it was for Senator Jenner, the symbolic enemy for Johnston was the bureaucrat/barbarian blend. The goal of global corporate policy was not to rig the game for the large businesses but simply to ensure that the game was played in a fair way by everyone around the world. One had to guard honest business against the predations of both the Socialist and the basic thug. Most important, as Socialism developed as a ripe alternative to American-style capitalism, it was crucial that well-meaning bureaucrats did not get the idea that it was alright to interfere with "the right of management to manage." This right was something close to sacred in the Anglo-American tradition and was worth fighting for if need be, as indicated in an interview on February 13, 1949.

Martha Rountree: Mr. Johnston, you said you thought we should guarantee democratic governments against military aggression. Do you think the United States is prepared to go to war tomorrow?

Johnston: Oh, I think if we are going to be successful, we are going to have to guarantee democratic governments, particularly those of Western Europe, against aggression, yes.

Rountree: Well, would we fight a war tomorrow if we had to?

Johnston: I think that we should—would have to, yes.

The United States would find itself at war quite often in this quest to protect the global business system, and Eric Johnston's perspicacity helps explain the reasons for it. The US Chamber of Commerce today supports the same line but without the benefit of the symbolic clarity that Johnston's strategic position in history provided him. In the aftermath of World

War II, Johnston didn't have to try to imagine what the vital interests and symbolic enemies of the country really were; these were self-evident. As Johnston put it, "You cannot secure the maximum of freedom of the individual without private enterprise," and if this meant that one had to go to war tomorrow, then so be it.

What Kind of Sacrifices?

Larry Spivak: Now, when you say we have neglected, when you and others say, we must make sacrifices, who must make sacrifices and what kind of sacrifices? What can the people do?

J. William Fulbright: We've rarely done anything, of any significance in the social reform of these countries. I mean land reform, improving the standard of living of the ordinary people there. We always thought this could be solved by military means, and this is a misconception, and we have not devoted enough attention to understand these people and to help them come along to a more civilized mode of life.

—After the Bay of Pigs invasion, April 30, 1961

We learn as much about the deeper values of a society by the way it reacts to dramatic news of a crisis as we do from the steady rhythm of its more prosaic conversations. One of those moments in the American conversation came with the launch of the Soviet satellite *Sputnik 1* in October 1957.

The long-term reaction to the *Sputnik* launch in the *Meet the Press* archive is unambiguous. Fears of the Russian threat and Communist infiltration had reached a fever pitch and were now subsiding, but after the launch a moral panic erupted about America itself and what kind of place it had become that matched in dramatic effect anything present in the data in the immediate postwar record. Therefore, it is startling that the immediate reaction to the *Sputnik* launch was not to book Douglas MacArthur or even the missile wizard Werner von Braun (at least not yet) for the October 6, 1957, episode; instead, it was to speak with the president of Harvard University, Nathan Pusey, as if to say, if science is the problem, then education is the answer. This was as clear an expression of the opportunity-based liberalism of the era as one could find.

As if to accent the tensions among civil virtues as America took its place in the sun, the *Sputnik* episode aired just over a week after President Eisenhower ordered federal troops to Little Rock, Arkansas, on September 24 to enforce the racial desegregation order of the *Brown v. Board* decision. Because of the leading role that Harvard plays as the symbol of educational excellence, Nathan Pusey and his reactions to world events at this moment can be used as a kind of proxy for one strand of American thinking about that tangled world and its effect on the unfolding democratic project.

Pusey appeared twice on the program, as did his predecessor at Harvard, James Conant, and these snippets of the television career of a great educator say a lot about the historical education that the country would experience as it passed through the 1960s and the Vietnam era. In the time between the two appearances of October 6, 1957, and May 4, 1969, we see in Nathan Pusey's transformation the fate of Progressive America in Camelot. The confident maturity of the Nathan Pusey who stood up to the challenge of Russian space technology is quite different from the heartbreak of an aging administrator forced into a repressive role in the drama of the occupation of Harvard's University Hall by the Students for a Democratic Society. In his post-*Sputnik* appearance of 1957, Pusey was a symbol of opportunity egalitarianism and the belief that education was the key to a democratic future. By 1969, appearing just weeks prior to the triumphant moon landing that was the real climax of the *Sputnik* era, Pusey was reduced to an apt representation of one key thread of the national mood—the retreat from egalitarianism to Hobbesianism. Where once Pusey stood as an emblem of equality and opportunity, circumstances forced him into the role of guardian of the peace against uncivil usurpers.

Nathan Pusey made his debut on *Meet the Press* with America in a state of moral panic. The country had won the war against fascism just over a decade before, but since then things had not gone as planned. China had turned to Communism under Mao, the Communists had fought the Americans to a stalemate in Korea, while at home the vigorous loyalty project had culminated in the "lumberjack tactics" and the national disgrace of McCarthyite extremism. Sober American elites despaired that a free society seemed incapable of competing with the regimented authority of their Communist adversaries. Fearful Americans wondered if they were to prove a match to the "slave society" of Soviet Russia. These conditions helped set the premise of the program on the *Sputnik* reaction.

Terry Ferrer (*New York Herald Tribune*): Dr. Pusey, the launching of *Sputnik*, the Soviet earth satellite, has caused some criticism in the last day or so that a slave or Communist society has been able to beat a free society in scientific effort. Do you feel that American education is lagging behind in the sciences?

Nathan Pusey: No, I don't think that's a proper conclusion to draw from this event of the last few days. The American science is not lagging behind; it has a very diverse goal in mind. It's trying to do many things. . . .

Ferrer: Then, in other words, you attribute the fact that Russia got there first to the fact that this was not a priority for United States science.

Pusey: Yes. I think that probably the way to state it would be the other way round. That it was a crash program for Russia.

But as is ever the case in American political discourse, any conversation about a slave society comes up against the brutal reality of the remnants of the slave society that flourished right here in such recent times. Pusey was quickly forced to pivot from international concerns to domestic ones, demonstrating how projects in support of individual, social, and cultural rights could be easily aligned in an environment like that of later 1950s America.

Leon Pearson (NBC): Looking to our South for a moment, would you say how long you think it might take to accomplish what you as an educator would desire to see accomplished, that is, a complete integration in our public schools?

Pusey: I suspect a long time, and certainly the events of recent days should give us all reason to believe it's going to take quite a long time to get this thing over the country. It's a sad and tragic business. There are so many conflicting feelings and points of view among people that you can't do it overnight. On the other hand, it seems to me that one can take heart; maybe I misread it, but I would say, take heart from the behavior of the young people in the South in this last period of crisis.

Pusey argued that if a truly egalitarian society is to be created, it would bridge the chasm of race, and this would demand increasing the federal commitment to the expansion of equality through a national system of education and the opportunities it could afford everyone. During *Sputnik* week, what a free society imagined it could do was to push more forcibly toward equality so that freedom might be safeguarded.

Pusey: The Russian people clearly are putting a great deal of money, a great deal of
    energy, into the training of scientists and building up the numbers of people
    who can work in this field. I feel that our real problem in the United States is
    to recognize how important not only scientists but all teachers have become
    in our society. Actually, you can't operate any part of America today without
    people who have had a great deal of education, and I don't think we place a
    proper value on the importance of the teacher in this. We have, particularly
    since World War II, been deeply interested, generously interested, if you will,
    in research, but we haven't asked ourselves, where do the people come from
    who do the research?

There in the opening moments of America's *Sputnik* moment, one could discern the outlines of the left-of-center take on ethical possibilities. Federal power could be used to expand individual economic opportunities in ways that clung assiduously to an ethic of intergroup tolerance. Pusey's pro-government views on education represented a powerful intellectual strain and was not going to fade fast. Others would find their voice on this front as well.

Appearing in the heat of the debate that would become the Defense Education Bill, on June 29, 1958, John Gardner, president of the Carnegie Corporation, appeared to discuss a major new report on education the organization had produced, which Ned Brooks introduced as "the most important of the studies by the Rockefeller Brothers Fund" that "calls attention to the imperative need for a major overhauling to meet today's challenge from the Soviet Union." Quoting the report, Brooks echoed the regnant social rights consensus: "Our very survival and the fulfillment of our goals depend on a solution of our educational problems." The solution that national elites were calling for involved massive reorganization of the American approach to education, involving difficult cultural change, as the Little Rock stand-off demonstrated, but also institutional adaptation to opportunity gaps. Little wonder that the slogan "a mind is a terrible thing to waste" would come to encapsulate it.

Dominant as this perspective was, not everyone was comfortable that the role of government had been validated in this way, least among them Larry Spivak. A sequence from that June 29 show demonstrates just how uncomfortable this confluence of social and cultural liberalism was for classical liberals to accept at the time.

Larry Spivak: Aren't you going to make it harder than ever to solve it if you keep handing out more money? Why don't you force the community to solve their problem? If they're not going to get more money from the federal government, they're going to have to solve the problem. They are never going to solve it with more money, do you think?

John Gardner: Yes, I do think they will. I'm all for not letting the patient die while you argue over his stubbornness. I think that you give the schools money and also hold them to standards.

Terry Ferrer (*New York Herald Tribune*): The communities, you say, should be helped; however, recent statistics show that, for example, in New York State, half of the school bonds have been voted down in the last half of 1957. So if the community refuses to appropriate the money, where is it going to get it? From the federal government? It's out of one pocket or out of the other, isn't it?

Gardner: It is, and I think it should be emphasized that the school districts receive the overwhelming amount of their money from the property tax, and tax experts, as I am sure you know, do not regard the property tax as a politically convenient or easy way to get money, and the school districts have to get it by popular approval. They have a very difficult tax road to follow.

As Gardner told the story, the need was to disassociate the quality of a school from the property values of the houses in the neighborhood around it. This was a bridge too far for the small-government liberal who found an awkward ally to oppose this expansion of federal power in education in the figure of the racial segregationist. Although there were movements toward a more centralized taxing authority for the education system, the furor over the local control of schools allowed for change only at a fairly slow pace, even in the face of Hobbesian threats to national survival.

If the joint forces of liberty and intolerance enjoyed guerrilla success in stalling the opportunity agenda of the *Sputnik* moment, the egalitarian liberal establishment was still quite capable of producing strident calls for progressive and egalitarian change that carried impeccable security credentials. In those days, the war-making vulcans of the day were less inclined to the libertarian persuasion than they were the egalitarian. One powerful example can be found in a January 13, 1960, appearance by the father of the nuclear submarine, Hyman Rickover, one of Jimmy Carter's commanding officers in the navy, who was then leading a kind of personal campaign for education standards.

James Reston (*New York Times*): What do you do about the kids that come out of good homes and where there is agitation for standards of excellence in the family, intellectually, and who go to good universities, and then they use this excellence in very secondary endeavors, whereas in Russia, which you are always quoting, they direct their brains to the place where the state needs those brains the most? What do you do about this problem?

Hyman Rickover: We can do the same thing here without state compulsion, if our values were not such that we gave material possession such a high place in our scheme of things—if we were taught now that this is really an affluent society where everybody has enough to get along on, that there are many other things in life besides possessions, filling our homes with new things. Every day the nursery rhymes on TV and radio urge us to buy new things. If we would learn that these things are thrown into the ashcan in a couple of years but what you put in a child's mind stays there forever, if we realize that the intellectual life, the life of the mind, is just as important as getting money and material things, I believe many of these youngsters would go on to intellectual endeavors.

Nathan Pusey was the representative of social rights liberalism as the nation passed the test of its *Sputnik* moment, but another fitting signal of the era is the decorated general Maxwell Taylor. Taylor was one of those near-great military figures, known well by those who shared the epoch with him, if largely forgotten by those born later. He is remembered neither as a villain in American history nor, to his chagrin, as one of its heroes. Taylor had distinguished himself in World War II and was army chief of staff in the Korean War. By the late 1950s he was one of those revered American tribunes who must have served as inspiration for C. Wright Mills as he penned *The Power Elite*.[9] Nathan Pusey appeared on the program that marked the reaction to the civil rights crisis in Little Rock, Arkansas, but it was Taylor whom President Eisenhower had ordered to command the 101st Airborne Division to enforce federal court orders to desegregate Little Rock's Central High School. No bit player, Taylor appeared on the program four times over a span roughly equal to Pusey's, and the grade of his descent is similar. If Pusey represented the nation's loss of innocence in the period, Taylor represented its humbling.

Taylor first appeared on *Meet the Press* on May 12, 1957, to describe how the modern military was to reorganize as it learned how to work its burgeoning stores of atomic weapons into its tactical repertoire. The goal was to resolve what would be hyped as the "missile gap" in the upcoming election. His last appearance was on March 31, 1968, amid wild speculation about what the president—to whom Taylor had provided crucial advice throughout the Vietnam War—would say in a nationally televised speech that night. We may have forgotten Taylor but will never forget what President Lyndon Johnson had to say, because it was then that Johnson announced, "I shall not seek, and I will not accept, the nomination of my party for another term as your president," effectively signaling his surrender to the Vietnam War and with it his legacy as the architect of the Great Society.

If a focus on social reform and educational investment was one of the transformative reactions to the *Sputnik* shock, so, too, was an investment in missile technology and atomic weaponry that would symbolically crescendo in the moonwalk of Neil Armstrong in 1969. It was against the background of a country intent on achieving superiority in space and missile technology that Maxwell Taylor entered the *Meet the Press* conversation in the spring of 1957.

Ned Brooks (moderator): Welcome once again to *Meet the Press*. This week we
join in a salute to the armed forces, and our guest is the chief of staff of the
United States Army, General Maxwell Taylor. At a time when all military
methods are undergoing radical changes, General Taylor has the responsibility for building the army of the atomic age.

. . .

Richard Wilson (Cowles Publications): General Taylor, as Mr. Brooks has said, the
trend in military forces seems to be toward smaller armies equipped with
nuclear weapons and guided missiles. I wonder if you can tell us whether in
the case of the United States these smaller weapons now exist in sufficient
quantity to create a really effective army on a nuclear basis.

Maxwell Taylor: We certainly have made great progress in recent years in developing atomic weapons adaptable to army requirements, and, as you know, we
are proceeding very rapidly in absorbing these new weapons into our current
structures. Our divisions are now being reorganized so that they will have
within them weapons that can fire atomic weapons on the atomic battlefield.

The first Taylor interview is striking in that it demonstrates how confident and even hardheaded were the top leaders of the American military in this pre-*Sputnik* moment. The accommodation to "the atomic battlefield" and the tactical use of nuclear weapons that Taylor advocates reveal that his views were not different in kind from those of figures like Curtis LeMay, who only a decade later would be ripe targets for *Dr. Strangelove*–type spoofs. The victory for freedom would be hard fought, requiring sacrifices that in retrospect seem almost apocalyptic.

Martin Agronsky (NBC News): General, do you think if you fight this limited nuclear war, which you say you must fight if we get into a Korea-type war—

Maxwell Taylor: Must be able to fight.

Agronsky: Must be able to fight, sir. Do you feel that could be confined to a limited war; wouldn't that almost automatically trigger off the larger nuclear war? Isn't that a real danger?

Taylor: It is a real danger, Mr. Agronsky, and we will never know it until the time comes. I still say we have to go on the battlefield prepared to use nuclear weapons.

In other words, in the fight for private enterprise all options were on the table. And beyond the catastrophic potential of the new realities of warfare, there were the concomitant realities of new costs that would come with the military-industrial complex. Conservatives might yearn for a time when government could be reduced to the size it once was before America became the celebrated "bulwark of freedom," but it was not clear when that time might come.

Richard Wilson (Cowles Publications): Then, if I understand your implications correctly, the time is just not near when there could be a substantial reduction in the cost of the armed forces.

Taylor: I cannot foresee one, Mr. Wilson.

Wilson: This ties very directly with what President Eisenhower said the other day when he said that there had to be a very, very great easing of the international tension before this country could look forward to a reduction of taxes. But from what you have said, whether the tension decreases or increases, it would be very difficult to look forward to a decrease in taxes.

Taylor: Of course, the question of decrease in tensions is really the catch, isn't it? To what extent can we really depend upon the peaceful intentions of the Soviet

> bloc? I, at this moment sitting here, cannot foresee the day when we can af-
> ford to disarm, counting on a decrease in tension.

As Oliver Wendell Holmes had argued, taxes were the price of civilized society, but civilization in Taylor's purview was predicated upon the reduction of international tensions as represented by the Communist threat. As tensions only increased over the course of the 1960s—Berlin, the Cuban missile crisis, and the Vietnam War—the commonsense opportunity agenda championed by Harvard's president and so many other establishment liberals would come up against its limits before it could reach its egalitarian goals.

When General Taylor appeared on *Meet the Press* on August 8, 1965, as the US ambassador to South Vietnam, he returned both with bad news on the state of the Vietnamese war effort and a sense of optimism because the argument he had consistently pushed to escalate the conflict seemed now to carry weight with President Johnson.

Larry Spivak: General Taylor, this week in private you gave the president and his senior advisers your conclusions on the serious and optimistic aspects of the situation in Vietnam. . . . And what do you consider the one or two most optimistic aspects of the situation there, if any?

Maxwell Taylor: By far the most optimistic element in the situation is the new broadened and deepened United States commitment to this country, indicated by the president's announcement of his intention to send additional forces to South Vietnam. This gave enormous lift to all of us, Americans, Vietnamese, all friends of South Vietnam, when this announcement was made.

                              . . .

Spivak: We will have about 125,000 American troops there by the end of this year. Some estimates say that we may need 300,000 to 400,000. Do those estimates meet with your understanding also?

Taylor: No, I would certainly not suggest the need for anything like 300,000 to 400,000. Bear in mind that we are really filling a gap in the indigenous Vietnamese forces by putting in our own combat ground troops.

                              . . .

Spivak: General, one more question: The American people are being told we are in for a very long war. Do you think that too from your experience of a year?

Taylor: It will be a long pull, yes, sir.

As is obvious in retrospect, the long, hard slog through South Vietnam did not turn out in a way that validated the optimism that General Taylor demonstrated in late 1965. By the time of Taylor's last *Meet the Press* appearance on March 31, 1968, the massive domestic reaction to the failing war effort, exacerbated by McCarthyite reactions, had poisoned the political atmosphere on the left to the point that Johnson's vision of the Great Society seemed to be evaporating before his eyes. When Taylor appeared on the program for the last time, Eugene McCarthy had nearly won the Democratic Primary in New Hampshire and Robert Kennedy had turned against the war. The speech given that night punctuated an era, closing with Johnson's famous Shermanesque statement on abdication.

On abdication day, the face the president chose to represent him on the Sunday-morning show, on which Johnson did not like appearing but couldn't help watching, was again General Maxwell Taylor, this time serving as special consultant to the president and president of the Institute for Defense Analyses. Unapologetic as ever, he conveyed the can-do spirit of the Hobbesian camp of the liberal establishment whose project to make the world safe for democracy had just suffered a damaging blow.

Robert Goralski (NBC News): General, a lot of people are trying to anticipate what disclosures the president will make tonight regarding Vietnam. Would you like to anticipate?

Maxwell Taylor: I don't think I would like to undertake to scoop the president, thank you.

Goralski: Sir, there has been a great deal of talk, of course, about a possible shift in basic strategy in Vietnam. Do you think a basic, fundamental change in strategy is called for at this time?

Taylor: I think we are seeing a fundamental change of strategy on the other side. I think the so-called Tet offensive was clearly a reversal of performance in the strategic area by the enemy, and consequently I think we have to adjust to that situation. . . . It certainly does justify a very careful rethinking of what we are doing in Vietnam.

. . .

Marquis Childs (*St. Louis Post-Dispatch*): You have been very closely associated with the strategy that has seen a buildup to, I believe it is 510,000 troops, today. Do you think that has been a successful strategy, General?

Taylor: Yes, I do. I think it responded to the three acts of escalation on the other
side, which I mentioned in response to Mr. Goralski, indispensable acts
unless we were going to give up on our basic objective of a free, independent
South Vietnam able to choose its own way of life.

It was as if the loss of Vietnam were a loss of America itself. Conflict abroad
had become an existential test of the principle of freedom. Although General Taylor, one of the men for whom the term "group think" was coined,
could not see it, the home front had already broken. Vietnam proved to
be catastrophic, and the country required decades of discourse to heal the
wounds to its honor and pride brought on by this unambiguous failure.

One can't help thinking that things could have been different. In his
appearance in 1960, Admiral Rickover, himself the inventor of the tip of
the spear of nuclear superiority, had responded to the two big challenges of
the *Sputnik* era by favoring an approach that placed social sacrifice in favor
of mass education over military sacrifice in favor of global superiority.

Larry Spivak: Admiral, do you think we are in a life-and-death struggle with the
Soviet Union?

Hyman Rickover: Why, of course, we are.

Spivak: And do you think education or military defense is more important in that
life-and-death struggle at the present time?

Rickover: Education is more important because military developments are transitory. They change every year or so, but education is permanent.

Sadly, the opportunity society imagined by the likes of Hyman Rickover
would not survive the pursuit of "the maximum of freedom" advocated by
the other side. Not all was lost for this cause. There had been a massive expansion of the federal role in education through the education initiatives
and the new role played by the National Science Foundation. Colleges
and universities had become larger and more vibrant places than they had
once been, and indices of economic inequality kept trending in the right
direction through the late 1960s into the 1970s.

But the era of social rights and the heyday of equality were largely
over. True, there was a new vibrancy in higher education, but much of
its energy was being directed against the war effort in Vietnam, and the
left wing of the democratic project was tearing itself off the bird. Student
riots and campus protests were widespread and intensifying, and street
protest and direct action appeared ever more legitimate than voting for

representatives of the two major political parties, who were involved in a contest to demonstrate which side was the true foreign policy realist. These intellectual currents made their way steadily to Harvard, which forced a less-than-graceful exit from America's oldest university for a man who had done much to promote the Progressive agenda that made the protests possible. The opportunity society exited in 1969 with him.

Larry Spivak: Dr. Pusey, you have come in for great criticism because you called the police to clear out University Hall. Now with the benefit of hindsight and for the benefit of other university presidents who may be in the same position as you were, do you really think that was the best way of handling such a situation?

Nathan Pusey: I did at the time, and I must say I still do, but you have to recognize that it was one of various possible alternatives. The others just seemed clearly to be more productive of long-range harm than calling the police at the time.

. . .

Spivak: [Now that] all this thing is over with at Harvard University, you have had a little time to put the whole thing in perspective. What do you now consider the issue which the university and the students and the faculty and the community face?

Pusey: To me the issue is quite plain. It is really a matter of tactics and what are acceptable tactics and not acceptable. There are many issues that deserve to be discussed, and they are troublesome. There is no denying that, but in the university community you simply cannot resort to force or coercion to try to have things your way without destroying the very nature of the university itself. This is what we have been trying to say, that there has to be a line . . . yet some small group of students keep pressing and pressing and pressing and do not accept the notion that you cannot use violent and disruptive tactics. I think myself that these people know what they are doing, and they are not interested in keeping the university alive as a place for free discussion. But that really is the issue: it is whether the university can preserve its nature and go about its business or whether it is going to become just a scene for politicking and squabbling.

What Pusey said of the nation's leading university was true for the nation itself. In the brief encounters we had with Nathan Pusey and Maxwell Taylor on this national stage, we can see key lessons of the American encounter with global leadership. It was a period of daring and dreaming with no shortage of disaster. The Kennedy inaugural address of January

20, 1961, crystallized the creed, "Let every nation know . . . that we shall pay any price, bear any burden, meet any hardship, support any friend, oppose any foe, to assure the survival and the success of liberty," but the challenge was to configure a free society to do it. As it turns out, neither Pusey nor Taylor had the answer, which the country struggled to find long after they departed the scene, when Jimmy Carter became president of the United States, thus opening a new chapter in the global adventure of American ideals.

The Principles of Human Rights and Civil Rights

I think the differences among our ideological categories of people have been removed; conservatives quite often in the past have been stigmatized by racism. That is no longer the case. I think many conservative people now are fully committed to the principles of human rights and civil rights and equality of opportunity.

—Jimmy Carter, July 11, 1976

In a sense, foreign policy after Vietnam may be thought of as a dialogue between Jimmy Carter and Ronald Reagan: post-Vietnam Americans instinctively side with the latter, while they always listen to conscientious appeals of the former. As a result of the Iranian hostage crisis and the economic slump that resulted from soaring oil prices, Jimmy Carter's presidency is now remembered as a kind of failure to be used as a symbolic shillelagh against future Democrats, and yet Carter's legacy would prove profoundly transformative. Carter's breakthrough in foreign policy, as unpopular and precocious in that domain as was Johnson's in domestic affairs, harnessed in the long run the ideological energies of the civil rights movement to a global cause.

It was Reagan whom we would remember as the victor in the Cold War, but Carter's human rights agenda provided the shadow theme of the era that dogged Reagan and his descendants. Carter's tortured path through history from "failed" president to "successful" ex-president is a result of the same ideological conditions that troubled his predecessor, Lyndon Johnson. If Americans were not entirely comfortable with a multicultural policy of social transformation at home, they were less so abroad. The ready equation of the Negro and the Viet Cong as agents of democratic revolution was hard for Lockean liberals and their supremacist allies to recognize. The typical American preferred the old ideas of victory for democracy in an Anglo-American frame and rationalized their otherwise fuzzy foreign policy ideas with what we now call American exceptionalism; the result was that when it was time to cast Ronald Reagan in the national drama, he came off like a founding father. Reagan undoubtedly trounced Carter's legacy in the short term, but because Carter's moral imagination was anchored in the global realities of cultural diversity and historic oppression, no amount of optimistic spin would smooth over the problems to which he drew attention like no one had before him.

Even though Richard Nixon distinguished himself in the realm of foreign policy, the big discursive shift in the foreign policy debate awaited Jimmy Carter. Nixon's foreign policy was sensible, breathtaking, and occasionally cruel. It was marked by the resurgent academic realism of Hans Morgenthau and Henry Kissinger and aggressive uses of power politics in places like Chile and Cambodia that still make us blanch. Carter had his realists on staff, too, as Zbigniew Brzezinski could attest, but his approach to the world was distinctive in his return to the plane of big ideas and the principles of ethical global stewardship that had been missing since Kennedy's assassination. Carter was not known for his foreign policy ideas before he took office, but he certainly was when he left it. He promoted an artful blend of antisupremacist ideas, American bromide, and postcolonial politics that he branded "human rights."[10]

The human rights doctrine was intended as a return to principled tactics in the fight with the Soviet Union, but it was much more than that in its rhetorical dimensions. Human rights diplomacy established a new mythos of the American idea in world politics. Under pressure from advisers like the civil rights icon Andrew Young, Carter deftly adapted the lessons of domestic racial conflict to the international scene. Few could quibble with the principle of human rights, but the meaning of the term was cast in the same forge as the contemporary articulation of civil rights. The focus of concern was directed toward the abuses of power of a dominant culture and the rights of the abused to seek redress for wrongs both novel and established. In practice, global human rights policy served as a major multicultural reframe of the democracy agenda that had long been a part the idealistic strain of American international relations. Given Carter's southern distaste for assertive uses of federal authority, he pivoted away from the social rights liberalism of his mentor Hyman Rickover toward a cultural rights reinterpretation of the American political tradition in world affairs. And his was an idea whose time would come. Tracing a circuitous path from the international sphere to the domestic and back again, Carter's metaphor of human rights as civil rights served as a continuous check on the excesses of American intervention in the Reagan era and beyond.

Despite the best efforts of private-enterprise apologists in the mold of Eric Johnston, the global human rights paradigm broadened the rhetorical span of global civil discourse in a way that maintained an exceptional role for the United States. In a difficult period of world history, Jimmy Carter did something remarkable and dangerous; he made himself the generalized instrument of the civil rights movement in a new democratic synthesis that transcended the specific origins of the perspective. The international human rights agenda that Carter adopted was responsive to the multicultural impulse demanded by scores of new nations emerging from their tutelage, but his efforts to channel the civil rights worldview into a human rights position to counter Communism was itself countered by the kind of organized skepticism and strategic scorn that can set the narrative for a generation. Jimmy Carter's gambit on global tolerance met the hard realities of a confluence of traditional small government liberal ideas that made it ever more difficult for any succeeding president to attempt to play the role of a Martin Luther King of the global south.

Carter's global vision was transformative and was surely a complex product of his life experience, but its proximate source and flavor might be traced to a single person, the Atlanta-based member of King's Southern Christian Leadership Council that Carter named as ambassador to the United Nations, Andrew Young. We can find no better symbol of how the Carter administration channeled the moral force of the multicultural left toward the challenge of developing a framework for the projection of American power in the cause of global rights than Young. Young, a civil rights leader who was on the balcony with Dr. King on April 4, 1968, when he was assassinated, who had interests in global affairs and impeccable credentials as a critic of American bigotry in all its forms, first appeared on *Meet the Press* in July 1976. In this episode, his role was the community healer who could vouch for Jimmy Carter's capacity to match him on the white side of the racial divide. Young was to Carter as Frederick Douglass was to Abraham Lincoln, a kind of outsider-equal who could provide the moral compass for the project of racial reconciliation. As UN ambassador he played a large role in shepherding a grounding rationale for American foreign policy that could address the worldwide problems of bigotry and ethnic marginalization. In that appearance just two weeks after the bicentennial of the Declaration of Independence, Young made the case for a deracialized domestic human rights agenda that would later prove to have global implications.

Douglas Kiker (NBC News): Mr. Young, you are described as one of Jimmy Carter's closest political associates; you are described as his chief black adviser. He has won the nomination. What advice are you giving him?

Andrew Young: Keep running and running hard. . . .

Kiker: You and others have claimed the black vote in the election for Governor Carter. If he does get that vote in the general election, as a black leader, what do you think that Governor Carter would owe to the American black people in return?

Young: Let me say that I think that Governor Carter owes the people of America something. He owes them good government; he owes them a sensitive response to the problems of the people of America, all of the people of America. I think one of the things you see how is that there are almost no specifically black problems, that black people get sick and have trouble paying the hospital bill, but so do the white people in a greater majority—in larger numbers than blacks. So that the things like health insurance are kind of deracialized issues. I think basically what black voters want is an end to a kind of lethargic economy, job opportunities, and a part of the American dream.

In forging his new synthesis, Young was taking a gamble that he could pair with Carter to heal the wounds of the civil rights era in the United States, while at the same time translating its ideals into a set of universal standards that could apply to people all over the world. This was Martin Luther King's ideal of the beloved community on a global stage. If there were no specifically black problems, then there were no problems that were specifically American problems. If there were no specifically American problems, the antisupremacist multicultural rights that had been tested in the crucible of the civil rights movement should apply to all the oppressed peoples around the world. Young appeared again on *Meet the Press* on June 3, 1979:

Andrew Young: You know, I didn't get in this job thinking I was going to win every battle. All I got in saying was, I would have an opportunity to continue the struggle. I think there will be a continued struggle in this, regardless of what the president decides.

Young's talent was to weave a universalistic human rights agenda into the narrative of respect and interdependence focused on particular abuses that was consistent with his civil rights past. In other words, he remained a national civil rights leader but became one fighting for the same cause worldwide.

Anthony Lewis (*New York Times*): Mr. Ambassador, you spoke to Mr. Monroe just now about the political realities in this country on Rhodesia, which you said had become clearer. It seems that, in fact, there has been a movement in the last few months toward Bishop Muzorewa, Mr. Smith, and so on. Were you suggesting something else, perhaps feeling in the black community?

Young: . . . I think we are now very hard-pressed to realize that the United States is really in an interdependent relationship with the entire world. We can deal as friends and as partners, but we have to deal on terms of mutual respect, and I think that to look at Rhodesia without considering the way everybody else in the African situation looks at it, not to consider the response of the nonaligned movement meeting in Colombo this week is to, I think, not take the full picture into perspective. I think that is the burden that is upon the president.

Timely and pressing as it was, the multicultural impulse did not win in every battle and faced challenges abroad as it did at home. Caught up in the narrative complexities of busing and affirmative action struggles, conservative whites were reluctant to embrace something overseas that they did not support right here. They surged back to power, many transforming themselves into Reagan Democrats in the process. Democratic leaders after Carter would thereafter fight for cultural justice just as they had once fought for economic opportunity a generation before. Carter had served as a pivot for the liberal narrative. It is not that Carter had jettisoned the class politics of the New Deal era, but he had helped to shift the accent of the liberal imaginary from equality to tolerance.[11]

The results of the Carter/Young pivot were pyrotechnic. Carter brokered a peace between formerly intractable enemies Israel and Egypt and cemented a new kind of democratic politics that was not simply about voting or economic opportunity. The global human rights agenda had multicultural roots that promoted interethnic conciliation as a central part of his new democratic project. Just as Carter imagined more humility among whites at home, he imagined humility among Americans abroad. The formula was common sense plus tolerance, inclusion, and diversity in international affairs. It was not Carter's lot in life to be remembered for his accomplishments in office, but on the level of ideas, his influence was considerable and long lasting. Andrew Young was eventually forced to resign from the Carter administration for having met with representatives of the Palestine Liberation Organization (PLO) against explicit government policy, but his impact on the foreign policy mood was decisive. It provided those on the American left with a satisfying answer to questions about their democratic identities after Vietnam and provided the world with a newly legitimated multicultural rhetoric through which to redress past evils. The legacy of Russian authoritarianism had stymied the liberal fight against bigwigs with the bogeyman of Marxist Communism, but America could still share its recent experience in overcoming bigotry with the riven world. As America passed through the bicentennial of its founding revolution, it was still playing out the implications of another revolution in cultural affairs that had produced in Andrew Young one of its most successful sons. When he reflected on these experiences on July 21, 1996, he put it as follows:

Andrew Young: I think what we were saying was—to the world—this is how we got here. We got to this point because of Martin Luther King's emphasis on nonviolence, on the emphasis on human rights growing out of Martin Luther King with Jimmy Carter, and these are messages we want to share with the world.

But what the human rights pivot added for the intellectual political culture on the left, it more than subtracted on the center right. Lockean liberals, racist or not, could not tell heads from tails when it came to this notion of group rights.[12] Where Alexis de Tocqueville had spoken of individualism as a fault, Americans of the "me generation" had elevated it to a sacred principle. The very idea that groups, whether considered in occupational or ethnic categories, could be recognized in democratic theory seemed heretical and dim-witted. This context helps make sense of an otherwise odd claim made by Howard Jarvis on June 18, 1978, in an appearance dedicated to the famous property tax revolt in California and explains why his Proposition 13 was as popular as it was.

Howard Jarvis: You hear the president talking all over this world about human rights, but he never says what they are. And the reason I think he doesn't say what they are is that so many countries we are trying to cozy up to don't have property rights, but we found out in the United States—and the people who wrote the Constitution of the United States said the people of the United States shall be protected in their life, liberty, and property; they didn't say "life, liberty and welfare," or "life, liberty and food stamps." They said "life, liberty and property." The ownership of property and the right of free people to acquire property is the most important part of human rights, and without that right we don't have any other right.

Or why George H. W. Bush could make a related jab at the human rights agenda when the humiliation of the American hostage crisis helped fan his presidential aspirations:

George H. W. Bush: Now what has happened? Our human rights people pushing for change . . . we are in an imperfect world. What we have got to do is spell out our interest in human rights, but not go in there and slap our friends around and be silent in the face of those adversary countries where we know we can't do anything about it.

It was not the problem of human rights violations that made conservatives uncomfortable; it was the human rights agenda that "goes in there and pushes way beyond what is required for change" that they condemned. If this sounds strangely reminiscent of the battles of the civil rights legislation of the previous decade, it should, but not because simple racism was the common cause. Instead, we see at work here two conceptions of democratic theory, one that recognizes the abuses of power of "the One" and another that fears more the abuses of "the Many," one based on antigovernment rhetoric and the other on antisupremacism. As post-Vietnam liberals riffed on variations of the multicultural theme, conservatives rediscovered the virtues and power of the tradition of classical liberalism.

The key to decoding dysfunction in this period can be found in the clash of liberal traditions that occurred. Given the small differences in what Republicans concretely proposed to do in a place like Iran, it was not so much the content of the foreign policy that wore on American aspirations but the way these conflicts were imagined and conceptualized. George H. W. Bush wanted leadership in America that would "reawaken a sense of pride by putting stars in the eyes of the kids in this country." Pop culture Lockeans like Howard Jarvis cared about the classical rights of property. For them, any leftie call for more multicultural rights had a ready answer—more market freedom. What applied in California was all the more applicable in Tanzania. Cultural and racial anxieties were linked with the positive vision for social change that Barry Goldwater had proposed in the form of victory for freedom. As in that fraught environment of the 1960s, liberal solutions were proposed in a spirit that transcended race in a formal way, but also in a way that could channel racial anxiety into legitimated forms of expression.

A policy that puts stars in the eyes is one that can trace the tribal story back to mythological time. It is what the conflict theorist John Paul Lederach describes as an unbroken story.[13] In November 1961, just days after John F. Kennedy provided his own Democratic stars-in-the-eyes speech on the "twilight struggle" between freedom and Communism, Barry Goldwater appeared on *Meet the Press* and developed an argument that later became the centerpiece of the Reagan revolution.

Earl Mazo (*New York Herald Tribune*): Senator, in his Seattle speech, President Kennedy condemned what he called the "frustrated extremists who cannot bear the long twilight struggle against Communists." Are you one of those "frustrated extremists"? What is your reaction to that?

Barry Goldwater: No, I am not a frustrated extremist. I think that had the president realized that he had one word in his statement right, he would have gone ahead and made the American people feel a little better who have that feeling of frustration. Americans are frustrated. . . . We have an enemy in this world, and the enemy is Communism. I think if the American people were told that we are going to win over Communism, no matter how long it took or how much it took or what it took, this feeling of frustration would disappear. We hear these eloquent phrases, but we are never told what they mean or what the purpose—what is America's purpose today?

After Vietnam and the new multicultural human rights synthesis supplied by Jimmy Carter, frustrated extremism was reborn as a kind of muscular liberalism in the classical mold. It was labeled "conservatism," but at its core one found more there of the liberal Richard Cobden than the conservative Edmund Burke. As Louis Hartz had argued, American conservatives were in fact small government liberals in disguise in foreign as well as domestic policy. Jack Kennedy's international social rights agenda had collapsed, and Goldwaterism was poised for a comeback. Americans were tired of backing down in their fight for freedom around the world, and even though they were convinced of the evils of intolerance, they were not entirely convinced that governments should take a more active role in promoting global diversity.

Then came the Iranian hostage crisis, and once again, all nuance drained from the American foreign policy conversation. When the Iranian foreign minister appeared on *Meet the Press* to defend his regime's arrests of members of the American embassy in early December, he channeled a global reform agenda that is reminiscent of Frederick Douglass's reflections on slavery and the Fourth of July in the United States absent the "quailing sensation" that Douglass felt in delivering it.[14]

Morton Kondracke (*New Republic*): Does the government of Iran respect international law? These forums, after all, are established in the international community. There is law involved here; there is a treaty involved between the United States and Iran, whereby differences between us can be settled at the World Court. Why create a nonlegal panel to do this sort of thing? Why not obey international law?

Sadegh Ghotbzadeh: It is astonishing that you constantly talk about the legality of things, the legal things, the laws, the orders, the international laws, international treaties that—since twenty-five years at least in Iran and for years, probably one hundred years, in Latin America, the United States government has violated every principle of the human laws and international law and international orders, and now all of a sudden they remember that there is somewhere around the world in some books, there are some laws that somebody has got to respect, but not the United States. The question is, where were you in the past twenty-four or twenty-five years to question the American government, why they have violated all these international laws, interfering in Iranian affairs, to put the tortures, to train the torturers—according to international laws to interfere in our affairs, to put the shah in the throne, to make a coup d'état against the government, to name practically all the ministers over there and to plunder the countries where—all according to international laws, and this time, only this time you all of a sudden remember there is someplace international laws are to be observed. That is a little astonishing to me.

This excoriating attack on the very idea of American liberalism in global affairs was painful and incendiary. Not only did it highlight American failure but it also mocked the American ideal. Carter's reputation would not survive the fire. The humiliation derived from these kinds of insults together with a failed rescue effort of the American hostages influenced the national foreign policy debate for decades. On July 27, 1958, May Craig had asked Kwame Nkrumah, the leader of Ghana, "Do you regard the United States as the shield of the free world? That is the way we regard ourselves. We have helped everybody." In 1979, the Iranian foreign minister could appear on American national television and accuse the country of being "the safe place for all these criminals and dictators who in the name of the United States do whatever they want in a country." By the end of the 1980 campaign, Ronald Reagan was describing Vietnam as "a noble cause,"[15] and Zbigniew Brzezinski was warning the Iranians: "Do not scoff at American power." The global human rights agenda that Andrew Young had shepherded from Martin Luther King's street protests into the core of the Carter Doctrine was on the ropes. But like the civil rights movement that had inspired it, it would have a lasting influence, even if only at times as a constraint on future projections of that American power around the world.[16]

Back on the Victory Trail

[We] need to get back on the victory trail if we are going to restore balance between the two parties. . . . I set out and for several months have been traveling around the state talking to people, answering questions, asking questions to find out whether there was an acceptability on the part of the people, and that is why I'm running.

—Ronald Reagan, January 9, 1966

All foreign policy after Vietnam has on some level been reduced to a single question: How can America act in a complex world as a force for freedom? Jimmy Carter supplied the Democratic Party's answer: America could stand against abuses of government power, while simultaneously standing against the institutions that supported cultural bigotry without making much of a fuss about concentrated economic power along the way. In this way Carter extended the lessons taught by the civil rights movement to a world of competing differences and complex histories of injustice and marginalization. But this is rather subtle fare; the conservative answer was more straightforward. The core of the perspective came not from a reformulation of democratic thinking after the disaster in Vietnam but rather from a return to Goldwater's muscular, laissez-faire anticommunism that he articulated before, as evidenced by this exchange from January 5, 1964.

Robert MacNeil (NBC News): You say, "Why not victory over the evils of Communism?" Could you explain what victory means in the Cold War context?

Barry Goldwater: Very simply—and I like to be simple—it doesn't mean defeat. The only alternative to defeat is victory. The problem we have in the world is a simple problem . . . will we be slaves ten, twenty years from now, or will we be free, and this applies to the whole world. And if the tentacles of Communism continue to spread across the world, then I am afraid that the answer is going to be slavery.

And the line between Barry Goldwater and Ronald Reagan was not hard to draw. Something of the Sarah Palin of his time, Reagan was ridiculed as a leader who was naïve at best and dangerous at worst, who spent much of his debut convincing the country that he was not a member of the reactionary John Birch Society. Martin Luther King had said that the arc of history is long and bends toward justice; we might say of Reagan that the arc of his biography was long but it bent toward victory. Even so, his victories came after much struggle and toil.

Reagan never had an easy time on *Meet the Press* either in his rise or during his reign. We can see the general tone in his first encounter with Larry Spivak on January 9, 1966.

Larry Spivak: Mr. Reagan, it is being said and written—this, for example, came out of the *Washington Post* this morning, and I would like to read it to you. It says your campaign "is an attempt to turn an actor into a believable candidate for governor and to make voters forget your right-wing views." You are going to have to meet that all through the campaign. How do you plan to counter such attacks?

Ronald Reagan: I think by simply telling the truth. If people listen to where I stand on the issues—and they will have every chance to find out where I stand, because I intend at every public appearance to allow my listeners to ask me questions—I think they will find out that this is a false image that is being created, or that they are attempting to create, with regard to me. That seems to be the modern dialogue in politics anymore, not to dispute you on what you honestly believe but to create a false image, to invest you with beliefs that aren't yours. As I say, I think the people, if they will listen to me, will find out the false image doesn't stand up.

Reagan was a deft critic of false images when they worked against him, but when they turned to his advantage, few could exploit "the modern dialogue" with greater force. Reagan had what even his adversaries would describe as the gift of symbolism, which also meant that he was a master of context. He could take the chance event and quickly turn it into a sound bite or a full-fledged moral tale. This was true of his "there you go again" quip to Carter in an important election debate and also of his very image, which conformed to the unspoken anxieties of the American people. As part of the context of his rise to power, the following commercial was played as he appeared on September 11, 1966, in a gubernatorial debate with incumbent governor Pat Brown.

Monday on NBC week, *The Road West*. [*man on rearing horse with rifle*] Man's greatest challenge, a journey that could make an ordinary man a hero or destroy him. Ben Pride took the challenge, and with his family sought out the rich fertile soil of the western plains. Not all was peace and freedom, however, and the road was often filled with danger and heartbreaking setbacks, and sometimes it was necessary to move on and build again.

To the television audience, Ben Pride may as well have been Ronald Reagan as he faced off against the less charismatic Brown in a *Meet the Press* debate that went as well for him as the later debate with Carter would. In fact, he might have been Ben Pride for the whole of his career, a frontier hero who could repair the story of America. People were so convinced that Reagan was not a person that they had to take seriously that he managed to clear the low bar that others set for him on policy matters while clearing new heights in semiotic presentation. For many, he fit the bill: Americans ate him up even as critics tore him down.

When he was finally elected president, to the horror of the cognoscenti, the ideological pressures on his administration and supporters were intense. His chief of staff, Howard Baker, appeared in an awkward interview amid concerns that Reagan's choice for secretary of state, Alexander Haig, was tainted because of secret tapes of his role in the Watergate scandal. When Haig himself appeared on March 29, 1981, he was confident and powerful in his first interview as secretary of state largely because he was managing a national crisis concerning a threat of a Soviet invasion of Poland. By the next day, he was subject to widespread ridicule for his claim that he was in charge at the White House after the president had been shot at the Washington Hilton. Reagan's first UN ambassador, Jeane Kirkpatrick (who will play a central role in our story), was asked on *Meet the Press* on April 5, 1981, if the administration was "as concerned with right-wing violence as it is with left-wing violence" in El Salvador, to which she gave a measured, complex response that was uncharacteristic of Barry Goldwater's appeal to "simple ideas." She was also asked if she was complicit in an attempt to discredit American nuns who had been murdered in that country the previous year. In May 1981, President Reagan's nominee to head the human rights post created by Jimmy Carter, Ernest Lefever, was successfully positioned as a right-wing ideologue and defeated because of his efforts to promote a "policy of quiet diplomacy on human rights in dealing with friendly nations." By late June, Carter's secretary of state, Cyrus Vance, made an appearance on *Meet the Press* in which he accused the administration of taking "more of a posture in many important areas" than a policy, which, he added, "is dangerous."

Reagan is remembered in his rise as a conquering hero, but he lived it as an embattled pioneer of traditional American liberties. As the *Meet the Press* record demonstrates, negative reception and a climate of attack were common themes throughout the Reagan era. As in other theatrical matters, Reagan's timing was perfect. In the lead-up to his reelection in 1984, the discussions about Reagan became steadily more positive, but the general tone of the Reagan reception was surprisingly negative throughout his two terms in office—especially on foreign policy.

The examples of anti-Reagan vitriol are unambiguous. One should never expect a particularly favorable treatment when one's former opponent for office gets a chance to speak to a national audience about your administration, but when former vice president Walter Mondale had his second *Meet the Press* opportunity to frame the Reagan presidency on November 30, 1986, in response to a genuine crisis in the Iran-Contra scandal, he was excoriating in his assault.

Al Hunt (*Wall Street Journal*): Mr. Mondale, when the Iranian regime played a role in bringing down your administration, Ronald Reagan and others were quite harsh in the way you all handled it. Now ironically, it seems to be threatening their administration. What lessons do you think we can draw from their conduct of foreign policy here?

Walter Mondale: I think they have had six years of very dismal performance. There has been erratic, ill-focused foreign policy. Now six years into their administration, they have accomplished nothing, no major foreign policy accomplishment, which is the good news. . . . The credibility of the administration with our allies—we told them not to sell arms to Iran, while we were doing it. We've been trying to get a—we were told [there is] a tough policy to fight with terrorists, and yet we've been trafficking with them. It's hard to know how foreign policy can be in greater disarray than it is today.

Other characterizations of the foreign policy agenda of the president on *Meet the Press* in this era were not much more favorable. In the middle of January 1987, Marvin Kalb introduced Secretary of State George Shultz as follows:

> Marvin Kalb [*on tape*]: The secretary of state, taking a break at an African game park, during a recent trip designed to show the flag and sell the virtues of a free-market economy. But at one point, his van got stuck in the mud, and even he couldn't help joking that maybe that van was really a symbol of American foreign policy, stuck in the mud of the Iran-Contra scandal.

Six months later, when the prime minister of Canada appeared, Kalb introduced him in a similar tone:

> Kalb: This is Parliament Hill in Ottawa, Canada, the site, starting later today, of the third annual US-Canadian Summit—two neighbors with an unguarded border, but with a growing host of economic and political problems. Today the Canadian view from—who better than the prime minister, Brian Mulroney, who has found that his close relationship with President Reagan is proving to be a political liability. He's our guest today on *Meet the Press*.

And as further evidence of the Ben Pride–like "danger and heartbreaking setbacks" faced by Reagan the conservative hero, in the June 14, 1987 episode, the weekend following Reagan's famous "tear down this wall" speech, the reporter Robert Kaiser asked Senator Sam Nunn the kind of question that reads more like a thesis:

> Robert Kaiser (*Washington Post*): Do you sense, as some of your colleagues do, that there's a general malaise in this administration, that there's a drift at work? I read an extraordinary quotation from Senator Moynihan yesterday. He said the possibility of awful mistakes looms on every horizon. There's a great anxiety here. A little Moynihan rhetoric. But is this a bad time for the United States in general?

In a final example of what I think may be fairly represented as a generally negative tone with respect to Reagan's foreign policy efforts,[17] I present the *Meet the Press* episode from January 1988, as the Reagan era was winding down, which featured historian Paul Kennedy of Yale University. It was not "morning in America" on NBC that Sunday. To put this excerpt in context, I note that to this point in the show's history, there had been no serious discussion of the United States as an empire (apart from concerns raised by foreign leaders like Ghana's Kwame Nkrumah), but with the release of Kennedy's book *The Rise and Fall of the Great Powers*,[18] empire was now a topic that could scarcely be avoided. And given Reagan's approach to the world as if it were a playground for private enterprise, the empire label attached to Reagan much like it once had to Andrew Jackson. Professor Kennedy ominously predicted the decline of the American empire along with its rival the Soviet Union, as well as the rise of China.

> Paul Kennedy: I am arguing that today's policy makers need to have a sense of the larger course of world history and of those historical precedents in which a number-one power has become so overstretched, refused to cut back on its commitments, and then found itself in some catastrophic strategical global juggling act in which it's impossible to send forces to all parts of the world where it's required to. . . .

> David Broder (*Washington Post*): Professor Kennedy, how does your theory apply to the Soviet Union? It would seem to me that they are even more overcommitted relative to their economic strength.

> Kennedy: . . . I think both hegemons are in a state of relative decline in world affairs. But the Soviet Union never climbed as high as the USA, and it is declining in a rather more fundamental, and I suspect rather faster, way.

Jimmy Carter had demonstrated that in the new fight for human rights, multicultural recognition and sensitivity to historical oppression were going to have to play a central part, which the American government would support. Conservative attempts to undo the Carter/Young synthesis were greeted much as were attempts to limit civil rights initiatives at the time, with rabid contempt and murmurings of racism. But for conservatives, the problem was not about race and culture at all; it was about the vital interests of America and the future of freedom, and as Eric Johnston had argued, that always meant one thing: private enterprise. American wars were not fought in support of some unspoken empire; they were fought for the empire of liberty, to secure corporate rights around the world. That was the American way. The job of defending this Johnstonian use of American power in a global economic system was a tough sell. It fell on an unknown professor from Georgetown, Jeane Kirkpatrick, an intellectual up for the job of rejuvenating Ben Pride's presidential prospects.

It is important to recognize that Kirkpatrick was a controversial figure, but she was also a dramatically powerful intellectual force. Her entrance came in an environment in which Johnstonian principles had been polluted with images of John Birchers and Goldwater extremism. Her president had been smeared as "Ronnie Ray-gun," and people now feared the coming of World War III. By the time that Reagan's morning-in-America campaign rolled along in 1984, she had become a darling of the Washington establishment. Here is how she was introduced in her *Meet the Press* appearance on March 31, 1985.

Marvin Kalb: And welcome once again to *Meet the Press*. In Washington, professors come and go. They bring their ideas, but they have no constituencies and therefore little power. It is the rare one indeed who leaves a mark. Henry Kissinger came out of Harvard in the late 1960s, and by the time he left eight years later, he was a major figure. The only other one who comes to mind is Jeane Kirkpatrick, who came out of Georgetown in 1981 and in only four years has become a kind of cult figure among conservatives both here and abroad. . . . Roger, in reviewing the clips for this program, one could easily have concluded that if this were a national election year, Jeane Kirkpatrick would be on some Republican's list for president or certainly vice president.

Roger Mudd (co-moderator): . . . She's an intellectual dealing mostly with bureaucrats, not to mention, of course, that she was a Democrat, and a welfare state Democrat at that, serving in a conservative Republican administration. But her speech at the Republican convention last summer made it obvious she wouldn't be a Democrat much longer.

Jeane Kirkpatrick [*on tape*]: Now the American people, proud of our country, proud of our freedom, proud of ourselves, will reject the San Francisco Democrats and send Ronald Reagan back to the White House.

What made Kirkpatrick such a star was her ability to take head-on the human rights frame that Jimmy Carter had institutionalized in a way that incorporated the powerful libertarian attacks on Carter's domestic program. We can think of her as the anti–Andrew Young of international politics, not because she attempted to bring a racist recast to foreign policy but because she undermined the human rights approach to interstate politics in a way that affirmed traditional and specifically American conceptions of liberty. In short, Kirkpatrick brought legitimacy and gravitas to a freedom agenda in matters of war and peace that was powerful enough to counter Carter's still-consolidating multicultural agenda.[19] There is no better example of this than the 1983 invasion of Grenada, which brought Ambassador Kirkpatrick to the *Meet the Press* studio on October 30.

Bill Monroe (moderator): Well, Mrs. Kirkpatrick, not a single nation except those allied with us in the action against Grenada have spoken up in our defense. The French and the Dutch voted against us in the Security Council; the Mexicans and other members of the OAS have criticized us. Can you cite a single provision of international law, the United Nations, the Organization of American States, under which we have the right to invade a nation like Grenada if we feel there's chaos there or we worry that some of our people may be in danger?

Jeane Kirkpatrick: Oh, certainly. And let me just say that I did that in my speech before the UN, in which I presented the US case. I said that the UN Charter does not simply forbid the use of force under all circumstances as an absolute. The UN Charter leaves very ample grounds for the use of force in protection of the other rights and values in the charter. Those other values include security and peace and democracy.

She made it clear that America might have to go it alone in defense of individual rights. The United Nations organization that it had helped create had now turned against it. The quest to secure the world for private enterprise was a lonely one, where the virtuous easily became the victims.

Monroe: Many Americans support the administration action in Grenada, but I wonder if you're saying that that action, that military success, had no moral cost, no public opinion cost, in view of the unanimity shown by nations at the United Nations, at the Organization of American States, against the action we took, with the exception of the US and the six Caribbean islands?

Kirkpatrick: Now wait a minute. Let's not say that there was unanimity, because there wasn't unanimity. There wasn't unanimity at all, and what there was, was a Security Council vote, which was heavily against us.

Monroe: Eleven to one.

Kirkpatrick: But let me remind you—with three abstentions—let me remind you that there are—the United States regularly loses in the United Nations, the General Assembly, and in the Security Council. No nation is more regularly both a loser and a victim at the United Nations than the United States except Israel, who is even more totally a loser and a victim. The United Nations is a political system, and it's a political system which is largely controlled by our adversaries. I've been talking about that ever since I've been there.[20]

Ideas have consequences, and Kirkpatrick supplied the Reagan revolutions with updated ideas to deal with the challenges presented to them by a global left that had been seduced to the Gandhi/King conception of the future as an inclusive, global, cultural bazaar. What is astounding in a review of the *Meet the Press* record is how successful this intellectual reaction to commonsense multicultural globalism was. Just as there were numerous episodes dedicated to Reagan's foreign policy gaffes and foibles during his presidency, afterward there is a singular interest in the stellar Reagan legacy. Like Dr. King, President Reagan has fared better in collective memory than he did in real time.

These memories of Reagan were no doubt the product of a fair amount of effort by reputational entrepreneurs. Reagan's legacy had become so precious by 1999 that two episodes devoted substantial airtime to the Reagan biography written by Edmund Morris, who when he appeared on October 3, was treated with as much gravitas as if the news item were a major foreign policy story.[21]

How much had changed about how Reagan was remembered comes through in a program dedicated to second-term scandals. On October 30, 2005, George W. Bush was facing a problem with a CIA leak investigation involving Lewis "Scooter" Libby, the vice president's chief of staff, who had resigned after being indicted. For the presidential historian Michael Beschloss, there was no better model for the embattled Bush than Ronald Reagan.

Michael Beschloss: Reagan was so secure, he didn't feel that he was jeopardizing
    that base in a serious way by doing the main thing he did, and I think this is
    the biggest lesson for a second-term president, and that is, in Reagan's case,
    he decided, "I'm now going to turn to my legacy. I'm going to do something
    important. I'm going to try to end the Cold War." That's the way he spent his
    last two years. That's the way historians remember him.

Similarly, future presidential aspirant Senator John McCain had the first opportunity to comment on Reagan on the occasion of his death in June 2004. His memories were not so different from those that Morris had described five years earlier.

John McCain: When I came home from a Vietnamese prison camp, and it was the
    first time—chance I had to meet him face-to-face. . . . When I came home
    from a time warp, from '67 to '73, America wasn't sure of itself. A lot of
    people think we'd lost our way. And he had an unwavering belief and faith in
    the greatness of the nation.

Ronald Reagan may have been an enigma as a person, but as a collective memory, he was a phenomenon. There is no better way to get a sense of this than to look at how he was contrasted in retrospect to Jimmy Carter. In an interview aired on April 22, 2001, Jimmy Carter's chief of staff, Hamilton Jordan, and Reagan's, Michael Deaver, appeared to explore the contrasting legacies of the two presidents. The exchange with Jordan is instructive:

Tim Russert: Hamilton Jordan, when you look back at the style of Jimmy Carter, as opposed to the style of Ronald Reagan, the presence of both men, how do you see it in hindsight, in terms of their presence and their ability to lead?

Hamilton Jordan: Well, President Reagan had some unusual gifts. He made complicated things look simple. . . . He had a gift for the symbolism of the presidents that I think is unmatched by any modern president.

Russert: "Gift of symbolism." Very well said by Hamilton Jordan. I'm going to show you two different speeches. One by President Carter back in '79 and then by President Reagan at the Berlin Wall. Here's first, President Carter.

[*excerpt from videotape, July 15, 1979*]

President Jimmy Carter: I want to talk to you right now about a fundamental threat to American democracy. . . . The threat is nearly invisible in ordinary ways. It is a crisis of confidence. It is a crisis that strikes at the very heart and soul and spirit of our national will. We can see this crisis in the growing doubt about the meaning of our own lives and in the loss of a unity of purpose for our nation.

[*end excerpt*]

Russert: The so-called malaise speech. Now, contrast that with Ronald Reagan at the Berlin Wall, and you'll see two different men and two different styles.

[*excerpt from videotape, June 12, 1987*]

President Ronald Reagan: Mr. Gorbachev, tear down this wall.

[*end excerpt*]

Russert: The president had often said—President Reagan—that you can't be a good president without being a good actor. He took it as a compliment.

Michael Deaver: Yes. I mean, I think he understood the importance of symbolism.

The gift of symbolism had a downside that Edmund Morris had noted amid the hoopla of his book's release:

Edmund Morris: He was by nature an actor. . . . Actors are trained not to focus
    too closely on their individual witnesses. . . . What Reagan saw through his
    myopic eyes was a general blur of smiling, affectionate, worshipping faces.
    That's how he saw his family; that's how he saw the American people; that's
    how he saw the world.

And that is how we see him today. Sensing the nature of symbolism, Ronald Reagan had escaped from his potential fate as a failed extremist. He
had placed America back on the victory trail, and after the fall of the Soviet Union the Ben Pride narrative became a kind of gift he could bestow on
his supporters. It was an America restoried and restored. Transformative
human rights globalism had been stymied abroad, just as the civil rights
movement had been at home. The scope of American government had
been limited, and the vision of an America that could project free institutions around the world had been sustained in the global frontier. Like a
forgotten western screen hero, Ronald Reagan was almost too good to be
true for conservative Americans rattled by the civil rights movement and
the culture wars. He presented the country with an opportunity to repair
its broken libertarian myth—to choose the global promise of the civilization of the cowboys over the lost, illiberal world of the Indians. The real
situation was often a good deal more complicated, but he performed his
role well, and few of his followers seemed to care about the contradictions.

With War on My Mind

I'm a war president. I make decisions here in the Oval Office in foreign
policy matters with war on my mind. Again, I wish it wasn't true, but
it is true. And the American people need to know they got a president
who sees the world the way it is. And I see dangers that exist, and it's
important for us to deal with them.

—President George W. Bush, February 8, 2004

It is a commonplace to claim that Americans were shaken by the failure of their efforts in Vietnam and adapted their foreign policy agenda and
self-image in profound ways in its aftermath. The reaction is often labeled
the "Vietnam syndrome" and can be used as a weapon by both hawks and
doves to suggest that the larger project of their opponent is tainted by a
kind of psychological hangover from that event. One side is blamed for
its unwillingness to support the American project to spread freedom and

individual rights, while the other is blamed for its attempt to overcome the humiliation of defeat through cheap victories. What is true of the people is often true of their presidents. Both Jimmy Carter and Ronald Reagan were desperate after Vietnam to discover a new global democratic project—to relive the American revolution in their own time. Carter took a more incrementalist and culturally sensitive approach to the post-Vietnam world based on his interpretation of the civil rights movement, while Reagan proposed grand projects of democratic liberation with updates in the mid-century chamber of commerce model. Where Carter would promote mutual understanding and cooperation, Reagan was intransigent in defense of the private-enterprise system against risks of coercive appropriation.

This has induced an ongoing dialectic between the narratives of human rights and democratic victory that has persisted even through the era of perestroika and 9/11. The main changes are the circumstances in which the perspectives are proposed. After 9/11, the victory argument was empowered to a degree that was previously impossible to imagine, and President Bush could launch two wars in its cause. When things went badly in Iraq after Abu Ghraib and the 2005 elections, the human rights argument found its legs. Across the subsequent history of political debate, these two democratic visions have contested with one another for dominance. In contrast to domestic questions, the struggle for civil power in international affairs hinges on what can appear to be a distinctive uncivil term: national interest.

When the United States inherited the pole position in the old Western race for global dominance after World War II, its leaders were unsure how to proceed. It was unclear if there should be an international body for dispute resolution between nations, if there should be an effort to maintain a massive standing army with the introduction of universal military training, if it was possible to coexist with the Socialist republic of the Soviet Union, or if American foreign aid should be used to reconstruct Europe. In each of these examples, the case for the use of American power in the cause of liberty was unclear, and therefore the political agenda of the American people was as well. Without an obvious framework through which to position novel events in democratic discourse, American leaders were befuddled. The old European language of power politics was the natural one for interstate relations, but this was not the American way. Even as specialized groups of elites became socialized to this worldview with the development of the field of international relations, American politicians looked for a way to square the circle of national interests within a larger quest to spread global democracy.

Partial salvation came in the struggle against international Communism, which helped the political classes across the ideological range to rally in support of the Victorian concept of private enterprise. But when the "evil empire" of Soviet Communism was defeated, American elites were once again at a loss about how to best formulate a project consistent with spreading democracy around the world. Was support for a country like Kuwait against the rapacity of its neighbor a sufficient threshold to unleash American coercive power with civil sanction? What about the examples of genocide in places like Rwanda, Somalia, and Bosnia? In the first case, American arms could be sanctioned in terms of the rhetoric of freedom; in the second, by virtue of forestalling the very kind of cultural atrocity that had originally triggered the multicultural human rights agenda. Often there was the possibility of resort to the language of security, and as effective as this was in practice, in theory it made Americans queasy. Too many Americans had internalized the old Franklin maxim that he who would sacrifice liberty for security deserves neither. Consider how strained this typical interview with Secretary of State Condoleezza Rice was on September 16, 2003.

> Condoleezza Rice: But the key here is you cannot put a price tag on security. Iraq was a threat. Saddam Hussein was a threat to the region, he was a threat to America, to American interests, he was a haven and a supporter of terrorism around the world, and he had launched wars, used weapons of mass destruction. He was a threat. He is now gone. The goal now is to put in his place, in the place of that horrible regime, a stable, prosperous, and democratizing Iraq. That will pay off many, many, many times over in security for the American people. What happened to us on September 11 should remind us that we have to fight the war on terror on the offense. We can't fight from preventive defense. It's fine to try to defend the country, but the president believes that we have to fight this war on the offense, and Iraq is part of fighting that war.

As Secretary Rice demonstrated in her virtuoso defenses of the increasingly fraught case that the Iraq War was part of a global project of democratic liberation, it was easy enough to see that Iraq might be plausibly characterized as a threat to the American people, but was it a threat to American democracy? Was it rationale enough for a foreign competitor to challenge our national interests, and if so, how were these vital interests tied to the larger democratic project?

Not all leaders could carry this logic back to principle, but those who could were almost guaranteed a space in the Republican leadership circle. As John Locke, the Constitution, and the rough draft of the Declaration had stated, America had vital interests in defense of their lives, certainly in defense of their liberties at home, but also in defense of their property, and the stock of American property was increasingly distributed around the global frontier. The most important lesson of the postwar period is that those leaders who rose to core leadership positions in the Republican Party never forgot this simple line of reasoning. Republican leadership over the course of the postwar period never gave up on its commitment to victory for the private-enterprise system over the forces that would put it at risk from political sources. This is the key insight of the Republican master narrative. The elder Bush's defense of Kuwait and even his son's doctrine of preemptive strike were simply the latest in a long line of arguments generated on the core theme that the chamber of commerce's Eric Johnston had elaborated back in 1949—"to perpetuate or to encourage private enterprise in the countries abroad."

George W. Bush was an authentic champion of democracy; it just happened that his conception of democracy was one that placed the accent on the liberty of large and productive enterprises over cognate concerns like economic equality and cultural recognition. This elaborated philosophy provided the substance of the second Bush inaugural address, which was also the main topic of *Meet the Press* on January 23, 2005.

[*videotape, January 20, 2005*]

President George W. Bush: We have seen our vulnerability, and we have seen its
    deepest source. For as long as whole regions of the world simmer in resent-
    ment and tyranny, prone to ideologies that feed hatred and excuse murder,
    violence will gather and multiply in destructive power and cross the most
    defended borders and raise a mortal threat. There is only one force of history
    that can break the reign of hatred and resentment and expose the pretensions
    of tyrants and reward the hopes of the decent and tolerant, and that is the
    force of human freedom.

[*end videotape*]

Tim Russert: Robin Wright, can anyone disagree with that?

Robin Wright (*Washington Post*): Not at all. But it's interesting how the second
administration really is redefining the war on terrorism to a war to achieve
liberty and to go after the regimes whose unjust rule has led to resistance
and the emergence of Islamic extremism. The one flaw in his speech or the
one limitation is that he defines it in terms purely of liberty, and he doesn't
really talk a lot about human rights law. And there's a big difference. Liberty
is achieving, you know, political change. But achieving it is often dealing
with the very regimes who are responsible for creating this extremist—Paki-
stan, Saudi Arabia, Egypt. There are a number of countries where the United
States faces a challenge. As noble as it sounds to take on the cause of liberty,
it's very difficult in practical terms to get regimes we count on for the war on
terrorism to actually undergo that transition.

George W. Bush would be largely misunderstood because the long decades of equating the cause of freedom with the cause of private enterprise
no longer required explicit justification on the right even as it was dismis-
sively demonized on the left. Critics might cry foul for leadership that
would trade "blood for oil," but most Americans had come to believe that
freedom was not like water; it mixed quite well with oil. The old Johnston
line that investment capital needed protection would find no more committed a champion for this American cause than in John McCain, who
carried the added burden of exorcising the ghosts of Vietnam for himself
and for the country. On October 19, 2003, McCain made one of his many
pitches to stick with the fight in Iraq so that freedom might spread around
the world. Wit and intransigence had been key elements of the style of the
why-not-victory narrative since Goldwater, and McCain was a master of
both.

John McCain: There's only two arguments you can make with regards to Iraq, is
we shouldn't have gone there in the first place and so therefore we should
pull out, or pay for and do whatever is necessary to win. It's not intellectually
honest to say that—to make an argument that somehow the United States
doesn't have to carry the burden here. Everybody here who thinks that the
French are going to contribute money and troops, raise their hands, please.
The fact is that we will, over time, get some international support, but, as
is always the case in these kinds of crises, the United States of America is
going to have to carry the load. And let me point out that if we succeed here,
and we must—this is not Beirut and Somalia where we can leave—when we
succeed, it will mean that democracy and freedom can flourish in a part of

the world where there is none today. It will send a message to the dictators, including the Saudis and the extremists, that their day is done. There's a huge amount at stake here. We can and we must prevail.

Victory for freedom was Reagan's answer to Carter's international cultural rights agenda as it had been Goldwater's to Kennedy's domestic social rights agenda. The Republican vision of democratic liberty was one that protected individual rights, not social programs and multicultural agendas. For many Americans, this simple idea was worth dying for, just as Eric Johnston had suggested it was, and if the facts did not conform with the theory, the facts were to blame.

Back in 1979, the architect of the human rights gestalt, Andrew Young, had said, "I think if we are only against killing by certain people, our position is compromised. The fact that we are against killing, we are against terrorism, that we criticize the terrorism when it is coming in by an airplane strafing people or when it is a bomb placed in a garbage can, I think, is the only way to approach the world." Young's criticisms of state terror were directed at dictators like the shah of Iran, whom America had supported as part of the freedom agenda of the Cold War, but he was not opposed to regime change when it was necessary for considerations of cultural redemption in places like Rhodesia and South Africa. Young was a proponent of nonviolence, but future human rights Democrats would whet their appetites for more aggressive regime change in cases involving ethnic hatred and cultural rights. After the end of the Cold War, the humanitarian basis for intervention would help Democratic leaders provide their own answers to the Vietnam question.

One of the leading figures in this movement was Secretary of State Madeleine Albright, who described the evolution of her thinking on the subject on September 21, 2003, on the release of her memoirs.

Tim Russert: There's a very interesting passage in your book, which I want to talk about a little bit. And I'll show you and our viewers on the screen. And this is talking about Kosovo and Bosnia. . . . "In the face of all his medals and prestige, I found it hard to argue with Powell about the proper way to employ American force. Even though I was a member of the Principals Committee, I was still a mere female civilian. I did, however, think then as now that the lessons of Vietnam could be learned too well." The lessons of Vietnam could be learned too well. Explain that.

Madeleine Albright: Well, what I thought was that we had—we were in kind of a mode of thinking that we were never going to be able to use our military effectively again. And I come from a different background. I—everybody has their baggage, and mine is Munich where, in fact, in 1938, the West did not stand up to Hitler, and, consequently, as a result of many steps, the country I was born in, Czechoslovakia, was dismembered, and, ultimately, Hitler had a free hand throughout Europe. So I believe in the goodness of American power, used properly. I also believed that bombing in Bosnia and later in Kosovo was an appropriate way to sideline a dictator who was involved in ethnic cleansing. It isn't easy to argue with Colin Powell, and I have the greatest respect for him, but there really was this sense in those meetings that the numbers put down were so high, and the cost of it so high, that it was done in a way that we would never use force. And I believed that we could use limited force in this situation to achieve what in the end we did achieve in Bosnia and later in Kosovo.

As Albright described, American power could be used just as it should have been used in World War II to stop the subjugation of the European states to German supremacy and the genocidal extermination of European Jewry. The breakthrough idea was only possible in the era of identity politics and multiculturalism. A cultural rights agenda in support of geopolitical tolerance and global diversity was itself compatible with American national interest. The rights of people to live secure in their ethnic identities had been coded as democratic for the American Left even if Republican free enterprisers failed to see where the national interest lay in other people's folkways.

These tectonic movements in the dialectic between the Carter and Reagan approaches to the world did not reach an inflection point until early 2011 when what was described as the "Jasmine Revolution" or "Arab Spring" shook the world of international affairs and the contra-genocidal human rights agenda was put to the test with the Democrats in power and a freedom movement spreading across the Middle East. The Arab uprisings confronted the American political classes with a dire test of their democratic convictions. The most stubborn problem was to make sense of how the old Hobbesian notion that underwrote realpolitik could be rendered compatible with evolving ideas of the interest of the American people in democratic reform. These challenges would prove to be as divisive and dumbfounding as they had been from the early days of the Pax Americana. President Obama started a third front in the larger war in the

Muslim world on terms that even members of his own administration could not understand. Both the secretary of defense and secretary of state (historically a potent and dramatic combination) appeared on *Meet the Press* on March 27, 2011.

David Gregory: Secretary Gates, is Libya in our vital interest as a country?

Robert Gates: No. I don't think it's a vital interest for the United States, but we clearly have interests there, and it's a part of the region which is a vital interest for the United States.

Gregory: I think a lot of people would hear that and say, well, that's quite striking. Not in our vital interest, and yet we're committing military resources to it.

Hillary Clinton: Well, but, but, but then it wouldn't be fair as to what Bob just said. I mean, did Libya attack us? No. They did not attack us. . . . They didn't attack us, but what they were doing and Gadhafi's history and the potential for the disruption and instability was very much in our interests, as Bob said, and seen by our European friends and our Arab partners as very vital to their interests.

No one seemed capable of explaining in a consistent way what the vital interests of the United States were. As with many questions in twenty-first-century America, it was David Brooks in the roundtable who recognized the intellectual challenges of the moment.

David Gregory: But there's going to be some conflict, David, between the fact that young people in the Persian Gulf states are going to look up and say, "Wow, the US helped get Mubarak out of there." They've talked tough about Gadhafi. We saw what happened in Tunisia. But when it comes to these Sunni monarchs, they're going to help them democratize, they're going to help them issue reforms, but they're not going to push them out.

David Brooks (*New York Times*): Right, and we're hedging, and I don't think we should be hedging. . . . And we—we're always hedging nuances that nobody else pays attention to that makes us look passive. The problem with Libya is we've gotten ourselves into a bad situation by imposing sanctions on Gadhafi, essentially saying, "You've got to fight to the death because there's no way out for you," but then not doing the second step, which was actually removing him. So we've put him—we've boxed him in, and now he's fighting back, and we're sort of doing nothing. It's a phenomenally difficult problem, but we've got to at least express our values clearly.

This business of expressing American values clearly in matters of foreign affairs was no easy thing to do; perhaps the most obvious point of neglect was a serious effort to ensure global equality in a world of fast-paced and unforgiving markets. Carter had reacted to genocidal and supremacist tendencies in global politics with his human rights agenda. Reagan had responded with an old-fashioned defense of contracts and property. Missing from American foreign affairs was a serious effort to transform the social conditions of ordinary people around the world so that they might participate in free exchange without risk of exploitation. It was too touchy to raise the specter of concentrated economic power, when it was so easy to associate it with Halliburton and Exxon/Mobil.

When Barack Obama was elected, it was as if he had become the surrogate leader for the world. People from every nook and corner of the globe reveled in the elevation of this son of a Kenyan father who served as a figurative representative of the global south, the first to lead a major Western power. He was a kind of super-Mandela who symbolized in his biography the triumph of tolerance and the progress of the human rights agenda. But the nation was exhausted by its own efforts to preserve freedom in this hopeful yet precarious world. The values underlying foreign policy remained as unclear as they had been for decades. The Republican conception of American vital interests abroad was wrapped up in the vigorous support of the private-enterprise system on which the global economy depended, but it often could be promoted without consideration of the social rights and general well-being of people liberated from formal despotism. On the Democratic side, the language of human rights could be used as a general check on the Republicans' dominant ideology and was particularly powerful when used to oppose cultural domination in its most egregious and genocidal forms. But the kind of long-term programs that had hope of promoting broad-based structural reform abroad were as unpopular in the country as they had been when Senators Jenner and McCarthy attacked the socialistic implications of the Marshall Plan. Democratic dysfunction had found its counterparts in the principles of freedom and tolerance. As with other aspects of the American story, not much of substance was being said about the secular trend toward economic inequality both within and between nations, irrespective of how consistently these problems presented themselves.

4

TAKING AIM AT THE NEW DEAL
To Restore the Idea of America

You know, when I first saw the Bush administration in action, I thought
that they wanted to undo everything Bill Clinton had done. Basically,
I took that a little personally because I thought that a lot of good had
happened during the 1990s. Then I realized that, you know, they're
taking aim at the New Deal. They really do have a mission in mind to
radically restructure the social safety net, the kind of consumer and
worker protections that have been at the base of building the American
middle class. I don't think anybody voted for that in 2000, and I regret
that it has been pursued so relentlessly.

—Senator Hillary Clinton, December 7, 2003

NONE OF US WILL SOON FORGET JAMES CARVILLE'S pithy phrase
"it's the economy stupid" that he posted in Bill Clinton's war room to
remind his campaign workers what the election was all about. What was
true in 1992 has been true in every other year as well. We live in an era
of sophists, economists, and calculators, as did our parents before us. The
condition has lasted long enough that, as a group, we have forgotten what
life was like before we knew the price, if not the value, of everything. Even
the great spectacle of war is in some sense resolvable to economics, which
supplies both the means to wage it and the ends for which it is fought.[1] As
Harold Lasswell has argued, politics is in some measure a fight over who
gets what, when, and how; it is a struggle over the institutions that govern
the economy.[2]

The epic battle between business and government as David Rothkopf has described it is a story one more of continuity than change.[3] Over
the slice of history contained in the *Meet the Press* record, the fight over
how mixed between public and private sources the mixed economy ought
to be was central. As was true in Victorian England before the rise of

the American megacorporations in the late nineteenth century, twentieth-century critics of concentrated economic power faced off against the laissez-faire, laissez-passer ideals of the merchant class. The issues were remarkably consistent: public debt, economic stimulus, and price stability; taxation and progressivity; social insurance and welfare supports; financial speculation and the business cycle; and concerns about workers' rights and consumer protections.[4]

Throughout the struggle the specter of Karl Marx haunted Washington. American critics of monopoly and oligarchic tendencies were never much moved by European social theory. Theirs was an intellectual world structured more by Thomas Jefferson than Jean-Jacques Rousseau. The American impulse toward social protection from market forces was uncompromisingly liberal and democratic from the Populists to the Progressives.[5] But as the heirs of the frontier-settling cooperative business enterprises after the Civil War glimpsed the threat of a workable future in the Socialist alternatives rising on the horizon of a new century, they doubled down on Victorian economic theories that had once been used to justify nineteenth-century British hegemony.[6] After the Communist revolution of 1917, the public part of the public-private partnership always reeked of Russian authoritarianism. In true American fashion, the captains of enterprise heaped Manichean scorn on those who even flirted with Socialist ideals. From Vera Cruz in 1914 to Moscow three years later to Havana in 1959, Americans experienced the Socialist alternative as a foundational threat to their democratic project and embraced a private-enterprise economy that provided the private-planning organizations we now call corporations unparalleled latitude in managing their internal affairs. Yet the productive power of big business brought with it economic inequality and insecurity on a scale previously unknown, along with the shadow of European class conflict.

In order to protect the country from the staggering class conflict he saw dividing Europe, the Progressive Republican Teddy Roosevelt advocated what he called the "Square Deal" and borrowed polluting imagery of business bigwigs from the Populists, Socialists, and anarchists of the nascent class movement for less radical purposes. He imagined that "malefactors of great wealth" were jeopardizing American freedoms while at the same time decried the threat to democracy posed by Socialists like Illinois governor John Peter Altgeld. In symbolic terms, Roosevelt blended the corporate boosterism of his predecessor, William McKinley, with the populist energies and egalitarian concerns of William Jennings Bryan into an idea that was a kind of mixed-economy American synthesis.[7] Today, Roosevelt is remembered as a historical oddity, but in the early twentieth century he was the personal embodiment of two potentially contradictory principles: private enterprise and the even newer idea that we now call the principle of social security.

Twenty years after TR's departure, the laissez-faire liberalism of the Herbert Hoover administration led once again not only to spiraling inequality but also the Great Depression, at which point the country was ready for a new Roosevelt who applied his cousin's ideas with a bold, experimental spirit, and after FDR, American capitalism seemed to settle into a new groove. Growth continued on the formula of private enterprise plus social protection; a New Deal countered the old. There would be no "Socialist" alternative, but people received the minimal protection they needed from the market and the economic oligarchs who dominated it.[8]

When the United States emerged exhausted from the European conflict of the 1940s, American elites were largely resigned to this Roosevelt mixed-economy synthesis. Wherever the self-regulating market and the visible hands that served to coordinate its functions undermined the very system of liberty that justified it, the government protected capitalism from itself and the American people along with it. But the New Deal institutions and the synthetic principle of social security that undergirded them were never very popular in certain segments of the business community. American business leaders were a new historical breed who imagined they had tamed the savage wilderness with a uniquely American form of economic virtue that had been passed down from the Founders. The tradition of limited government was for them part of their ancestral domain and spoke to what it meant to be an American. The Great Depression and the New Deal then represented a tragic interruption of the liberation narrative that they could trace from Lexington and Concord through Appomattox to the Chicago Haymarket. For these displaced and disaffected barons of industry, Hoover's "rugged individualism" was the story of America: period. Their enemies were government bureaucrats, and there was no need for augmentation with concerns about bigwigs or bigots. They maneuvered through long years of accommodation with the New Dealers to a point where they could break the stranglehold of the social securocrats in order to repair the narrative of an America unburdened by European social categories.

Toward this effort, the cultural oppression of African Americans provided classical or neoliberals with an unlikely opening. Ironically, the clear battle lines of the protracted economic struggle between capital and community were complicated to the point of confusion by the maturation and eventual success of the civil rights movement. Because African Americans (who had seen progress as a group only when governments were strong, as under Lincoln and Franklin Roosevelt) were never enamored of the antigovernment rhetoric of the Adam Smith / David Ricardo / Richard Cobden set, as a group blacks were disproportionately unmoved by the return of the Victorian economic mind-set that groups like the US Chamber of Commerce and the National Association of Manufacturers promoted after the war. This meant blacks would disproportionately support the programs for social protection that were the cornerstone of the New Deal and would be disinclined to demonize the state and its potential role in securing economic justice. By symbolically linking government intervention in support of expanding economic opportunity with that of promoting racial inclusion and cultural recognition (polluted with illiberal images of dependency and backwardness), the neoliberals could marry the two root causes in the public mind and disconnect some part of the commitment to social protection from the New Deal coalition.

Republicans set out to seduce white southerners to the cause of unregulated enterprise, using threats of an internal "barbarian other" as a wedge, thereby undermining the foundations of the social democratic project of Roosevelt's welfare state. It worked. We remember this masterstroke as the invention of the Reagan Democrats or as Nixon's Southern Strategy, but it was in the making from the first days of the Allied victory. Its eventual success plunged the country into novel confrontations from which we have not recovered.[9]

In this dramatic realignment of the party system of the old South,[10] free-market philosophy had of necessity become coded with racist imagery, but as the most central proponents of this antigovernment libertarian impulse from Ronald Reagan to Jack Kemp to Ron Paul knew, the race coding was only an expedient toward the larger goal of restoring the idea of the independent American that, for them, had lost its purity in the Progressive and New Deal eras of the early twentieth century. As Reagan claimed at the time, Reaganism was not about racism; it was a return to "what it once was like in America when men were free,"[11] but after Governor Reagan, opportunists from Richard Nixon to Newt Gingrich would use sometimes vicious symbolic confections of black barbarism and social dependence to stifle any murmurings of an anticorporate agenda.[12] Put simply, for contingent reasons, free markets and coded white supremacism developed after World War II along paths of elective affinity.[13]

The worst part of the situation was that the most powerful groups on both the left and the right had an interest in confusing the public on the issue. For fear of losing momentum, the resurgent classical liberals did not want the persuadable American—those voters who were cast adrift in this chaos of the culture wars—to see that their laissez-faire agenda would by design undermine the gains toward economic equality and social security made under Democratic leadership. Similarly, cultural liberals did not want the ambivalent to see that their multicultural agenda had co-opted the larger part of the egalitarian moral force that once supported the rise of unions, social protection programs, progressive taxes, and corporate regulations. On this score, Left and Right were united. The people should not be allowed to see inequality; they should see either intolerance or despotism instead. In this state of confusion and paralysis, as Los Angeles mayor Antonio Villaraigosa put it on June 19, 2011, when people spoke about the economy, it is as if people were "living on a different planet," and in some sense they were.

Richard Hofstadter had said that America was a place that had no ideologies but rather was one;[14] it was in the abstractness of this idea of freedom where the conservative-who-was-really-a-liberal located his domain, and this he could trace back through Locke, to Augustine, and to Christ himself. For the classical liberal, who after the war knew himself as a conservative, the Socialists and the multiculturalists were desecrating this idea that was the domain of his ancestors. The historian Rick Perlstein has described this phenomenon as Nixonland, where a mean-spirited politics infected the body politic, but it was something else as well—it was an angry and desperate reaction to the loss of the idea of America—what Lederach had described as "a narrative broken."[15] These conservatives were going to take their country back, and their process of narrative repair has distracted us these many decades.

Unscramble the Omelet

I. F. Stone (*The Newspaper PM*): Mr. Churchill, if your party, the
conservatives, come back to power, will you liquidate the Socialist
enterprises—the Labour Party? What kind of policy would you apply
in the economic sphere?

Randolph Churchill: Well, of course, as it has been often said, you
can't completely unscramble the omelet. But on the other hand,
there are still quite a number of eggs left in the private chicken
roosts, which we might be able to safeguard.

—February 6, 1948

In the late 1940s, a historic opportunity opened up for the visionaries of a world made safe for private enterprise. Although the Democratic
Party had been in power for more than a decade, explosive tensions were
roiling within it that promised to compromise the coalition that Roosevelt had strung together. Moreover, a political void had opened in the
world order itself, and other than the Red Army, only American business
was poised to fill it. Although many industry leaders had benefited from
their connections to the effusive and popular FDR, they suddenly found
themselves on a platform from which they could promote their interests
worldwide.

One of the leaders tasked with extending this platform was Herbert
Brownell, chairman of the Republican National Committee. In a meeting in late 1945, Brownell had given a speech at a committee meeting
in Chicago. His appearance on *Meet the Press* on December 14, 1945,
was perhaps the first example of the campaign function that the Sunday-morning shows would play in our culture that might be labeled the
"Russert Primary."[16]

At that point, the strategy of the Republicans was not clear, and
their reasons for hope seemed limited, but Brownell and his fellow Republicans recognized that there were forces at work in the country that could
propel them back to power, and the key was to harness them. What the
Republicans needed was an iconic symbol with which to bludgeon the
Democrats, thereby pulling off key portions of their reliable constituency.
The obvious candidate was the imagery of Socialism. First, the United
States was confronting a daunting competitor for influence in Europe that
had gone through a Socialist revolution. Second, Socialist appeals were
catching on across Europe, where even England had thrown out the victor

of the Battle of Britain, Winston Churchill, and replaced his Conservative Party with a Labour Party that had become energized, in part, by the writings and organizing efforts of a professor from the London School of Economics, Harold Laski. "Socialism" was mud that had been successfully thrown in the past for Republicans and might stick on the New Dealers as well. Brownell explained how this approach in civil positioning might work again.

Larry Spivak: Mr. Brownell, you seem unwilling at the present moment to speak for the Republican Party, but I'm sure you'll speak for yourself. In your speech at Chicago, you were quoted as saying that if the American people do not believe in Socialism, then they should vote for the Republican candidate. Do you really believe that Truman, Byrnes, Vincent, Wallace, Hannegan, Patterson, and the other men around Truman are Socialists?

Herbert Brownell: You should have read the next paragraph in my speech.

Spivak: I did.

Brownell: In which I said all the Democrats are certainly not Socialists or in favor of Mr. Laski's philosophy, but the Democratic Party being made up today of the southern bloc, which maintains itself in power by denying the right of franchise to a substantial majority of the citizens in the South, the big-city machines, and the radical left wingers cannot obtain a majority of the people of this country without those radical left wingers, and they have to compromise with them in order to maintain themselves in power. And that means compromising with the people who believe in Laski's philosophy.

As this passage makes clear, the Republicans flirted for a time with using their inheritance as the party of Lincoln to shame the Democrats on their racism and maintenance of an abusive caste system. However, the willingness of the Truman administration to reform on its own, with programs and arguments like those that would eventually produce the great civil rights legislation of the mid-1960s, brought other forces into play that emphasized the utility of the rhetoric of freedom from government interference toward destabilizing the rhetoric of the equality of the common man.

The key focus of the Republican attack was on the very mechanisms of economic management that had made it possible for Franklin Roosevelt to push his equality agenda. The Republicans would make clear to the American people that more radical schemes like the full employment bill that Secretary of the Treasury Henry Wallace was pushing through

Congress were incompatible with the principles of the free-enterprise system. They would also show that the taint of Socialism extended to even the less invasive schemes of government financing that made practical the New Deal philosophy of social security, broadly considered. As Brownell explained in anticipation of Minnesota congresswoman Michele Bachmann, Keynesian deficit spending was the gateway drug to Marxism.

Larry Spivak: Well, who, who are the groups that they have—you think they have to compromise with—and what sort of socialistic planks they're going to have to accept or that they are accepting?

Herbert Brownell: Well, they're typified here in New York by the American Labor Party policies.

Spivak: Well, what, for example, what socialistic program has the American Labor Party here put over, through the administration?

Brownell: Well, the basis, the basis of Socialism, uh, is deficit financing, and that is the basic theory of the American Labor Party, Henry Wallace, left-wing, uh, branch of the Democratic Party.

Arnold Weischman (*The Newspaper PM*): That wouldn't be Marxian Socialism, would it, that you're referring to?

Brownell: It's the, it's the indispensable intermediate step.

Weischman: Would you say then that the deficit spending of President Roosevelt over the—during his administration—was socialistic? That's what they did—deficit spending.

Brownell: Uh, when it's carried farther and farther as the present tendency seems to be, Mr. Weischman, I'd say that that was the indispensable, intermediate step toward, toward, uh, Socialism in this country and radical left-wing tendencies.

Spivak: Wasn't a good chunk of the money that was voted, uh, approved by the Republicans in Congress, and wasn't most of it for the war?

Brownell: A good chunk of it was for the war, and that which was well spent, nobody thinks—[would have] had it otherwise; a good chunk of it was wasted by the bureaucrats in Washington and the government, and the Republicans didn't approve it and they never will.

The pieces of the postwar Republican critique were already clearly in place: deficits equal Socialism; guns are affordable, but butter is not. The story was clear enough. What the Republican establishment lacked was electoral votes to live it, and it just so happened that many of these were recently put up for grabs given the racial conflict brewing in the American South.

A great example of the forces that were suddenly in play for the Republicans is the January 9, 1948, appearance of Lee "Pappy" O'Daniel, the Democratic senator from Texas who had won the seat in the only election contest that Lyndon Johnson ever lost. O'Daniel was also a grain trader and opponent of rationing and price control who led a hillbilly band of some repute.

It was a typical feature of wartime economics to impose wage and price controls on key goods and services that made it possible to direct scarce resources to their most efficient uses. These operations were managed by the Office of Price Administration (OPA). OPA had ceased operation by 1948, but Senator O'Daniel had been riled to action by threats made by Secretary of Agriculture Clinton P. Anderson on *Meet the Press* the previous week. Anderson had suggested that in response to abusive practices in the agricultural markets he might "name the names" of the big meat speculators, effectively branding them as enemies of the public good. Many traders like O'Daniel saw this use of federal power as abusive, and he was one southern businessman who was unafraid to stand up to the "pinko" New Dealers right to their faces in the public square. The show's host introduced him as follows:

Albert Warner: Facing the press table is Senator W. Lee O'Daniel, Democrat of Texas. From the grain and flour business, he turned to politics. Using his own colorful tactics, including a liberal application of hillbilly music to the whole Texas landscape, he jumped into the governorship of the state, with a clear majority over twelve opponents—the first victory of this nature in the history of Texas. . . . The senator has been a storm center in Washington and in Texas—a Democrat, he has often voted with Republicans, not too easy for a Texan. He became a foe of the New Deal. He did not endear himself to his congressmen recently when he said the government was filled with senile old men. Some have called him reactionary, but his friends say he is an independent businessman looking for efficiency and standing up for individualism.

The O'Daniel performance did not disappoint. His was an early example of the colorful influence of the Texas businessman on American political culture. He quickly made clear his opposition to any return of price control or rationing.

Larry Spivak: Senator, you come from a great cattle country. Do you think meat rationing is necessary?

Lee O'Daniel: Well I, uh, I not only think it's, uh, not necessary; I know that it's not necessary. It's wholly unwanted and it's un-American and it's not needed, and, uh, we'll get into a lot of trouble if it's adopted.

O'Daniel had a natural grasp of the American liberal system, and he needed no Austrian economist to help him articulate the moral stakes involved in protecting it.

Sarah McClendon (Washington correspondent for eight Texas newspapers): Senator, before OPA died, I believe you and other senators said if price controls were removed that the price of beef would go down. Would you care to say why this failed to happen and today we have high-priced beef in the market?

O'Daniel: Well, I'm one of the gentlemen who didn't say anything about prices going up or down, either one; I didn't. I didn't use that argument because I didn't believe in that argument. I argued against OPA because I believe in our American system of free government. I believe the people should be free, and I was arguing for their freedom and their liberty. So that if anybody has anything to sell, why as a free American citizen, they can sell it for whatever somebody wants to pay for it.

Resistance to expanding the role of the federal government for the reconstruction of Europe or for the control of domestic prices was bolstered by the classical individualist idiom of democratic politics. In the hands of colorful figures like Lee O'Daniel it would raise national attention, but even in less musical language it would bolster a conservative reaction to the programs of the New Deal era. The continuity in thinking and in figurative reference from these early Republican efforts to the present is quite stunning, as the following sequence from an interview with the Republican representative from Minnesota, Harold Knutson, demonstrates. The episode aired on November 11, 1947, in reaction to President Harry Truman's speech in support of European recovery that would become the Marshall Plan. Note the resistance to income taxes on the matter of principle, the reference to Karl Marx, and the coining of a term, all of which rather directly herald the coming of Ronald Reagan.

Phelps Adams (*New York Sun*): I am particularly interested in their [Republican] suggestion, their very strong suggestion, that there be a ceiling, a 50 percent [ceiling] on income tax rates so that the government would never take more than half of a man's earnings in any year. Do you approve of that one too, Congressman?

Harold Knutson: Uh, in principle, yes. Of course, we've got to recognize the fact that the income tax was first, uh, advocated by Karl Marx as a means for drying up the source from which we draw venture capital to start new businesses. In his book he outlines it. One of the requisites for bringing about, uh, uh, socialization of the world is, uh, imposing such heavy income taxes as to drive industry into the lap, or into the fold, of the government.

Adams: In that connection, Congressman, isn't it true that ever since the income tax amendment was adopted back in 1913, I think that was . . .

Knutson: That's right.

Adams: Every time we've reduced tax rates, the yield from taxes to the Treasury has increased?

Knutson: You're absolutely right, Mr. Adams. Back in the '20s we had four tax reductions, and each one resulted in increased revenues.

Spivak: Mr. Knutson, is there any chance that we can get you to introduce a bill to do away with the income tax altogether?

Knutson: No, we can't do away with it, but at least we can use it in a manner that will be least hurtful to our economy.

. . .

Albert Warner: Mr. Congressman, you've used the term "do-gooders" that seems to be a favorite term with you. I think you used it also in hitting at the State Department for its, uh, its, uh, Geneva trade conference agreement. What is a do-gooder?

Knutson: Oh, a do-gooder is one who would rather think of his neighbors than his own family.

[*laughter*]

The list of concerns of these enemies of the New Deal was clear enough: hanging on to the old Democratic Party, supply-side tax cuts, do-gooders, and deficit financing as an intermediate step to Marxism. Reaganism was in the air in the opening scenes of the Pax Americana even while Reagan was still pursuing his acting career. The New Deal was well entrenched after four consecutive Democratic presidential terms, but its ideas seemed weakly supported and easily attacked by those who could remember the virtues of the small-government American system. The goal was to frame the Democrats as the party of class struggle and group rights while reminding the American people that the American way was to promote a free and independent society of self-motivated individuals. The trick was to pull this off in an environment in which giant industrial bureaucracies had taken over most sectors of the economy and routinized the work life of millions of Americans. In response to the rise of the multinational corporation, the New Dealers thought of their role in terms of what John Kenneth Galbraith would call countervailing power. The goal of Republican leaders was to convince the people that these corporations had no power to countervail.

The confidence and ideological purity that one finds in Republican leaders and the occasional southern Democrat in the 1940s may help explain why the victory of Harry Truman in the 1948 election and the coming of his domestic program in 1949 were greeted with such alarm and disdain. The key features of Truman's Fair Deal (central among them universal health care) were attacked consistently on *Meet the Press*, much as one would expect such programs to be attacked today if they were proposed. The flavor of this opposition becomes clear in this introduction to the first appearance of Senator Paul Douglas of Illinois, a University of Chicago economist who served as a stalwart liberal on both welfare legislation and civil rights issues right up to his defeat in a Senate run in the wake of the Chicago Freedom Movement in 1966.[17] Douglas was introduced on a radio version of the program on July 15, 1949, in voice-over tones seemingly drawn straight from Eric Johnston's masterwork, *America Unlimited*:

Announcer: The world is in the midst of a great struggle, and no man can say which side will win. The struggle is between the individual and the state. The issue is ages old, but of pressing significance now. How can man in our complicated society get greater security without sacrificing his freedom? Can he do it through the Socialist state or by some variation of it? The Russians have gone all out for Socialism, and the individual has paid for it by the loss of his freedom. England's goal, too, is Socialism. But thus far she has moved slowly and kept most of her major freedoms. Here in America we, too, are searching for an answer. We know that men cannot divide more than they produce. We believe that security at the price of liberty is too great a price to pay. Is there enough wisdom in our people and among our leaders in business and labor and government to keep us free and bring us plenty? Today we have greater security and greater freedom here than anywhere else in the world. Can we keep it? Or must we, too, travel the road of the totalitarians? Here now to give you his answer to those questions is Paul H. Douglas of Illinois.

Even without the dramatic opening music, no *Meet the Press* introduction can compete with this one for intimidation value. But Senator Douglas was used to pointed questions; in fact, he had said that his experience in the Senate was "like a bull among the darts of the matadors." What distinguished Douglas's line of critique from much of what we now see in public debates about the economy and social welfare policy was the willingness with which he located and named the enemies of equality and how clearly the principles of the Progressive era framed his perspective. Douglas recognized clearly that to stand for an idea in the civil sphere, one needed to stand against something as well. These attitudes were on display in a televised version of the program from September 24, 1949.

Richard Harkness (NBC commentator): Senator Douglas, you're in the vanguard, shall we say, of the Fair Deal. Mr. Herbert Hoover has called the Fair Deal collectivism—

Paul Douglas: The welfare state.

Harkness: Uh, Mr. James F. Byrnes has called it statism. Do you think that those are scare words?

Douglas: Well, I think they're highly inexact. I don't quite know what they mean. And insofar as they're scare words or designed to be such, I think that they are false. I suppose you are referring to the fact that these gentlemen seem to regard it as improper for the federal government to act on matters of welfare. Is that right, Mr. Harkness?

Harkness: No. That wasn't it at all. I was merely quoting them and asking, asking your reaction. Uh, well, let me ask you this then, uh, since we're dealing with words, Mr. Douglas. You're an economist. As a Fair Dealer you say that the, eh, government can deliver welfare to everybody without the federal Treasury going bankrupt.

Douglas: Well, I—

Harkness: Let me finish my question. Please, sir. Uh, would you say then that, eh, the words "Fair Deal" are catchwords for voters?

Douglas: Well, uh, [it] seems to me that uh, if one goes back to the Constitution, you find that uh, the promotion of the general welfare is one of the four fundamental purposes for which the federal government was formed.

Harkness: The general welfare, that's right.

Douglas: Namely, to establish justice, ensure domestic tranquility, provide for the common defense, and promote the general welfare. And that is stated not only in the preamble of the Constitution, but it is stated in Article One, Section Eight, which lays down the powers of Congress. So I say that any government that's worthy of its salt, any American government, should legislate for the general welfare. What else should it legislate for but the general welfare?

Harkness: In other words, we've had a welfare state [*almost laughing*] since the Constitution was ratified?

Douglas: That's right. Only in times past, the federal government has passed legislation to help propertied groups, such as granting of land for railroads, protective tariffs, patent rights, RFC [Reconstruction Finance Corporation], and so forth, and no complaint came from Mr. Hoover or from the progenitors of Mr. Hoover when the federal government was asked to act in these respects. It was only when the federal government began to help the unemployed and to take care of health and try to provide housing for the people without property that this was said to be dangerous.

As confident as Douglas's midwestern Progressivism was, unreconstructed New Dealers like himself were taking heat from the proponents of big business armed with Victorian economic ideas old enough to seem new. In an appearance on March 26, 1948, during the height of that tax battle, the supply-side argument for economic stimulus comes through rather clearly, even as its spokesman, Republican senator Eugene Milliken of Colorado, proposed it in a less sure voice than Reagan surrogate, David Stockman, would on the program many years later. Incentives to "risk investment" would outweigh risks of budget deficits.

Ernest K. Lindley (*Newsweek*): Senator Millikin, it's rather hard to be harsh with you tonight since we've all probably been computing how much we're going to save through your tax cut if it's passed, but I want to ask you a more serious question about it from another angle. Isn't it likely that this tax cut combined with the increased expenditures for defense, which are now in the offing, will throw the budget into the red next year?

Eugene Millikin: I would not say that it's likely, Mr. Lindley. Uh, I think it is, uh, a measure in aid of not going into deficit spending. Uh, the testimony before our committee, uh, indicated that, uh, investment capital is drying up, especially risk investment capital. Uh, the testimony was to the effect that we required tax reduction in order to stimulate risk investment to, uh, uh, uh, to stimulate risk investment. Uh, uh, history also shows that under conditions similar to the present, uh, an income tax reduction bill, uh, does not, uh, have the effect of reducing revenue. Uh, it has, uh, certain stimulating effects, uh, particularly when it, uh, uh, as I said before, uh, increases the incentive for, uh, risk investment.

Senator Millikin stuttered in his defense of what would one day come to be known as supply-side economics; later cohorts would speak with more authority and confidence. This was a crusade on which all keepers of the faith had to remain patient. And if the risk investment/flatter taxes piece of free-market rhetoric was already in place in the immediate postwar context, so, too, was the fear of planning and the kind of corporatism that John Kenneth Galbraith would advocate.

To get a sense of the fear in play of government economic planning and something like a new class of government bureaucrats who had taken over Washington, we can find no better example than that of the second of five appearances on March 16, 1949, by Truman's vice chairman of the newly formed Council of Economic Advisers, from which I quote at length:[18]

Larry Spivak: Mr. Keyserling, I have before me a UP release, in which Representative Noah M. Mason, Republican of Illinois, has said that you were the most powerful and most dangerous man in America today. Would you care to comment on that?

Leon Keyserling: Well, I can comment on that, Mr. Spivak, by asking the people who are, uh, listening to this program and seeing it just to look at me [*placid and homely voice*]. Do I look like the most dangerous or the most powerful man in the United States?

Spivak: No sir, those are the things that are in your mind, not on your face, Mr. Keyserling. You have a very benign and very pleasant face and a very nice smile.

Keyserling: Thank you, sir.

. . .

Warren Francis (*Los Angeles Times*): Well, uh, Mr. Keyserling, there is a great deal of wonder about what position you occupy and what the advisory Council of

Economic Advisers does. Are they going to tell Americans how to spend their money and make America over?

Keyserling: Why, certainly not. Nobody wants to make America over. It's a grand country—by far the most wonderful country in the world. We want to make it better; all of us do. Nobody wants to make it over.

. . .

Spivak: I want to ask this question before I read some of these things. Do you think that the Spence [economic stabilization] Bill will contribute to greater freedom in our economy and in our democracy? Do you seriously think that?

Keyserling: [*pause*] Well, I certainly do.

Spivak: You think that by giving powers to the president, uh, like those given to him in the Spence Bill, over prices and wages censorship, powers to acquire enormous property, to set up government corporations, powers to buy and allocate unlimited amounts of commodities—you think that that's going to make our economy freer?

Keyserling: [*pause*] Well, I really think that [*broken voice*] . . . I really think that you know that those questions are not very penetrating. Every government operation that has ever been undertaken has involved either the setting up of a corporation or some other agency.

. . .

Spivak: Well, Mr. Keyserling, would you trust this bill to any president—would you, for example, have been glad to have this power in the hands of a Harding, or a Huey Long, or anybody of that kind? I mean, remember, we are in a democracy and presidents change. Would you give a general bill with all of these powers to one man without the the, uh, uh, uh, checks that we ought to have in a country like ours?

Keyserling: Well, I wouldn't have liked to see Huey Long invested with the powers invested in the president of the United States by the Constitution of the United States. And that reveals the slant of your question, doesn't it, Mr. Spivak?

Spivak: No, but I'm speaking specifically about these powers themselves, which you say you had a hand in preparing. Would you have had these powers in the hands of many presidents that you knew?

Keyserling: Would you have wanted Huey Long to have the powers which you think a president of the United States appropriately has?

Spivak: No, but the only thing—in a democracy you take the chance that you someday may have a Huey Long, and for that reason you have protective laws. Isn't that your understanding of a democracy—that you have checks and balances to make sure that no *bad* man can do *bad* things to the country?

Keyserling: My understanding of a democracy is that it is not contemplated that the president of the United States have only those powers which a bad man would misuse. I certainly have much more faith in that democracy. A bad man shouldn't have any powers. A bad man shouldn't be president of the United States.

Martha Rountree: Mrs. Craig.

May Craig (Portland, Maine, *Press Herald*): But Dr. Keyserling [*tone rising*], if you forge the weapon of centralization, the dictator invariably comes and grabs it; that's what happens everyplace else. It could happen here.

Once you have seen enough of the *Meet the Press* archive, you know that when you see May Craig jumping on a line of argument with emotion, it is clear that middle America had just been moved as well. It must have appeared in those grim days of British Socialism, tax-cut rollbacks, and Chinese Communism that the planners, bureaucrats, and do-gooders of the Fair Deal were quite close to achieving their goal of establishing a Socialist dictatorship right here at home.

Among the unrealized Progressive dreams for social security, the fight for health care stands out.[19] One of the most entertaining episodes to highlight the way that libertarian (or at least laissez-faire) doctors successfully forestalled its realization was a radio program from December 9, 1949, during the push for Truman's medical insurance program. The guest was Morris Fishbein, who had just been forced into retirement from his position as editor of the *Journal of the American Medical Association*. He was introduced as "the most controversial figure in the medical world today."

Larry Spivak: Well, Dr. Fishbein, I'd like to get down to the nub of this question. As I understand, your objection to national health insurance is first because it's compulsory, second because it's socialistic—whatever that may mean—and third because it brings bad medicine. Is that essentially true?

Morris Fishbein: I would say that those three points are essentially true.

Spivak: Alright. Now, on the compulsory end of it—is this medical—the AMA against compulsion for compulsion's sake?

Fishbein: I think they believe that those nations which hope to be democratic must place as much responsibility on the individual citizen for the conduct of the intimate affairs of his life as can be placed upon him.

As a demonstration of how this single aspect of the conversation about the management of economic affairs has not changed much over the course of this debate, I offer this final exchange between Larry Spivak and Dr. Fishbein.

Spivak: Well, Doctor, isn't it true that under the army you had complete socialization of medicine and you had a pretty high order of medical—

Fishbein: Now, I answered that one time for Senator Pepper, so it's very easy to answer that one again.

Spivak: Don't give me the same answer though.

Fishbein: Oh, th—it served with him. Now, the answer is simply this—that in the army the doctor had absolute control over the patients. If you are willing that the doctors of this country shall tell everybody in the country exactly what they shall do when they're sick, and that they shall do that and nothing else—give the doctors the kind of almost totalitarian control over people that they had in the army in times of sickness—why then, of course, you abolish freedom entirely.

Earlier in 1949, the freshman senator Hubert Humphrey was grilled for, among other things, his support for the coming health legislation of the Fair Deal. In this interview Humphrey demonstrated his creativity in a way that points to his rise as a Progressive leader in the era of social legislation that followed. As only a few key figures in that period could do, Humphrey used the language of the Progressive Left to invert the line of attack that his questioners directed at him toward the program of social rights for which he was known.

Glenn Neville (*New York Daily Mirror*): Senator, what I want to know is, is there anyone among you Democratic Progressives who is interested in keeping the cost of government down instead of increasing it all the time?

Hubert Humphrey: I am definitely interested in economy in government. And economy in government to me does not necessarily mean spending little. It means spending what you have and spending it well. Just as economy in a home doesn't necessarily mean spending a little. Now, I am interested in governmental reorganization. I want to see as many dollars saved as can be humanly saved in terms of increasing government efficiency. But this curtailing of services is not governmental economy. It's a governmental type of extravagance. It's social extravagance.

Neville: Where do you get your money? You get your money from the people and simply redistribute it, adding on an administration cost, do you not?

Humphrey: Yes. That's true. We must, of course. All the money in this country comes from the people, and let's not have business forget that either. Money, and the American national incomes, comes from the people. People produce the goods and services. And I want to say that an educated child that develops—matures—into manhood is a much better producer than one that has been denied the opportunities of education. A healthful child that grows into healthful manhood or womanhood is a much more productive citizen and will increase his productivity as he goes into the areas of industry. And a soil that's taken care of, sir, is a much more productive soil. Now, that isn't an expenditure of money in terms of what you call extravagance; that is an investment. This is an investment in the future and the present day of America.

C. Norman Stabler (*New York Herald Tribune*): Why, Senator, in connection with those last two questions, I wondered just where you'd stop in the welfare state. You would have so many things done for the people and then tax the people to pay for them. Why not buy shoes for them and their clothes? Where will you stop short of a totalitarian government?

Humphrey: May I say that the best way to evade a totalitarian government is for the organized community, known as the nation, be represented by its government to take some vital concern in the welfare of the individuals.[20]

Thomas Jefferson was rolling over in his grave. His agrarian vision for the Democratic Party had been replaced with a newer ideal. For young Humphrey and his ilk, a business enterprise was itself a bureaucratic operation, one that had fallen into ill repute because of its unfair and monopolistic tendencies when the great industrial trusts were invented in the late nineteenth century. Concentrated economic power had to be checked with another power, that of the "organized community known as the nation."

From the perspective of the US Chamber of Commerce this blend of nationalism and Socialism could only remind them of their recently defeated enemies. The Republican Party was desperate to find a way to limit the tragic implications of the New Deal. In 1932, *Time* magazine ran a piece on a Soviet political purge titled "Stalin's Omelet," in which a party official, Lazar Kaganovitch, reportedly said, "Why wail over broken eggs when we are trying to make an omelet!" Later, Walter Duranty, in a dispatch from Moscow in March 1933, described a famine induced by Stalin's collectivization of farms with the lines, "But—to put it brutally—you can't make an omelet without breaking eggs." In the 1940s, the captains of American enterprise thought that Roosevelt, too, had broken too many eggs in the making of his New Deal. The principle of social security had become enshrined in the hearts of the people alongside the free-enterprise ideal of the gilded age, and there was a need to unscramble this omelet, even if it took the patience of Job to do it.

The Middle of the Road

Henry Gemmill (*Wall Street Journal*): I am almost too awed to question an economist who advises the president; I respect you all, present and past. I suppose you have noticed that two of your sharpest critics are Leon Keyserling, who advised Mr. Truman in the same role as you have, and who seems to feel, if I correctly interpret him, that you have really done nothing at all that the Eisenhower crowd didn't do under similar circumstances, and that we are headed for stagnation and another recession. We then also have Arthur Burns, who held the job for President Eisenhower. He seems to criticize you from precisely the opposite direction, that you have been doing too much fiddling with the economy and that we are headed right straight for another inflation and balance of payments crisis. Are these gentlemen bad economists or good politicians? What do you have to say?

Walter Heller: I have to say first of all that the position of the man in the middle is always difficult. I have to say secondly that apparently we are hitting somewhat a middle of the road between two extremes.

—September 3, 1961

In 1960, Nixon had lost to Kennedy in a nail-biting election in which many blocs of voters could have tilted either way, and it seemed that if either candidate could have appealed more effectively to the practical needs of organized groups, the election might have gone the other way. When the Democrats returned to power under John F. Kennedy in March 1961, they had learned many of the lessons of the Eisenhower era, namely, that there had been an "exhaustion of political ideas," as Daniel Bell had described it in the subtitle of his book *The End of Ideology*.[21] The McCarthyites and John Birchers had been tamed and in the process had neutralized any remaining leftist threats. In the "Mad Men" era, American elites were distressingly sane. They had settled into a kind of smooth accommodation between capital and labor that seemed secure under either a Democratic or a Republican administration. The name of the game in the New Frontier was to conquer the middle and to win over groups with well-defined interests.[22]

Accommodation was in and extremism was out. Even Nixon would later demonstrate, as President Eisenhower had before him, that he was perfectly happy to engage in fairly aggressive interventions into the free market in support of the welfare state. As John Gerring has argued, the Kennedy administration was represented by the arrival of a new kind of Democratic ideology that had begun back in the early 1950s with the campaigns of Adlai Stevenson. What these Stevenson Democrats were missing was a nose for finding villains for economic problems. Unlike either Roosevelt or Truman, neither Stevenson nor Kennedy conveyed in his public message any clear sense of the economic threat to democracy that the private-enterprise system posed to average Americans.[23] These were not the kind of Democrats who were overly exercised over the power of the Few.

Kennedy pivoted away from the rhetoric of class struggle toward that of the "rising tide" that lifts all boats and sensible and professional macroeconomic management. Under his stewardship, the solidaristic energies of the Roosevelt persuasion were turned in new directions when they were not lost altogether. Kennedy-era villains were supplied by what were almost stock characters, like the race-baiting governor of Alabama, George Wallace; the self-parody of an anticommunist Robert Welch of the John Birch Society; and the made-for-television gangster union boss Jimmy Hoffa. Where Roosevelt had likened the rule of organized money to that of an organized mob, Kennedy joined the revenue proposals of the investment class with cutting-edge ideas drawn from the best economics departments in academia. It was a politics of consensus: the middle between two extremes.

The best example of the exhausted ideas that marked the New Frontier era is an interview with Charles Percy, chairman of the Bell & Howell Corporation, who in 1966 replaced Paul Douglas as senator from Illinois in a racially charged election. In 1959, Percy had been busy crafting the message of the Republican Party, even if by today's standards he looks more like a New Democrat than any stripe of Republican. Percy first appeared on *Meet the Press* on October 18, 1959. In this post-*Sputnik* environment, anxieties were directed toward the Soviet military threat and the notorious "missile gap." Percy had prepared a strategic document for matching the Soviet threat with an economic growth agenda that included a liberal dose of social welfare spending. This document served as the basis for the 1960 Republican platform on which Nixon ran and for the moderate ideological position that Percy called "dynamic conservatism."

Roscoe Drummond (*New York Herald Tribune*): I would like to raise another aspect of controversy within the party and put it to you frankly: Many people, I think, honestly feel that one reason the government is not making greater headway in closing the gap in scientific weapons with Russia is the budget ceiling. You have stated, and we have all read in the report, that you definitely would not let the concept of a balanced budget stand ahead of achieving that. Would you, then, be frankly saying that at this point this is a significant departure from administration policy?

Charles Percy: There is no question but what the expenditure for [the] military will increase in future years. What we have simply said is that we must cut down in some areas to emphasize other areas.

Drummond: No, but haven't you said that you would put the priority objective of closing the missile gap ahead of the priority objective of a balanced budget?

Percy: Absolutely.

. . .

Jack Bell (Associated Press): We have another sizable gap, too, in space. Your report says that we are planning to transport a man to the moon by 1970. Don't you think we will find a Russian colony already existing there if we wait until 1970?

Percy: We said certainly by 1970 this is possible. I think we would all be very disappointed if this were not possible before that date.

. . .

John Steele (Time-Life): It seems to me that almost every recommendation in your reports was qualified with a "but," seemingly to limit the role of the federal government. It was true of your recommendations on housing, education, and social welfare. What is this fear and trembling about the growth of the federal government?

Percy: I don't think we have any fear or trembling about it. I think we have made a very clear-cut statement right in our preface that we believe that we should have strong, efficient, central government. I think there is a misimpression that Republicans are against central government. We are not. We think there must be a strong government to carry out our military policy, a strong government to carry out our foreign policy, which only can be carried out by the federal government.[24]

Even as the democratic class struggle faded,[25] the era of big government had only just begun; Eisenhower had carried it to term and Kennedy was its midwife. The ideas of the dynamic conservative were contained in a six-teen-year plan that the Republican idea man Charles Percy had proposed, and the plan was quite compatible with what would become the Kennedy program, complete with attention to military superiority over the Soviets and a man-on-the-moon program by decade's end. It made no more sense at the time for capital and labor to demonize one another than it did for whites and blacks to do so. The idea was to split the middle, to find the best ideas on all sides, and to reach a consensus.

Among the best representatives of the spirit of this new age of post–class antagonism was the economist Walter Heller, Kennedy's chairman of the Council of Economic Advisers. Heller was a centrist Keynesian who eventually enjoyed the distinction of having appeared more times than any other economist on *Meet the Press*; his appeal was due partly to his successful triangulation of issues in the dynamics of class and economy. Heller began as a hero of the moderates while he held office but was later celebrated on the right for his support of investment-focused tax cuts.

In 1963, President Kennedy proposed a stimulative tax cut that would not be matched with spending cutbacks.[26] It was a Keynesian intervention into the economy that sent Washington into a tizzy. What was then known as the "Heller tax cut" was not passed until the Johnson administration in 1964, but the subsequent surge in economic activity that followed it brought the idea of fiscal stimulus into the mainstream of economic thinking, even in Republican ranks. Seven years later President Nixon, following Milton Friedman, famously declared that "we are all Keynesians now." But at the time, the prospect that the government would voluntarily incur a large deficit to stimulate the economy was somehow dumbfounding to large parts of established opinion. Making matters worse for the logic of government activism, in an effort to sell the plan, Heller had made a provocative argument in support of it. In part of a complex shift in the Left's demonology from class to culture,[27] Heller suggested that the only thing holding Americans back from promoting a healthy and thriving economy was the Puritan ethic, the very complex of ideals that many people credited with establishing the values of the country. This curious rhetorical pivot gave critics of deficit financing an opportunity to mount a delaying attack on the president's plan that was successful until after Kennedy's tragic assassination.

Kennedy demonstrated his inborn centrist tendencies in selecting Walter Heller, one of those superdelegates of the zeitgeist whom most of us have forgotten. He is best remembered for his central role in promoting the fabled Kennedy tax cut, which has become one of the most powerful scripts in the social rights drama that has defined the parameters of economic reform. Without the Kennedy tax cut there might have been no Reagan tax cut and subsequently no Bush tax cut and eventually no "fiscal cliff." It was around Kennedy's example that Republicans often rallied. What they saw in the plan was something that Heller had advocated, but from a very different point of view; the big money behind the Republican Party saw that they could advocate a less progressive tax structure on the theory that this would stimulate the job creators to use their money more energetically, thereby reframing the Heller tax cut as one of the best examples of supply-side economics.

The first brush with Heller's civil positioning of deficit stimulus through tax cuts came on February 10, 1963, as the tax-cut proposal was under consideration.

Richard Harkness (NBC commentator): Doctor, I suppose that most of us translate government budgets and economic policies in terms of our own families or own businesses. For instance, I am quite sure the Harkness family could not reduce its income, as you would by reducing taxes, and spend more. I am sure that we'd end right up in the poorhouse, and I think a lot of people in this country think that the government is headed the same way. What is your comment on that?

Walter Heller: My comment on that is that many a business has headed into riches precisely that way. How did Henry Ford, for example, accomplish what he did? Namely, by lowering the price of his product and by increasing volume, and by cutting taxes now and invigorating the economy and increasing incentives, the president is convinced and his advisers are convinced that we will stimulate additional activity, and we will get more revenue in the long run and get the balanced budget sooner that way.

. . .

Vermont Royster (*Wall Street Journal*): Dr. Heller, I'd like to return to this question that seems to be bothering the Harkness family so much. You have proposed that we cure a long succession of government deficits by deliberately planning the biggest planned deficit that has ever been incurred in peacetime by this or any other country, and I believe that you have complained that the American people have difficulty in understanding this because they are imprisoned in a "Puritan ethic." That is, people aren't smart enough to understand why big deficits financed by inflation aren't good economics. In your opinion, Dr. Heller, what is wrong with the Puritan ethic?

Heller: . . . As to the Puritan ethic, let me say first of all that I was citing in an admiring tone, not as a slur, not suggesting for a moment that the American people don't have the capacity for understanding. What I was saying was this, that because essentially of the Puritan ethic they are willing to deny themselves tax cuts unless and until they are convinced that they are in the national interest. And our job, it seems to me and the administration, is to show that they definitely are in the national interest, that the stimulus to jobs, to incentives, to profits, to production, will more than make up the lost revenues. And as I said to Mr. Harkness, the best outlook for a balanced budget is to get up to a prosperous level, cut down unemployment, cut down unused capacity, and get the revenues that go with a fully prospering economy.

And the attack on the Puritan ethic did not end there. Over a month later, on March 17, 1963, the voice of middle America, May Craig, came after Heller in an interview with a Republican skeptic of the stimulus idea, Congressman John W. Byrnes of Wisconsin.

May Craig: Dr. Heller, the president's economic adviser says that people who think you shouldn't cut taxes without cutting spending are suffering from a basic "Puritan ethic," and you said that you are more of a "a Puritan than a Heller." What do you think a Puritan is, and what do you think a Heller is?

John Byrnes: Of course, I was making my reference to Mr. Heller on the basis of his fiscal philosophy of planned deficits. Whereas I think the basic Puritan ethic that he was complaining about—and there is no question about what he was complaining—was that as far as people generally are concerned, they resist the idea of going into debt. They resist the idea of increasing spending at the same time you are decreasing your revenue during a period when you are already progressing at a high debt level each year.

Although the pivot to tax-cutting stimulus was a big success for Heller and for Kennedy's economic legacy, the net result may have been to reinforce the idea of Democrats as big spenders. Moreover, with his pejorative reference to the Puritan ethic as the adversary of Democratic economics, Heller replaced the imagery of class antagonism that had justified the spending programs since Roosevelt with a cultural interpretation on the crest of a wave of cultural change that would fragment the New Deal coalition and undermine its social protection narrative.

At the height of the Fair Deal Leon Keyserling had argued on March 16, 1949, that the success of the economy lay in the hands of a wise business class, a line that implicitly placed the blame on a foolish one. "I think one of the biggest reasons why we have thus far been spared from the kind of economic relapse that we had in 1920 and 1921, is that the managers of our business system as a whole are wiser, more farsighted, more appreciative of the interests of the economy as a whole than they ever were before." But Heller's story, like those told by many liberals in the period, had no villains and consequently no heroes. In an otherwise forgettable episode in the history of civil positioning, Heller revealed the spirit of liberal management in the period by impugning the very Protestant ethic that Max Weber had lionized as the spirit of capitalism. As cultural revolution became an ever more irresistible pull for lovers of more expansive notions of liberty, the Democratic Party was going through its own cultural evolution. FDR had once crowed that the previous "do-nothing" government had promised social welfare that would not cost a thing. Under Heller, Kennedy seemed to be saying that the only thing we have to fear is Plymouth Rock.

The major theme of the theatrical side of Kennedy's management of the economy was to pivot away from Roosevelt-era class politics and toward a conception of economic democracy predicated on courting business, managing macroeconomic risks, and overcoming outdated folkways. It is astonishing that the succeeding administration under Lyndon Johnson promoted social welfare legislation on a pace to rival that of his hero Franklin Roosevelt, while adding little or nothing to the collective repertoire of literary supports of the equality agenda.

As Robert Caro had said, Johnson was a master of the Senate, but this did not imply he was a visionary of the moral imagination.[28] Instead, when it came to a grand vision, he relied primarily on the Kennedy bequest. As he said in his speech to Congress upon Kennedy's death, "My fellow Americans, let us continue." Johnson was not a kind of drudge workhorse who was averse to public debate and the political power of well-placed social drama. He had an ear for the show business of politics and is remembered for the ennobling rhetoric he presented in several powerful and important speeches. Bold as he was, however, from the standpoint of democratic theory his administration was to the Kennedy administration what Truman's was to Roosevelt's. Johnson spent his abundant energies and legislative skills to find ways to implement and justify Kennedy's initiatives and ideas: national aid to education, medical insurance for the elderly, and civil rights.

Johnson was an implementer, and when he implemented, it was at an hectic pace. In almost every place that Kennedy failed to produce legislation, Johnson succeeded. Yet if one looks at the record of the national conversation as contained in the *Meet the Press* archive, one finds very little focus on the major social welfare legislation of the period.[29] Johnson just did not make the theory of the case for Medicare, and in origins we discover destinations. In the place of an argument for social protection there was constant and energetic discussion about race, civil rights, and Vietnam. Thinking about the bitter public drama that surrounded President Obama's Affordable Care Act, one would expect, looking back, to see similar arguments about the passage of Medicare, education, extension of Social Security, and other similar initiatives, but it simply did not happen. Perhaps as a consequence, the public was never bonded to the New Frontier social policy as they had been to that of the New Deal.

This raises the question, Why did Johnson make so little public hay about what would be some of his career-defining achievements? Part of the answer is simply his political realism. Johnson's preference was to provide results and to resort to talk only when it looked like he was likely to lose. The Medicare bill had the votes in 1965 that it did not in 1962, so it produced little public discussion in the former case, while it produced a lot in the latter. But things go deeper than that. My sense is that in the flush 1960s there was simply no clear sense of democratic peril represented by economic inequality: bigwigs made for bad villains in a bipartisan consensus.

This even held for the poverty program. In the 1960s poverty was something that for most Americans happened to other people, while in the 1930s it was something that was likely going to happen to you. Consequently, in the War on Poverty, there was no obvious threat to American liberty; there was only a moral imperative, and in the absence of villainous threat for the people to rally against, it was bound to fail.

In Johnson's Great Society speech, there is no explicit mention of democracy, freedom, or human rights. The same is true of his special address to Congress in which he announced the War on Poverty on March 16, 1964. Instead, he presented a call to commitment to share the abundance of a free society with others. The idea was redistributive; it was not framed as compensation for past exploitation or the abuse of concentrated economic power. For reasons that have much to do with inflammatory racial animosity, Johnson did not promote his poverty plan as Roosevelt had done, with an unambiguous story about how his enemies would thwart him in his efforts to bring justice to the mass of the people. Instead, he sermonized and shamed his following to action. As David McCullough narrates in a popular history of the subject, "Johnson would make war on poverty and there would be no casualties. Everyone would be a winner, even big business."[30]

Most revealing, however, is that Johnson could summon the artistry of high drama when he found it necessary. As Daniel Bell has admitted, the end of ideology was little more than a transition in ideology to new objects.[31] The literary constraints on Johnson's support for social protection could not find a greater contrast with those of his Voting Rights Act speech on August 6, 1965.

I speak tonight for the dignity of man and the destiny of democracy. I urge every member of both parties, Americans of all religions and of all colors, from every section of this country, to join me in that cause. At times, history and fate meet at a single time in a single place to shape a turning point in man's unending search for freedom. So it was at Lexington and Concord. So it was a century ago at Appomattox. So it was last week in Selma, Alabama.

The irony of the Great Society is that it was not received for what it was, the realization of Hubert Humphrey's dream to use the public power to ensure both social and cultural rights in a way that did not compromise individual liberties. Instead, it was billed on the national stage as a divisive drama in which one civil virtue (freedom) was pitted against another (tolerance). The moment demanded that Johnson pit his bigwig rhetoric against their bureaucrat rhetoric, which he chose not to do. It was Lyndon Johnson who had the chance to live Humphrey's dream, and it quickly turned out to be a nightmare.

We Can Start a Prairie Fire

I believe we have been going down a dangerous road in this nation.
Now I have an opportunity to put these views into practice. . . . We can start a prairie fire that will sweep across a number of states.

—Ronald Reagan, May 26, 1968

It is easy to see in retrospect that the Kennedy pivot from the rhetoric of equality to something less threatening under the influence of academic economics and the US Chamber of Commerce was a major change in the national conversation about the economy. With no clear class enemy to fight as Roosevelt and Truman had, the Democratic Party shifted its energy to other concerns and other narratives of liberty and repression. Opponents of the Kennedy-Johnson pivot, like Barry Goldwater and Ronald Reagan, faced a difficult ideological challenge. They had to position themselves on the other side of pending civil rights legislation of the mid-1960s in a way that was consistent with a vision of the future of individual liberty that could in some way transcend the divisive founding prejudices of the nation.

To do this, Goldwater, and Reagan would have to step once more into the breach to combat the expansion of the social security state. Because the politics of the time were so dominated by the avowed and irrefutable dramatizations of injustice by civil rights activists, Goldwater and Reagan and the conservatives who followed them were typically portrayed as enemies of tolerance and inclusion. But the strength of their hand was that they knew that the political realignment under way would allow them to channel the support of the cohorts of racial reaction toward their larger goal, to redeem the politics of the vanquished forces of Herbert Hoover and the Victorian economists. Democrats fought the leading movement conservatives by often depicting them as racists, which on the whole they were not. Less attention was paid both then and now to what they really were—champions of unregulated private enterprise that rendered them enemies of group rights of all sorts. The transformative Republicans were not racists but laissez-faire irredentists who were not afraid to exploit the divisive innuendo. In this way, the energies of cultural conservatism could be directed toward a larger project, to salvage the cause of freedom in the world through the mechanism of a private-enterprise system unshackled from the social and cultural rights agendas of Franklin Roosevelt and Hubert Humphrey.

Because of the fierce urgency of the time and the rather direct way that leading conservatives flirted with the established forces of American race pride, the libertarian focus of the conservative movement is often mischaracterized as somehow essentially bigoted. But the free-market fundamentalism that conservatives began to rediscover in this period was only incidentally connected to the supremacist ideal. Reaganism was a simple extension of postwar Republican politics, which, as Chairman Brownell had clearly stated, was opposed to "denying the right of franchise to a substantial majority of the citizens in the South." Just as George Wallace standing in the schoolhouse door in 1963 became an indelible image of racial oppression, Barry Goldwater's "extremist" courtship with southern race baiters has left the impression that conservative economics was little more than coded racism. But for all the semiotic continuities between the property gospel of a Ronald Reagan and the states' rights cynicism of a Strom Thurmond, the virtues of the free market for the Jeffersonian American transcended race just as clearly as Adam Smith transcended Scotland.

Although Nixon is known for implementing the race-charged southern strategy, it was originally Barry Goldwater's idea. There is a paradox in the Goldwater southern strategy that we see him first begin to articulate on *Meet the Press* in a 1955 interview.[32] The southern strategy was both a cynical ploy to gain segregationist votes and a kind of Fabian (and perhaps far-fetched) plan for the redemption of American original sin. Some may wonder at the awe with which Ronald Reagan is approached in conservative circles, but it can be explained by his heroic efforts to recover a robust faith in the Founders—by his project of narrative repair. In the height of the status revolution, Reagan discovered a way to reaffirm the Jeffersonian commitment to what in 1966 he called "the individual's right to the disposition of his property," while simultaneously opposing those people he described as "infected with the sickness of prejudice and discrimination." Racial anxiety could be used as a wedge to disrupt the class warfare and groups rights heresy of the tumultuous era of the New Deal, while at the same time promoting a great awakening of neoliberal spirit.

For more than a generation, figures like John Tower, Barry Goldwater, Ronald Reagan, and Newt Gingrich played off Friedrich Hayek against Gunnar Myrdal, balancing a turn against ethno-supremacism with a turn against government and its central instrument, taxation.[33] They capitalized on an opportunity to save the souls lost to Roosevelt's seductive class politics, while tolerating racial animus only insofar as it was necessary to accomplish the larger goal of promoting freedom. This led to conflicts in self-concept that were coded, complicated, and incredibly corrosive, and they are just as consequential fifty years later. We still confuse a preference for laissez-faire economics with racism.

The problem of race coding was both a boon and a challenge for the rise of conservative economics. It provided the Republicans with a ready cabal of colorful and gifted politicians from the South like the heirs to Pappy O'Daniel, but it also placed them clearly on the wrong side of history in regard to promoting the ethics of tolerance. To manage this dilemma, the Republican leadership required intellectual as much as political leadership. One model for a way forward was the example of the conservative academic John Tower, who became the first Republican senator from Texas since Reconstruction after taking over the Senate seat once held by O'Daniel and Lyndon Johnson. By playing with the nostalgic idea that the ideals of classical liberalism had become something of a conservative creed in America, the so-called economic conservatives could promote a liberal and even radical agenda under the rubric of preservation. Professor Tower appeared on *Meet the Press* on June 18, 1961.

Robert Abernathy (NBC News): Senator, you have been described as a man whose political philosophy lies somewhere between that of William McKinley and Alfred the Great. You call yourself a conservative. As a former professor of government, can you give us a brief definition of what you mean by the word "conservative"?

John Tower: Of course, in the field of academic and political science there are several accepted definitions of conservatism that apply in different cases. Our peculiar American variety of conservatism would, I think, go something like this: I believe that the conservative in the United States is one who wants to preserve our existing constitutional and legal system, one who wants to preserve our capitalist economy, one who wants to preserve the federal character of the republic. He is one who believes that—to perhaps simplify it a little bit—as Thomas Jefferson, that government is best which governs least. He opposes the centralization of too much power in the hands of the national government. He favors the devolution of power and responsibility on state and local government. He opposes high taxation and high spending. His concept is one that is basically libertarian or with the accent on liberty rather than with the accent on equality.

. . .

Raymond Brandt (*St. Louis Post-Dispatch*): Senator, four or five times during this interview you have used he word "preserve." Preserve everything. You have said nothing about looking forward, which seems to put you in the same category as the John Birch Society. Did you get the support of the John Birch Society?

Tower: I don't think that I got any formal support from them. . . . We believe in progress. We don't believe in status quo or standing still. We believe in progress, in sustained progress, but we think that progress can best be accomplished within the framework of free institutions. . . . We believe that economic growth should be regarded as the achievement of a free people, not as the function, the duty, the assignment of the national government.

It is with John Tower that we begin to see the truly muscular opposition to the concrete agenda of the civil rights movement from within a libertarian civil frame, along with built-in media hostility to the conservative movement. In the early days of the 1960s there was a great deal of confusion about how to manage the problems of cultural difference within the framework of democratic laws. Figures like Tower proposed an answer that would make it possible to join North and South in a new power bloc of conservative opposition to the expansion of the activist state, all based on a limited government interpretation of the moral economy.

Where someone like Ronald Reagan would prove diffident about his opposition to the concept of public accommodations in the 1964 Civil Rights Act, Tower was confident in his denunciation in his July 7, 1963, appearance in the role of chief strategist to the Goldwater campaign. What is so artful in his performance is his ability to blend in principled opposition to group rights in both forms—diversity and equality—in a single pass. Tower was one of the first to see how classical liberals could use the taint of multiculturalism to unscramble the omelet by using the new branding of the word "conservatism." With Tower and others like him, we begin to see the modern form of antireformist liberalism at its best.

Frank Van der Linden (*Nashville Banner*): Senator, you are the only Republican who sits in on the meetings on strategy held by the southern senators, led by Richard Russell of Georgia, and you predicted a long filibuster against President Kennedy's civil rights bill. Could you tell us, sir, do you think any part of this bill will be rejected by the Senate, and which part that might be?

John Tower: Which part will be rejected by the Senate? I think the part most likely to be rejected by the Senate is the so-called public accommodations provision, the one which would make it illegal for private business establishments to practice discrimination. I think that perhaps a good portion of the president's program might ultimately pass, but I think that that section will most probably be rejected.

. . .

Van der Linden: What about the proposal that is soon to come out of Adam Clayton Powell's Labor Committee in the House? That is for an FEPC [Fair Employment Practices Commission]. Do you think the union people will go for that, the workers themselves?

Tower: Again, I don't know just what the reaction is going to be. I personally intend to oppose the FEPC idea, because I don't want to see the federal government getting into the business of dictating employment practices. I think that some of this civil rights legislation has implications that go far beyond the pure matter of civil rights. It is a matter of extending government controls. It is a matter of drawing nearer and nearer to the establishment of a police state.

This is the line of thinking that Barry Goldwater carried into his disastrous 1964 campaign against Lyndon Johnson and that conservatives carried to victory decades later.[34] The key was the image of "dictating employment practices," an image that linked the politics of redistribution and that of recognition. To committed liberals, having recently witnessed Bull Connor's strong-arm tactics in Birmingham, Tower's logic might have appeared like a ruse of a covert racist, but it was something more as well. For the neoliberal conservative for which Tower was the model, the bureaucrat and his dictates (and later taxes) posed more danger to democracy than did the bigot and his hatred.

Barry Goldwater would lose the 1964 election in a landslide and after the emotionally bruising campaign, the Goldwater brand was in the dumps, as was anyone associated with it. But when Reagan, having won the gubernatorial election in California in 1966, tried his hand at presidential politics in 1968, enough had changed in the field of cultural politics to recommend the John Tower brand of antigovernment opposition to robust civil rights legislation. Much as Tower had counseled placing the accent on liberty rather than equality, Reagan could place the accent in his message on freedom over tolerance—property over propriety. It worked, and others noticed as this interview of May 26, 1968, demonstrates.

James J. Kilpatrick (Washington Star Syndicate): Let me then inquire about two
or three specific issues, if I could, Governor. Where do you now stand
on open occupancy housing legislation either at the federal or at the state
level?

Ronald Reagan: I stand where I stood all the time. I have always been opposed
to discrimination and prejudice. I have been opposed prior to the time
that it was against the law—against restrictive covenants. I am opposed
to them morally on the ground that I deplore anyone who does practice
this. On the other hand, I have to tell you that I believe there is a limit
to what we can do in solving these problems with legislation, and I don't
believe we serve any useful purpose either for the people we are trying to
help or for the rest of society here if we embark on the dangerous precedent of allowing government to interfere with the individual citizen's
right to the control and disposition of his own personal property. And I
say, this is something that can come back to haunt us in the future. I am
opposed to that.

. . .

Larry Spivak: Governor, may I check what you said a moment ago on a matter of
open housing? I understood—at least there has been a report that you have
changed your position about repealing California's open housing law, the
Rumford Act. Is that true?

Reagan: . . . No one has ever advocated that you wipe this law off the books completely and not replace it with necessary legislation to make sure that you do
all that can be done to curb the practice of discrimination. My only change
is, I believe we can do better. . . . The part of the bill that the people of California tried to change has to do particularly with the individual homeowner
and the government's now having a control on that individual and his right
to property, and believe me, this is the issue in California and I believe in
most people's minds—not a racism or a desire to discriminate, but a belief
that there is something dangerous, that there is a great tie between a right to
personal property and individual freedom.

With Tower and Goldwater's assistance, Reagan had discovered the product that would sell, but the Nixon victory in 1968 upended the conservative project just as it was hitting the market. In the lead-up to the Nixon presidency, Reagan demonstrated how one could pivot from bigotry to freedom by sublimating the white backlash. Counter-anti-discrimination policy could be articulated to Lockean liberal ideals to great electoral effect. But Nixon was no true believer. Just as he would frustrate jingoistic expectations by going to China, he also instituted wage and price controls to deal with the nagging problem of inflation in August 1971. What this meant for the kind of free-market purists who were becoming more vocal in the Republican Party was to signal how dangerous the climate had become for liberty. Neil Young had written the famous song "Ohio" about the shootings at Kent State the year before. A close student of Friedrich Hayek probably could have adapted the lyrics of that song to his own cause. It seemed that libertarians were finally on their own. As a practical expedient, Nixon had embraced the radical egalitarian agenda of John Kenneth Galbraith, who as a result of Nixon's actions was elected in 1972 as president of the American Economics Association. Things could hardly be worse for the classical liberal.

Given that Nixon had not only gone over to the Heller camp but had embraced what was seen as an abusive and intrusive government takeover of price and wage policy, the only hope for the laissez-faire neoliberal seemed to lie with the stark alternative of Austrian economics. Lucky for them the Nobel Committee would use its newly constituted prize for economic science to promote the classical economic model that had long ago fallen out of favor. Midway through the Ford administration, Hayek appeared on *Meet the Press* on June 22, 1975, to celebrate his reception of the prize and to promote an alternative point of view. As Hayek's reception made clear, the free marketers had a lot of work to do, but with gangster government as a constant threat, it was worth the effort.

Hobart Rowen (*Washington Post*): Dr. von Hayek, you talked in response to Mr. Levine of a painful adjustment of the unpleasant effects that we would have to endure in order to beat inflation. With all due respect, sir, aren't your theories somewhat unrealistic in a political sense? Do you visualize governments today being able to take such steps as you recommend?

Friedrich Hayek: Perhaps I'm unrealistic. As long as people do not fully realize the danger of inflation, they may well pressure for more inflation as a short-term remedy for evils, so we may well be driven into more until people have learned the lesson. What it means is that inflation will still do a great deal of harm before it will be cured.

By 1975, it had become as respectable to be a conservative as it was to listen to country music. Goldwater had claimed in his appearance of November 19, 1961, "When the history is written, my brand of conservatism is going to be called liberalism." Fourteen years later, history had already been written, and Goldwater was proving prescient. John Tower conservatives had opposed the key provisions of the Civil Rights Act of 1964, particularly the second and seventh titles, because they represented a threat to freedom supported under the guise of ethnic tolerance. Radical neoliberals like Hayek and Milton Friedman were now making it respectable to oppose even the most moderate versions of the Democratic economic agenda and did so on battle lines established in the era of nineteenth-century laissez-faire. As Brownell had argued thirty years earlier, "The basis of Socialism is deficit financing."

These influences were slowly metabolized through the political culture so that by 1978, the wave of respectable conservative thinking was beginning to crest. This was the year of the tax revolt in California and of more conservative economic thinking inside the Beltway in both major parties. Jimmy Carter was to lose his bid to promote a comprehensive energy policy, and antiracist thinkers with free-market agendas were all working on reinforcing projects of economic liberalization that would place significant pressure of the legacy of the Great Society and the tradition of activist government that Democrats had worked to establish for generations. To see how racially coded messages were purified of the taint of the prior decade, consider the steady set of appearances in 1978 by Alan Greenspan, Howard Jarvis, Jack Kemp, and Milton Friedman. All four of these power players promoted a tax-cutting line that built on the political efforts of the other over the course of the year. Together, they almost presented a unified front. The watershed event was California Proposition 13, which would limit property taxes to an increase of 1 percent of the full cash value of such property per year. As a by-product, the tax revolt would also make it difficult to fund the social protection programs that had been so popular in both parties.[35]

The racial conflicts of the Johnson administration had joined the ideas of poverty and race in the public mind, and Jarvis campaigned for the proposition in loosely coded language. This exposed him to attack for his use of the cultural subtext, even as he promoted a new libertarian line of proto-American thinking that persevered for the next three decades in the rhetoric of the Republican Party.

Bill Monroe (moderator): *Time* magazine quoted you a few months ago as saying the Constitution talks about the right of "life, liberty and property" but not "food stamps, illegal aliens and welfare." Doesn't that suggest that you are talking about the property owners getting back tax revenues specifically at the expense of poor people and minorities?

Howard Jarvis: We think that the people who own homes in the United States are the most important people in this country. We think that the most important thing in this country is to preserve the right to own private property because it is the number-one extension of human rights in the United States. Without the ownership of private property in the United States, freedom will disappear.

Jarvis was direct and intemperate in his willingness to use anticivil stereotypes of African Americans to promote his free-market ideas, but the other enemies of recent trends in tax policy revealed what the true motivation of the Goldwater-Reagan camp had been all along. The idea was to use the racially coded concerns about the welfare state to undermine the very idea of government intervention itself. In this sense, race could be used to undermine the class arguments of a host of Democratic leaders from William Jennings Bryan to Lyndon Johnson. Staunch antiracists like Jack Kemp supplied the policy tools and political cover to realize the Goldwater strategy, and committed professional libertarians with racially Progressive views like Greenspan and Friedman provided the intellectual firepower to soften the opposition for the Jarvis assault. These following excerpts are from appearances from April 9, September 17, and November 12, 1968, respectively.

Irving R. Levine (NBC News): The president has proposed a $25 billion tax cut. Some Republicans would like to see a larger tax cut. Early in his administration, President Carter proposed a $50 tax rebate, which he withdrew when the inflation rate began to rise. In view of the inflation picture at this time, is this the moment for a tax cut?

Alan Greenspan: It is always the moment for a tax cut in the sense that taxes are too high and, I think, do inhibit investment in this country, and I think to the extent that we build up taxes, it causes an extraordinarily heavy burden by curbing the rate of growth in federal spending. If you ask me, do I think that we should allow federal spending to rise indefinitely and cut taxes indefinitely, I would say that is playing a shell game with the American people and that while they may appear to have a tax cut, the inflation which would occur as a consequence would be the much sharper implicit tax on their real incomes.

. . .

Levine: To return to your tax proposal, you often cite the 1964 and 1965 tax cuts under John F. Kennedy, which resulted in increased economic activity and larger tax receipts, as underscoring the validity of your own proposals. But the Kennedy cuts came at a time when the inflation rate was at 1.4 percent, far below the present 7 to 8 percent inflation rate. Isn't that a major difference that you fail to take into account in your public statements?

Jack Kemp: I haven't failed to take that into account. In looking for an economic policy that would both be bipartisan and help get America moving again, as you look back in history, certainly in the experience under President Kennedy we had a very positive application of these incentive/effect–type economic policies that I have been talking about, along with Senator Roth and the vast majority of the Republican Party. There are differences to be sure, but one thing that is true today that was true then is that high tax rates are a burden on the American people and that they are discouraging the commerce and the market activity and the investment and work opportunities for all the American people.

. . .

Bill Monroe (moderator): Our guest today on *Meet the Press* is Dr. Milton Friedman, the Nobel Prize–winning economist who has been called an intellectual leader of the tax revolt. Dr. Friedman endorsed the original Proposition 13 in California and several tax-limiting initiatives that were on state ballots last Tuesday. An adviser to Republican presidents, he is now a senior research fellow at Stanford's Hoover Institution. Dr. Friedman, there were a good many tax-limiting initiatives on state ballots last Tuesday. Some of them passed; some of them did not. How do you interpret the results?

Milton Friedman: Most of those that did not should not have passed. They were not good amendments. On the other hand, most of those that did pass were of the kind that were desirable. I interpret the result of the election as a clear indication that the American people are getting fed up with having too much of their money wasted by government.

What Reagan had said of the Birchers on *Meet the Press* on January 9, 1966, he could also say of the Wallacites he was attracting in the era of busing and affirmative action: "I figure that any individual who elects to go along with me and vote for me has bought my philosophy, and I haven't bought his, and that is the way it is going to be." As a signal of how much things had changed since the mid-1960s in this debate, by 1982 it was those who exposed the racial implications of the laissez-faire approach who were now vulnerable for playing the race card, as noted in this exchange on July 25.

Rich Thomas (*Newsweek*): I would like to turn to the subject of Proposition 13, the California initiative in which the voters massively rolled back their existing property taxes and which seems to have found a responsive echo across the country. In a speech before a government employees union, you recently said this was a racist act, and I am wondering if this isn't something of a cheap shot in view of the fact that everyone else has sort of seen it as a simple demand on the part of a large segment of the California voters—passed sixty-seven to thirty-two or something like that—simply because they felt their taxes were too high. They have been going up very rapidly.

John Kenneth Galbraith: You mustn't be so solemn. I didn't say that. What I did say was that attacking bureaucrats is the only form of racial discrimination that is still permissible in this country. If one—if that is a cheap shot, why, it is going to be impossible to engage in conversation from now on.

Galbraith was right that it had become respectable to attack bureaucrats while playing the race game. The Reagan revolution depended on these dynamics as southern states and southern leaders slowly moved through the clarifying period of realignment into the Republican column. The goal of the transformation had little to do with race per se but with class—the class accommodation of the Roosevelt era that conservative opponents of the New Deal had never accepted. The welfare state was out of control, and if Reagan had to break a few eggs to unscramble the omelet, he would do it. The subsequent debates about the state and the economy from the late 1970s to the election of Bill Clinton were steeped in this murky brew of ideas. As Galbraith correctly predicted, it had become impossible for liberals like himself to engage productively in the conversation from then on.

Not the Old Democratic Ideology

Tim Russert: Will the vice president [Gore] listen to his fellow New
   Democrats or continue to embrace the old Democratic ideology?

William Daley (Al Gore's Campaign Chair): It's not the old Democratic
   ideology.

—August 20, 2000

Bill Clinton is too often remembered as a philandering, political moderate who was too eager to cut a deal with the hard Right of the *National Review* crowd. These things are true, but he was also a tough-talking innovator of the rhetoric of economic equality. Strange as it may sound, what was distinctive about Bill Clinton was that he brought class politics back from decades of neglect. Of course, the class he favored was not the blue-collar, organize-down-at-the-auto-plant variety, but a new middle class grounded in postindustrial realities and modern-day inequalities. When Franklin Roosevelt rallied the nation in the cause of the nation's poor and working people, these people represented the middle portions of the occupational structure. By the early 1990s, occupational upgrading had moved those middle portions of the structure into formerly white-collar occupations. It was these new workers and consumers of the middle rank to whom Clinton would appeal but with resonant images of business bigwigs from the American political storybook.

In contrast to Jack Kennedy, Bill Clinton told economic stories with economic villains in them. His message was confrontational. As a campaigner, Clinton envisioned villainous foes of democracy and civil society who stood in the way of social justice and preyed on those who "worked hard and played by the rules."[36] Clinton was moderate in issue selection, sphinxlike in his associations, and crafty in his political maneuvers, but he was also transformative in his economic influence, which tends to be overlooked given the subsequent history of his presidency. Clinton's achievement is overshadowed by the decades of ideological trench warfare that ensued as he implemented his vision, but insofar as *Meet the Press* serves as a record of salient public discourse, it becomes ever more clear that Clinton's administration was as big a break toward an opportunity agenda as John Kennedy's was away from it, even if it is the frustration of Clinton's ambitions, more than his transformative capacity and egalitarian vision, that we remember.[37]

Even two decades later, we are only now beginning to see the full flowering of the Clinton pivot toward a middle-class class politics. Bill Clinton is awaiting his Lyndon Johnson, and to some extent he has him in Barack Obama. Faced with an economic meltdown and soaring deficits that were the result of a financial crisis spawned in an environment of limited regulation and oversight, try as he might, Obama could not avoid the class politics of the middle class that Bill Clinton had brought back into the mainstream in his 1992 campaign. It was carried into his program by figures like John Edwards and Hillary Clinton. We remember the breakthrough 1992 campaign with the James Carville line "the economy, stupid," but he might have added, "a rising tide no longer lifts all boats," because his boss campaigned as if this were the message.

Clinton first appeared on *Meet the Press* as one might expect him to have, as a cautious moderate, unwilling to cozy up to his coalition partners but careful not to offend them either. He first appeared in September 1987 opposite the fiery and provocative secretary of education, William Bennett, without producing much in the way of sound and fury. Clinton distanced himself from the teachers' unions in modest ways but without signaling any kind of profound break. In 1991, he appeared as the chairman of the Democratic Leadership Council (DLC), which was formed as a centrist alternative in the wake of the defeat of Walter Mondale. But when the chips were down and the kid needed a comeback, Clinton turned on the class politics. Here is Bill Clinton fighting for the Democratic nomination on January 5, 1992, in the buildup to the New Hampshire primary.

Lisa Myers (NBC News): Everyone agrees that the greatest threat to the nation's long-term economic health is the massive budget deficit. Are you prepared to promise that if you are elected, you would balance the budget within four years?

Bill Clinton: Well, I don't want to get into a promise that's like "read my lips," that I might not be able to keep. . . . Keep in mind that two-thirds of the deficit this year and next year is paying for S&L and bank failures. I've offered a plan to reduce bank failures. If you do that, you'll cut it by two-thirds on an annual basis. Then if you do the other things I've talked about—control healthcare costs, reduce defense, at least in five years, it'll be a $90 billion a year peace dividend, minimum, maybe more.

. . .

Myers: Let's talk about entitlements for a minute. There is a report this morning that the administration's budget, the president's budget for this year, will propose a means testing for Medicare. . . . Couldn't you accept some sort of means testing for the wealthy?

Clinton: I could if they were going to get something for it. . . . But this is—keep in mind this is in the context of George Bush's plan, which is, charge the elderly more for the same old health care, give working people a tax credit. It's all a bonanza for the big health insurance companies and the healthcare bureaucracies. It'll be a disaster. It won't do anything to control costs.

Bigwig villains abound: false promises, S&L bankers, health insurance companies, private bureaucracies, bonanzas. With these images, Clinton was attempting to articulate a vision of how to grow the pie as well as how to distribute it fairly. His gift was to blend the imagery of the struggling middle class with the cutting-edge analytical devices of the moment. Clinton did not always govern with the populist spirit on which he campaigned, but the wave he rode to office owed much to the old Democratic ideology.

The crucial conceit of Reagan's Jeffersonian vision was to ignore the fact that sometime after the 1880s, the seat of economic activity had transitioned from the family firm to the corporate bureaucracy. Most of the economic activity in the twentieth century was managed in complex supply chains that had at their core some large, centralized firm strategically positioned to maximize its profits and minimize its risks by controlling activity in the chain. This is what the business professor Michael Porter had called, following Joseph Schumpeter, competitive advantage.[38] The giant bureaucracies of the day were the very kinds of firms that Fair Deal economists like Leon Keyserling had worried would act unwisely. What Clinton recognized, when giving access to his more progressive advisers such as soon-to-be secretary of labor Robert Reich,[39] was that these giant bureaucracies were inherently placed in unfair competition with both their workers and their consumers.[40]

The challenge Clinton faced in reviving a social rights agenda after the Reagan revolution arose from complications introduced by the other big story maker of the 1992 campaign, Ross Perot. When we review the objective record, it is challenging to make sense of what exactly made Ross Perot such an exciting candidate in that election. It certainly had little to do with his first appearance on *Meet the Press* on May 3, 1992.

When he appeared on the program, it was in the midst of the Rodney King–inspired Los Angeles riots of 1992, and his interpretation of these was tough yet sympathetic, with hints of Daniel Patrick Moynihan's old interpretation of the fragile black family in his answers. Perot would not take a stand on affirmative action and embraced feel-good and work-based social programs like the Civilian Conservation Corps as a pathway out of poverty. Perot was deeply concerned about the deficit, as he would famously demonstrate with his pie charts and witticisms of the campaign, but his defense of his positions failed the Russert test in as dismal a fashion as one could imagine. He simply had no grasp of the numbers to support his plan and had not prepared for the interview in that way. Were it anyone else, he would have been rated as not ready for prime time, but Perot's reception was quite different, as is clear in the wrap-up of the Perot debut.

Tim Russert: Albert Hunt, do you think we have a presidential candidate here?

Al Hunt (*Wall Street Journal*): I'm not from Vegas, Tim, but I'd say it's ninety-five to five.

Russert: What about the situation in Los Angeles? How is that going to play out in terms of affecting the presidential campaign?

Hunt: Usually when race becomes an issue, it tends to help Republicans; it tends to help conservatives—it has for twenty-five years. It may again, this time. I think that's probably the least important thing, Tim. You know, I just hope that we don't get hung up in that old liberal-conservative fight here. I hope we listen to people like Bill Bradley and Jack Kemp, who said, "Hey, it's time to think now about what works."

Russert: Lisa, do we have a presidential candidate here?

Lisa Myers (NBC News): Oh, I think definitely.

Russert: You're a hundred to one.

Myers: Yes.

Russert: Sign me up with the Myers-Hunt club—one hundred to one. And I also will predict, Albert, that in the weeks to come, you may see Mr. Perot perhaps even passing President Bush in terms of the polls. As he has to become more and more specific on the issues, that will be a real test of the viability of his candidacy.

Hunt: He's already running ahead in a couple of states—Texas, New Mexico.

Myers: And he should pass Bill Clinton in the national polls within a couple of weeks.

Russert: I think he has, Albert.

(The DLC had recognized that Americans craved a kind of "third way" path out of Reaganism and away from the bad and racially coded memories of Johnson's Great Society. Perhaps Perot filled that gap. Perot was attractive, it seems, simply because he was some kind of quirky blend of the two existing parties and he could tell a good story. He would labor to make his signature issue, the deficit, that "crazy aunt that nobody in the family talks about," the central social drama of the 1993 governance season with the aid of every literary aid he could devise. Perot had convinced America that it was the deficit that represented the core threat to democracy and freedom. Perot had provided the enemies of the social protection agenda exactly what they needed, a new master story with which to bludgeon the proponents of equality; the story line would be simply, "We're broke."[41]

Much in the same way that the Vietnam War debt hindered President Johnson's attempt to create the Great Society, the debts that Reagan had incurred to pressure the Soviet Union out of existence hindered Clinton's dreams of a middle-class tax cut and a national healthcare system. Clinton would be remembered for his governance in times of economic growth and for leaving office with a budget surplus, but his larger postindustrial class project remained largely unfulfilled. By the time that Gingrich's Republican revolutionaries rolled into town in 1995, Robert Reich was largely alone in his use of class thematic reasoning and soon to be "unlocked" from the cabinet.[42] The following is an example from January 15, 1995, which represents the typical rough treatment that Reich received on *Meet the Press*.

Robert Reich: We've got to make—again, if you're working hard and you're playing by the rules—this is something the president said in 1992; he says it over and over again—you ought to be able to get ahead in this country.

Tim Russert: You said—we have about a minute left. You have been accused of trying to start a class war between the rich and the poor. And one of the evidences people point to: "Reich says cut corporate welfare too. Eliminate tax breaks for farmers, for corporate advertising, for airlines."

Reich: Come on, Tim, this isn't class warfare. Look at—

Russert: But let me read what some of us—has the administration adopted your attempts at eliminating so-called corporate welfare?

Reich: The president's budget is going to be out on February 6. You will see, the president is actively interested in cutting unnecessary subsidies to corporations. There is—at the same time that we are trying to cut welfare and make sure we get people into work, we ought to take a look at aid for dependent corporations, and there's a lot of it in this country.

Russert: Senator?

Nancy Kassebaum (Republican, Kansas): Aid for dependent corporations—well, I'm not sure about that. But let me say I certainly believe that a cut in the capital gains tax, structured the right way, helps the economy. It doesn't hurt it—structured the right way. I think that's important.

Reich: Senator, with all due respect, there's a lot of evidence that shows that that does not increase investment and it only, basically goes to the pockets of the very, very wealthy, and that's what the Republicans are trying to do.

The deep irony of the Clinton administration was that it had always billed itself as aggressively centrist and maddeningly triangulating with respect to the old divisions of Left and Right. Clinton was portrayed as a kind of class traitor who broke the heart of the Left who dared support him. Yet the transformative appeal lacking on the operational side of the Clinton agenda was present on the level of ideas. Under the influence of figures like Robert Reich, Clinton had taken a new kind of middle-class politics into the mainstream. Where Kennedy had pivoted to the right in his class politics thirty years before, Clinton pivoted left.

Before Clinton, Democratic circles thought of the middle class in light of the middle-class experience of the twentieth century. After Clinton, the middle-class society itself seemed in jeopardy. The challenge of the Kennedy era was to bring people out of poverty and into the stable and flourishing middle class, to prevent people from pulling up the ladder behind them. The challenge of the Clinton era was to ensure that there was something at the top of the middle-class job ladder for those who could climb it. This intellectual contribution, quite apart from his policy accomplishments, in which Clinton opened a new frontier in debates about social rights and protections for a group that once seemed not to need them, was his true bridge to the twenty-first century. It is not that these arguments were in any way new, but Clinton made them respectable, even commonsensical, in a way they had not been before.

The Republican Party fought the latent logic of Clinton's style of New Democrat policy with a message so simple and heartfelt that it could have been lifted from Reagan's 1964 "A Time for Choosing" speech. The clarity and moral power of this Republican narrative made it both remarkably flexible and easily believed by large numbers of voting Americans. Having been shamed off their Reichian risk-reducing, postindustrial class politics, Democrats found themselves no match for their opponents, who felt they were finally in a position to unscramble the omelet of the welfare state. In the early months of the Republican Contract with America, a face-off between the chairman of the Republican National Committee, Haley Barbour, and the general chairman of the Democratic National Committee, Senator Chris Dodd of Connecticut, from January 22, 1995, provides an ample summary of the dynamics of the national conversation for the following decade.

David Broder (NBC News): In 1992 the voters of this country ended twelve years of Republican control of the White House; 1994, the same voters turned around and—forty years of Democratic control of the Congress. What do you think the voters are trying to say? What is it that they're sore about, Senator Dodd?

Christopher Dodd: Well, I think it is the anxieties that people have talked about in terms of their own economic situations, the personal anxieties when they see crime rates and the like, and that sense of unease about what tomorrow may bring. . . .

Broder: Economic anxiety the basic cause?

Haley Barbour: No, I don't think so, Dave. I think the difference between 1992 and 1994 is that in 1992 the American people did not perceive that Republicans were for anything. People who had voted for us because they were for smaller government, lower taxes, less spending, and fewer regulations in '80 and '84 and '88 didn't change their mind about those things in '92. They changed their minds about us. They decided in 1992 we hadn't been adhering to what they thought they had voted for. The New Democrat seemed to be somebody who understood the limits of government. But by 1994 the American people saw, once the Republican Party was back and absolutely right on the issues about the relationship of government to our people, that government—we saw that government's too big for its britches and people are not getting their tax dollars'—their money's worth for their tax dollars now; that taxes ought to go down, spending ought to go down, the federal government ought to get smaller. There ought to be a devolution of power away from the federal government and back to the states and to the people, as the Constitution intended. And they also saw, from the other side, that Bill Clinton was not a New Democrat, but in fact, a big-government liberal who believes that government is the answer to every question, who believes that if people will just give the government enough of their money in taxes and enough control over their lives and businesses that government can solve all their problems.

Broder: Let me—

Barbour: The people know that's not right.

John Kasich, then a congressman representing, but later to become governor of, Ohio, may have provided the anthem for the conservative movement when he said on April 14, 1997, "A Republican Party that does not believe in tax cuts is a Republican Party that has lost its soul." Even apart from the rise of the religious Right in their caucus, the Republicans were in no mood to hazard their souls to compromise with the likes of Bill Clinton. This line of thought carried through the Bush tax cut as well as the attempts by the Bush administration and later by Congressman Paul Ryan of Wisconsin to introduce plans to replace the Social Security and Medicare programs with individualized options. The key objective was to reduce spending and to reduce taxes as both an economic stimulus and a pressure tactic on social welfare policy.

One strange feature of Clinton's discursive transformation is that it was so successful that it went largely unnoticed in the Democratic Party itself amid the climate of relative abundance of the late 1990s. It was clear why the Republicans pushed their tax-cutting, small-government solutions, but the Democratic narrative lacked both coherence and a natural policy domain. Democrats would often remember their populist roots during campaign season but pivot back to corporate realism when it was time to govern. Even in the hot contest of the 2000 Democratic primary, with serious challenges facing him to his left, Gore could not channel his inner Clinton to capitalize on the new postindustrial problematic.

The campaign of 2000 may have been a critical moment for developing the social drama of the declining middle class into a coherent narrative that could be placed against the one that Haley Barbour and most of the other Republicans had been telling since Clinton took office, but Al Gore himself seemed lonely in the Democratic establishment in his recognition of the potential power of the middle-class narrative with corporate villains. Despite Gore's best attempts in the general election with George W. Bush, he could not get his populist line out from under the cloud of Clinton's character issues, campaign finance scandals, and detailed questioning about his change of heart about the point at which life begins. The reason may have been that he had lost credibility in his commitment to bring a concrete plan together with his populist rhetoric, as his evisceration of the Bradley healthcare plan demonstrated, or it may have been that he redirected the language back into an older idiom with phrases like "working families" that seemed more like special cases of people who hadn't prospered than a central threat to democratic civilization.[43]

Whatever the reason, when the challenges facing the middle class became an issue, the Washington establishment didn't seem much to care. Certainly Tim Russert was not impressed. In the July 16 interview with Gore, Russert directs much more heat at the abortion question than at Gore's populist interpretation of the contrast between himself and George W. Bush: "That's the difference in this election. They're for the powerful, and we're for the people."[44] What Dick Gephardt had said on *Meet the Press* on July 2, 2000, two weeks earlier, about a Republican prescription drug bill seemed to be what people thought of an egalitarian political project led by the Democratic Party: "It's a sham. It's a hoax. It's public relations. It's electioneering." In their powerful December debate on *Meet the Press*, Bill Bradley himself had condemned Gore in fairly scathing terms that demonstrated that Gore lacked the key ingredient of success—authenticity.[45]

Bill Bradley: You know, for [the] ten months that I was running for president, you ignored me. You pretended I didn't exist. Suddenly I start to do better, and you want to debate me every day. It's ridiculous. We're having debates. We had a debate the other night in New Hampshire. We're on *Meet the Press* today. We're going to be in Iowa and New Hampshire the first week of January. The point is, Al—and I don't know if you get this—but a political campaign is not just a performance for people, which is what this is, but it is rather a dialogue—

Al Gore: That's not what I'm doing.

Bradley:—with people, Al. It's a dialogue with people where you listen to their stories, where you listen to what they have to say about their country's future, where you seek to engage them and convince them that the direction that you want to take the country is the right way. That's what a campaign's about.

Of course, Al Gore lost the election of 2000 to George W. Bush, but the effect this would have on the future of rhetoric of inequality was difficult to predict. In an interview dedicated to "the Nader factor" just days before the election, Tim Russert provides some insight into Nader's motivation for staying in the race.

Tim Russert: Bill Kristol, Ralph Nader sat right at this table after his interview
and he said, "You know, this is the equivalent, basically, of the conservative
coalition," his Green Party; the conservative coalition trying to drive the
Republican Party to the right, if you will; his Green Party is going to drive
the Democratic Party to the left, more Progressive values. And if Al Gore
loses, so be it because it makes the Green Party a real force for the year 2004.

But unlike the ways that the challenge from the Right represented by Barry Goldwater in 1964 or the threatened defections of right-wing groups
later were celebrated, inside the Democratic Party the blame for the loss
in 2000 was placed squarely on Nader's shoulders. The best summary of
the Democratic establishment's reaction to Nader's gambit can be found
directly after the election by the pundit and political consultant James
Carville.

James Carville: Well, I will not speak his [Nader's] name. I'll just call him an
egomaniac. And if he ever walks into a room that I'm in, I'm just going to
quietly walk out. If he walks up to me, I'm just going to turn my back on
him. I'm going to shun him. And any good Democrat, any good Progressive,
ought to do the same thing. Don't be rude to him; don't do anything. Don't
do—he's an egomaniac. He's self-absorbed. He obviously cost us the presidency. I will not speak this egomaniac's name. Not for the next four years.

It appears that in Democratic circles, extremism in defense of equality was
a powerful vice indeed. What Carville had said about Ralph Nader might
have stood for all of those discontented Progressive extremists in the party
as well—they would be ignored. Bradley had felt ignored by Gore until he
was a real threat for the nomination. Nader's following had been ignored,
yet when the threat was realized, ostracism was the solution. There was a
fundamental asymmetry across the American political spectrum. Squeaky
wheels on the right got oiled, but not those on the left. Accordingly, the
window of respectable opinions shifted in the direction of articulated extremism on the right. The challenge of an imperiled middle class was becoming a more central part of the social drama of the American Left, but
its champions seemed to lack the radical exit option that the Right had
used to such powerful effect.

The Edge of Insanity

The probability of default on Treasury is zero. It's the safest asset in the world by far. But we've just gone through an experience that anybody looking at it has to say, "Whoa, maybe somebody might actually default in the future," if we were going to go to the edge of, of insanity.

—Austan Goolsbee, outgoing chair of President Obama's
Council of Economic Advisers, August 7, 2011

Randolph Churchill had said in the opening acts of this drama that one could not completely unscramble the omelet of the welfare state and the social rights that were embodied in it. As the middle-class experience became more precarious, the risk-buffering properties of such systems became all the more important, even as the challenge of paying for them increased under conservative pressure for economy. The problem for the country was that Americans were both unerringly committed to the programs that ensured social protection from the global market and to the need to reduce taxes and cut spending in support of market liberalization in roughly balanced proportions The national conversation had turned since the 1960s toward both a preference for supply-side investment tax cuts and for the landmark programs in defense of the principle of social security that Roosevelt, Kennedy, and Johnson had championed. The accommodation was unpopular and unsustainable. Therefore, revenues were short and macroeconomic conditions were unstable. The Democrats had few policy options available to them, while any moves that they did take came preframed in the anticivil package of big government and its characteristic atrocity, unrepresentative taxation. These were the challenges encountered by the new face of Democratic politics, Barack Obama.

Even though most government debt burdening the ambitions of the Obama administration had been piled up under the Bush administration in times of war, the Reaganesque themes of the read-my-lips Republicans were ready for use in confrontations with the new president, who had taken power in the wake of the greatest economic catastrophe to confront the American people since what Karl Polanyi described as the Great Transformation.[46] By 2009, the private healthcare system that lobbyists for the medical industry had defended against reform so effectively since the Fair Deal was bankrupting the nation with costs well above those in any other developed country. As Obama pushed for the debt-containing plans for universal health care that he had promised in his campaign, the champions of the rhetoric of freedom were ready to pounce. Economic populism was once thought of as a creature of the Left, but after Reagan, the spirit of populism had shifted to the right and its arguments were presented with a largely libertarian flavor. With the Tea Party movement having just organized a Tax Day mobilization event in April 2009, a *Meet the Press* panel attempted to narrate this novel development.

> Nina Easton (*Fortune Magazine*): Well, I, I would—first of all, I, I think the media underestimated this as an animating force, a tax—the potential of tax increasing. I think, I think that there is—it's an animating political issue. It's something that the Republicans can hang their hats on. I would recall [the] 1993 Contract with America, when Democrats didn't take that seriously, either. I think tax-and-spend issues are a real, are a real animating issue for Republicans. I think there's also been a little mini–Tea Party on the Hill, in that we saw moderate Democrats have already declared, basically, dead on arrival the, the Obama proposal to limit deductions for wealthy households giving charitable contributions. There's concern about the cap and trade, which is the energy plan that's, that a lot of Republicans are countering as a—they're calling a tax increase.

> David Gregory: Right.

> Easton: And some moderate Democrats are agreeing. So I think that—I, I do think the tax thing, I think the Democrats underestimated at their own peril.

> Dick Armey (FreedomWorks): If it's so patriotic to pay taxes, why not include everybody? Why shouldn't every American who's working, making—an adult American—share in the tax burden, distribute it more evenly? You can get rates down, and it can encourage growth.

As the Tea Party movement developed and became more threatening to the president and his agenda, older arguments with lingering racially redolent themes had energized a broader antigovernment movement, which never saw itself in racial terms even as it benefited from half-forgotten associations between free markets, white workers, and a responsible work ethic. These associations were anything but forgotten on the left and by the 2010 election cycle, amid frustrated street protests, the Tea Party was widely condemned as rife with bigotry as it became the subject of race-themed reporting. Powerful as these arguments were in channeling attention and outrage among Democrats and liberals, in the larger conversation they had only limited effect. The Goldwater-Reagan-Hayek narrative had sufficiently inoculated the neoliberal activists from accusations of racism. For the antitax, enterprise libertarian, the bigotry attack had become something like a disease that would come and go, inflicting minimal damage on the host. The way that Senator John Cornyn of Texas responded on July 18, 2010, to this attempt to pollute the movement shows how powerful the racially purified rhetoric of freedom had become after four decades of defending the barricades.

David Gregory: I want to talk about the Tea Party as well, Senator Cornyn. . . . There are some real debates going on about the role of the Tea Party and whether there are racist elements within the party itself. The NAACP [National Association for the Advancement of Colored People] had its meeting this week and talked about—called on the Tea Party to really stand up to some of those forces. This is how it was reported in the *Kansas City Star* this week. The headline, "The NAACP Resolution Addresses Tea Parties." The organization "passed a resolution Tuesday calling on all people—including tea party leaders—to condemn racism within the tea party movement. . . . The resolution asserts that tea party supporters have engaged in 'explicitly racist behavior, displayed signs and posters intended to degrade people of color generally and President Obama specifically.' The tea party movement is not just about higher taxes and limited government, the resolution says, 'but something that could evolve and become more dangerous for that small percentage of people that really think our country has been taken away from them.'" Is this a problem?

John Cornyn: Well, I think it's slanderous to suggest that the vast movement of citizens who've gotten off the couch and gotten—showed up at town hall meetings and Tea Party events, somehow to smear them with this, this label, it's just, there's just no basis for it. But I think the—what the Tea Party movement demonstrates, and I think the, the, the enthusiasm that we're seeing from independents and Republicans, is that if Washington isn't going to change itself, then we're going to change Washington.[47]

Ronald Reagan had won this round. As he argued at the height of racial tension in 1966, antibureaucratic conceptions of freedom were not racist: they were holy. From the housing-equity fights of the late 1960s, to the tax revolt in the late 1970s, to the Contract with America, to the experiment in refounding represented by the rousing of the largely white Tea Party movement, the freedom defense was effective against charges of racism and intolerance, even when it didn't carry the day.

In December 1949, the health industry advocate Morris Fishbein had said in his attack on the "socialized medicine" proposal of Truman's Fair Deal, "Those nations which hope to be democratic must place as much responsibility on the individual citizen for the conduct of the intimate affairs of his life as can be placed upon him." Not much had changed in American rhetoric over the sixty years that Democrats had fought to realize the dream of universal health care. What had changed was the willingness of the advocates of private enterprise to take their argument to the brink of chaos.

Foreshadowing a showdown that would imperil the credit rating of the country for "the first time in history," in a *Meet the Press* episode dated October 25, 2009, John Cornyn turned a debate about a vote on the Affordable Care Act into one about the capacity of the government to honor its promises.

John Cornyn: David, the majority leader is a, is a good vote counter, but I think even he was surprised when thirteen Democrats voted with the Republicans to reject $300 billion in additional red ink in the form of the Medicare reimbursements for doctors vote that occurred last week. I think the majority are recognizing that he has big problems keeping Democrats together, much less attracting Republicans to vote for it. And the reason is we have maxed out our credit card as a government. We are at a $12 trillion debt limit; for the second time in the Obama administration the Democrats are going to ask Congress to vote to increase the—that debt limit.

Although Washington reacted to this tactic as if it were novel, this wasn't the first time in history the full faith and credit of the federal government had been put in jeopardy. As Representative John Kasich of Ohio explained in a December 3, 1995, appearance on *Meet the Press*, when polarization had led to one government shutdown that year and threatened to trigger another, the stakes were too high to give up in the fight for freedom.

John Kasich: There's just one other point I want to make because I know that when people see this fighting going on in Washington, they believe that it's just these politicians because most fights in Washington, frankly, are too political. But about balancing the budget, this is something that we feel passionately about; it's one of those things that we don't think we should compromise. And rather than Americans thinking it's just a bunch of kids in the sandbox, these are people fighting on some of the most important principles that we have ever argued about in the history of our country.

The country was in store for an almost exact replay of the epic govern-ment-shutdown debacle of late 1995 and early 1996. Then as later, the in-surgent Republican House raised an alarm about the unsustainable costs of the welfare state, proposed tax cuts as part of a balanced budget deal, refused to offer a "clean vote" on the debt ceiling, and raised the specter of impeachment if the administration played its hand badly. This last item, of course, proved to be significant once the debt battle failed to turn out as the Republican leadership had planned. The core features of the Republi-can playbook were on display in a representative example of the confronta-tional tone of that deficit standoff in a *Meet the Press* interview on January 7, 1996, with the Republican majority whip, Tom DeLay of Texas.

Tim Russert: Will you raise the debt limit so that the secretary of treasury can bor-row the money to pay the country's bills?

Tom DeLay: The president vetoed the debt limit—raising the debt limit ceiling in December.

Russert: But you're willing to—will you pass a clean debt limit . . . ?

DeLay: No, we won't.

Russert: You won't?

DeLay: No, we won't.

Tim Russert was incredulous throughout this period of Republican in-transigence. He had trouble imagining that Republicans would take this fight against the principle of social rights/social security to the point that "for the first time the United States of America may go into default."

Russert: But you're willing to allow the country to go into default?

DeLay: It won't go into default.

Russert: Why?

DeLay: Because no president in history has allowed it to go in[to] default.

From the Fair Deal to the fight against Obamacare, whatever the problem was, the answer for Republicans was less government and freer markets. Bureaucrats were the enemies of democracy, and the principle of social security in all its insti-tutional manifestations was a cover for tyranny and servitude. The Republicans who led the Gingrich revolution had rejected the synthesis of William McKin-ley's private enterprise model with Theodore Roosevelt's principle of social secu-rity, and they were eager for a confrontation to break it apart.[48]

The Gingrich confrontation did not work well. Clinton sailed to reelection in the 1996 election that followed the 1995 debt fight, but this may have had something to do with the nature of the candidate Republicans chose. Bob Dole was the 1996 Republican nominee, but he was unpopular among members of the liberty league, as Mitt Romney would be sixteen years later. Still smarting from debt debate, one of Dole's rivals, Senator Lamar Alexander of Tennessee, spoke for his fellow conservatives when he appeared in a tough-talk interview on January 28, 1996, and volunteered a relatively accurate prediction of the outcome of the coming election.

Lamar Alexander: Oh, that's the way it's going to work this year. We're either going to go the Democratic way or the Republican way, which is why we need to nominate a Republican who can help reelect the Congress. The people outside Washington are really fed up with the bickering here. And I think people are going to say, "We're either going to give it to Clinton or we're going to give it to the Republicans." Which is why Senator Dole's performance Tuesday night, I think, caused so much conversation in Iowa and New Hampshire. We got a preview of what we hope we don't see in October.

Tim Russert: What was the conversation regarding Senator Dole's response?

Alexander: He's not the man to be in that debate with Clinton in October.

Russert: Why?

Alexander: Clinton was faking a marvelous vision. Dole was too decent to fake a vision that he obviously doesn't have. And in a vision contest between Dole and Clinton, Clinton wins.

The Republican Party would never again nominate a candidate who couldn't fake a vision, and the core features of that vision were not hard to discern. One could find them ascendant in Republican rhetoric from William McKinley to Herbert Hoover. Neoliberalism, the long-standing and deep-seated suspicion of economic management by the government, had developed into a philosophical divide that appealed to "conservative" Americans in almost sacred terms. It served as a ready Republican answer to the problems of middle-class stagnation that the Democrats were struggling to bring to the surface.

By midsummer of 2011, even those who had not been paying attention recognized what a chaotic mess Washington had become. Republican leaders were keenly aware of how deep were commitments to both the private-enterprise system and a framework for social security that protected people from it, and they quickly derided Democratic attempts to frighten the country with suggestions that they planned to "privatize" or "gut" the signature programs of the welfare state. Representative Paul Ryan of Wisconsin emphasized this in his big opportunity to take his case to the nation on May 22, 2011.

Paul Ryan: We're being sensible, we're being rational, and we're saving this program. And you cannot deal with this debt crisis, David, unless you're serious about entitlement reform. And, unfortunately, I think we're going to have "mediscare" all over again, and that's unfortunate for the country.

Yet the logic of the Republican approach was to move toward a privately managed system for all of the social needs that Roosevelt's New Deal had highlighted. Whether it was saving for old age and bouts of unemployment or in managing the risk of ill health, the Republicans of the twenty-first century were as optimistic about the unlimited possibilities of limited government as were the Democrats of the nineteenth. The Republican political consultant Mary Matalin put this clearly in her defense of her chosen hero of the day on June 3, 2007, as she retold the story of the Republican debacle of 2006.

Mary Matalin: The last election [in 2006] was a repudiation of Republicanism, but it was not a repudiation or even a diminution of conservatism. So what Fred Thompson connects to, and the country connects to, is our heritage of limited government. To us that means something. It means unlimited possibilities in this country and the principles of the Founders. And, you know, that's not big—good chatter for Sunday-morning TV, but that's what's missing in the field, and that's what's missing with the country.

The goal was to wean the public off the New Deal much as one would a junkie off a drug. This was articulated in a representative way by another political consultant, Anthony Castellanos, on August 7, 2011, the *Meet the Press* episode after the debt ceiling meltdown.

Anthony Castellanos: But I think something Mr. Greenspan says is important and that is that this is not going to be without pain. There's a reason alcohol, drugs, and promiscuous government spending are all addictive. They feel good at first. When you stop doing them, it's going to feel less good.

It is not hard to see the cultural allusions in that statement. The direction of change was clear. For Republicans, the New Deal was over. It was high time to move back toward the old one. Only in question was the pace and how much pain the people could take.

The profound irony of the downturn of what economist Paul Krugman called the Lesser Depression was that after seven decades of mass education, the laissez-faire wing of the Republican Party was now in a position to take advantage of the crisis of democratic capitalism to begin to undo the New Deal and its signature principle that shared a name with its most memorable program, Social Security. As was always the case in the United States, England was the model. Writing for the *Guardian* in a Britain wracked by riots brought on by the policy of "austerity," the columnist Janet Daley wrote what the Republican leadership could only speak in hushed tones in the smoke-free rooms of the Washington establishment: "The idea that a capitalist economy can support a Socialist welfare state is collapsing before our eyes." Ideas in the twenty-first century were exhausted, but without any semblance of consensus.

The fight had been long, but the goals were clear. As Barry Goldwater had surmised, the value standard around which persuadable Americans would rally was Isaiah Berlin's concept of negative liberty[49]—freedom from the interference of others in one's life. In an era of cultural upheaval, he rightly guessed that tenuous progressive notions of group rights and robust conceptions of the use of government were vulnerable to those who would promote a new founding. This ethic was anything but sterile. Emerging champions like Representative Paul Ryan would arise to face president Obama, who embodied the inclusive interpretation of the American creed. These new figures, many of them white and midwestern like Paul Ryan, would invoke the power of the political storybook, particularly the chapters on free markets as founding principles, to divert the steady flow of polluting accusations of racism coming from their stymied opponents. In truth, they cared little about race per se; this was all business. They would use Lockean principles—individual in contrast to group rights—to derail both Socialist and multicultural tendencies in a stroke, thereby celebrating their conception of the American idea. Hayek would check Myrdal. Conservatives would be true to the Founders, standing athwart history as long as it took to do so, even to the brink of insanity in extreme defense of the principles of liberty. What they knew in their hearts was that in the big rock-paper-scissors game of democratic demonology, government tyranny seemed to trump cultural intolerance time after time.

5

THAT REDEMPTION WE DREAM OF
The Tangle of Intolerances

The first reaction of the oppressor when oppressed people rise up against the system of injustice is an attitude of bitterness. But I do believe that if the nonviolent resisters continue to follow the way of nonviolence, they eventually get over to the hearts and souls of the former oppressors, and I think it eventually brings about that redemption that we dream of.

—Martin Luther King Jr., April 17, 1960

ONE OF THE MOST INTRIGUING CONVERSATIONS in the United States is the one about how we cannot have a conversation about race. On the surface, it appears that Americans simply do not like to talk about race and, when confronted with the problem, want to move on to other more comfortable subjects. But the national story is imbued with color, from Crispus Attucks to the March for Jobs and Freedom, from the Civil War to Barack Obama. Race is certainly a tough subject to manage in American politics, but as the *Meet the Press* record shows, it is far from underrepresented in the national dialogue. We Americans talk about the problem a lot, although we tend to talk past one another. Even worse, many times one finds an issue at the center of the social drama of Washington politics that has everything to do with race, even though no one wants to say exactly how. To even begin to understand the politics of American dysfunction, we will have to decode the race debate.

Through a character in his play *Race* (2009), David Mamet suggests that race "is the most incendiary topic in our history," and although much of what is said about it is characteristically misleading or even offensive, it has been anything but avoided on the airwaves of *Meet the Press*. On March 19, 1948, one of the early moderators, Albert Warner, had put it in terms that seem strangely contemporary: "Any talk about racial problems and discrimination is difficult, but better to have it openly explored. Silence in any event is impossible." He was right, and we have kept talking, but because most of our conversations are steeped in deep codes and distracting symbolism, it is difficult to even see the problem clearly or to advance any novel ideas in the area.

This is unfortunate for the democratic project, because decades of strategic thinking and the accidents of political history have conspired to make it hard to identify precisely where Americans disagree about race-related policy. For example, Americans of this generation are clearly more tolerant than they were in previous ones, but after the divisive debates of the civil rights era, economic ideas have been infused with racial implications; it is sometimes difficult to know where a person's free-market convictions begin and racial presuppositions end. A leader like George Wallace may once have adopted libertarian ideas as a simple cover for his supremacist agenda, but today the same arguments may be advanced by an African American, like presidential aspirant Herman Cain, or a true fan of social inclusion and cultural diversity like the late congressman Jack Kemp. The labored symbolism of this foundational divide in American politics makes it likely that we may never know where this line might be objectively drawn.

One thing that is well known but poorly understood is how the policy focus of the civil rights movement has drifted through discursive currents. Although the root cause of racial injustice is concentrated cultural power, supremacy of racial status can and has easily translated into state oppression and economic exploitation. Bigotry begets problems with bigwigs and bureaucrats. With successive victories over the symptomatic corruptions of racial power, civil rights came to refer less to concerns about personal freedom or economic equality per se and instead settled on the basic problem: promoting racial tolerance, social inclusion, and respect for difference. The meaning of the movement changed as it developed. It grew beyond just stigmatizing direct threats to freedom like lynching and the poll tax and began to address group disparities in other areas like segregation in schools, public accommodations, and discrimination in employment. Soon it became obvious, as it had been in the 1870s, that it was not possible for a despised minority to live in a state that resembled liberty without some provision in the civil sphere to ensure against populist tyranny. Accordingly, at root, people were fighting for what we might call cultural rights—group identity, cultural survival, heritage, and a sense of belonging. Overcoming the structural barriers and abuses of the legal system that represented the concrete stakes of the movement was a means toward a larger end.

As Gwen Ifill, a reporter deeply invested in the racial conversation on *Meet the Press*, once described it, "People just have this core of pain in them." That pain is the problem. From the way people talk about these issues today, we may assume that the civil rights movement was primarily about discrimination, but it is better thought of as a fight to validate people of African descent as valued members of democratic civilization and as Americans as original as the revolution. What was in play during the civil rights movement was an ongoing revolution in the field of cultural rights that pointed toward a status revaluation, a situation in which no one, black or white, had to look at his or her heritage with a sense of dread and embarrassment.[1] This tendency is exactly the issue Martin Luther King Jr. described in his first appearance as "a basic problem of human relations," which the movement he led would rectify.

What remained unclear was how this triumph in the revaluation of cultural traditions would translate into structural reforms that might eliminate the economic inequalities between and among race/ethnic groups. One reason was that an outcome of the status revolution was that many whites who were once sympathetic to a progressive economics and an economic or social rights agenda had become more skeptical of the expansion of government into matters of regulating social status between groups. This sentiment was bolstered by the anticivil coding of the cultural rights agenda itself as bigoted and intolerant—so-called reverse discrimination. This adverse coding, used to incrementally marginalize the most vocal advocates of racial equality like Stokely Carmichael, Al Sharpton, and Jesse Jackson, had the perverse effect of making it more difficult to implement programs of social protection for disadvantaged minority communities and therefore more difficult to alleviate the institutionalized problems that perpetuated cultural stereotypes.[2]

Symbolic confusion on the left presented an opportunity for tolerant neoliberals like Ronald Reagan, who pressed this advantage into a rout for the forces of group rights in general. After decades of well-organized pressure illustrating the group rights connection between race and class talk and the illegitimacy of each under premises of strict constitutional liberalism, the persuadable American had forgotten over time why she liked FDR in the first place. What she had not forgotten was that when

Johnson initiated his joint effort to combat discrimination and poverty, the cities had burned.

These developments were a boon for the enemies of the welfare state. By the 1990s, neoliberal champions like Secretary of Education William Bennett and anti–affirmative action crusader Ward Connerly were confidently undermining even race-neutral / race-sensitive social programs like those promoted by the sociologist William Julius Wilson under the guise of support for traditional individual rights and through the rhetoric of color blindness. Conservatives' cry of "identity politics" had tainted the concept of cultural rights (lifestyles and folkways), which extended to social rights (protections for workers, consumers, and the environment) as well.

What was true of people once described as Reagan Democrats was in all likelihood more durably ensconced in their descendants. As more people were socialized in an environment in which multiculturalism had joined Socialism as the iconic adversary symbols of a free society, it was easier to turn them against any project that could be associated with either. Moreover, as more whites repudiated the philosophy of the New Deal and embraced their Jeffersonian roots, the tolerance and equality agendas could be played off one another in a competition for a narrower slice of national attention. The fight for social justice as cultural rights could be used to undermine the gains for social justice achieved as social rights. Treating the symptoms had given the disease opportunity to adapt; culture eclipsed class in elite rhetoric.

Eventually, the terms "race" and "class" became almost synonymous shibboleths in the American political lexicon, a phenomenon that the tragedy of Hurricane Katrina made painfully clear. On the left, race/class was a consecrated cause to fight for. On the right, it was a dangerous liberal heresy that perverted the message of the Founders.

A troubling outcome of the conflation of race and class for advocates of structural reform was that institutional inequality could in this way be reduced to a problem of personal morality. If these ideas were conjoined and racism was a problem of recognition withheld, the challenge became not so much to change the rules of the economic game but to change the way one looked and felt about other people.[3] Class—the word—was therefore less about the occupational structure and more about the status system. Racial justice demanded a status revolution and a campaign for intergroup tolerance, not a class war that institutionalized economic equality irrespective of ascriptive characteristics. In fact, the term "equality" came to imply equality among ascriptive groups more than it did equality among individuals.[4] Although this ran counter to the intentions of the reformers, the champions of private enterprise had in this way reached one of the political goals they had been striving to achieve for decades; they had neutralized Roosevelt's class rhetoric and the equality agenda that came with it, thereby opening the doors to the renewed accumulation of great fortunes by what would come to be known as "job creators." In the twenty-first century, the Republican Party stands for freedom, the Democratic Party stands for tolerance, and even though the people yearn for equality, it is not clear which party will help them realize it.

The Progress of Civilization

We think that the white race is the greatest race of people inhabiting this earth; we think that we have contributed more to the progress of civilization than any other race; we do not subscribe to this theory that is advanced in many quarters that pride of race is an evidence of Hitlerism, because we don't deny any other person any right.

—Richard Russell, senator from Georgia, July 30, 1948

When African Americans returned from fighting for their country in World War II, they were not disposed to accept the same conditions at home they faced when they set out on that titanic struggle. It is often now forgotten, but the famous March on Washington for civil rights was first planned by A. Philip Randolph in 1941. To avoid this divisive embarrassment, President Roosevelt had established a Fair Employment Practices Commission (FEPC) by executive order. What this commission amounted to was the admission by national leadership that discrimination in employment of the kind sanctioned by law in the South and passed down through "the custom of centuries" elsewhere was losing its claim to legitimacy. Nowhere was this turn in social norms felt with more urgency than in the Deep South, initiating a massive political realignment that would push southern Democrats into the former party of Lincoln in a way that would transform and confuse American politics for more than seventy years. What was true in civil war was true in uncivil politics—the southerners had better generals than did the North. Like modern-day Robert E. Lees, southern supremacists artfully deployed their strategic imaginations to delay and disrupt the northern democratic project on both the cultural and social rights fronts. It was, after all, on the Virginia plantations where the doctrine of individual rights had been conceived, and it was in the South where it would be defended against all reasonable demands for reform.

The case of the state of Georgia provides a telling example. In 1946 the state was governed by the affable and intimidating Eugene Talmadge, affectionately referred to as "Ol' Gene." First elected to the governor's office in the landmark and realigning election of 1932, Ol' Gene Talmadge became widely known as a leading example of the type of southern demagogue who made much of the rest of the country cringe. To a northerner, Talmadge came across as the very model of affable despot that animated the mythology of the civil rights era. Described by the historian William Anderson as a "champion of the mythical little man" who offered him little but "the security of the past that made the way into the future a little easier,"[6] Talmadge was perhaps only surpassed by Mississippi senator Theodore Bilbo as candidate for lead villain in the civil drama of postwar racial politics that would play out in the South over two decades.[7]

On August 2, 1946, just four months before his death and in the midst of his contentious fourth campaign, Talmadge made his only appearance on *Meet the Press*, which was then still an emerging hit radio program on the Mutual network. Ol' Gene made the political scene at a moment when his brand of unvarnished populist supremacy was both enough to secure his election in the Deep South and to engender broad-based contempt in the northern press. In these early days of *Meet the Press*, this was the third show that could be said to have been dedicated to the race problem, but it was the first to deal with the most troubling aspect of racial relations that traveled under the catchphrase "lynching." Eight days before the radio program, "four negroes were seized from a car . . . lined up abreast and killed" in a crime that was still making news for having gone unsolved as recently as 2008.[8] As with many of the early programs on race, this one began with a congenial introduction and a playful conversation that was quickly combined with philosophical gravity and the pointed questions for which the show became so justly famous.

Announcer: The man who has accepted the challenge of the press is seated this moment in our Atlanta, Georgia, studios. In a special two-way hookup between Washington, D.C., and Atlanta, Georgia, the press will fire questions at Eugene Talmadge, who recently won the Democratic primary for the governorship of Georgia, which assures his election for a fourth term as governor.

After a brief discussion about how he would handle the developing sto-ry of the four murdered African Americans, Talmadge was confronted by Larry Spivak. Talmadge used this exchange to attempt to ground his political project in a larger democratic tradition. He compared himself to Andrew Jackson, claiming that "a positive man as an executive is always criticized." Larry Spivak, incredulous that Talmadge had deflected the question about his nonchalance in the face of a grisly crime committed in his state by referencing similar critiques that were directed at Andrew Jackson, pushed back.

Larry Spivak: Governor, are you suggesting that the criticism that has been leveled against you and against Georgia is in exactly the same category as the
criticism that was leveled against Jefferson [note that Jackson has become
Jefferson]?

Eugene Talmadge: Over a different subject, but the sentiments behind it were practically the same.

Spivak: Do you believe that Jefferson would have been on your side in this question
of the lynching, Governor?

Talmadge: On my side in a question of lynching? I'm against lynching! And I presume that Jefferson would have been against lynching.

Talmadge's slow drawl was offset by a menacing emphasis in his state-ments. *Newsweek*'s Ernest K. Lindley built on Spivak's line:

Ernest K. Lindley: Pursuing that, Governor, do you regard lynching as a crime?

Talmadge: Why certainly [*emphasized*] I do, and I hope you do [*drawn out*].

Lindley: I certainly do [*lifted emphasis is condescending*]. I want to ask you next eh,
em, eh, if the killers of those Negroes in Monroe, Georgia, have not been
apprehended and brought to trial by the time you become governor, what do
you propose to do about that crime?

Talmadge: We always have officers out in Georgia for people who have violated the
law. Sometimes it requires several years to apprehend them and bring 'em to
court and to trial. I remember one trial in Georgia, when I was a student at
the University of Georgia, where they caught a murderer [who] had . . . committed [the murder] forty years before that and they tried him and convicted
him.

What is so striking about this episode is not that Talmadge revealed his cruelty in his willingness to casually play in public with the investigation of four gruesome murders as a cat would with a mouse, but that the tone of the national debate had already settled into its first stable postwar pattern. Eugene Talmadge's style of overt, brutal racism had become an adversarial point of focus for the conscience of the nation, much as Gunnar Myrdal suggested it might only two years earlier. Concerns about the systemic character of what the local church in Monroe who had raised the alarm on this crime called an "outrage against humanity," namely, state-supported racism, were becoming established in the public mind in a way that would soon disrupt the southern way of life. Talmadge was clearly received on the program as a kind of undemocratic ogre who was willing to abuse his power to cover a racially motivated crime. The reporters were uniformly repulsed.

This pattern continued. On the very next Friday occurred what probably remains the most infamous performance that *Meet the Press* has ever produced. The guest was Senator Theodore Bilbo, who had recently distinguished himself in the Senate for his uncompromising support for a racial caste system in the South. Bilbo's nickname was "The Man," and he was as good a candidate as any to play that role with all the connotations that later cohorts of African Americans would attach to it. The show is best remembered for the fact that Bilbo admitted on air that he was a member of the Ku Klux Klan (part of a local unit that appeared to be named for him), that it was not possible to leave the Klan once he had joined it, and that he expected strong Klan support in the upcoming Senate election in November 1946. Along the way, Bilbo managed to use the only broadcast example of the *N*-word in the history of the show, to dismiss the Fourteenth and Fifteenth Amendments as frauds, and to admit to engaging in racially targeted voter intimidation: "Further, it was the duty of every white Democrat to resort to every means within the law to keep the N— from voting in our primary because they were not qualified to vote." In contrast to Eugene Talmadge, who was somewhat embarrassed by the uncivil excesses of the political culture in Georgia, Bilbo was defiant in his defense of what even then were seen as outrageous invasions of civil liberties. Little wonder Mississippi would burn.

While Bilbo's Klan membership was known in certain circles at this time, the public, personal, and defiant announcement of Klan membership on a national radio program was enough to transform Bilbo into an icon of all that was wrong with the status system of the South (while doing a lot for the ratings of the still new radio program on which he made his announcement). Here was the condensed image of incivility, an unrepentant "Johnny Reb" against whom it was possible to struggle again. The fact that Bilbo was at that moment campaigning for office and won even after this media firestorm only reinforced the point. Images of angry mobs, supportive sheriffs, enabling senators, and unconcerned governors solidified into a single image of a tyrannous majority in a South that was largely immune to reformist energies. The moral case against the segregationist South was as old as the Constitution, but in the immediate postwar period, these new pieces of widely circulating public performance made it more difficult for forces outside the South to ignore the unruly and undemocratic forces at work there. Bilbo was a symbol of intolerance with national reach and implication.

It is difficult for a contemporary viewer to enter the moral universe portrayed by southern reactionaries like Gene Talmadge and Theodore Bilbo. They are the caricatures of the southern bigot who seem, in retrospect, to have been sent from central casting. They appear to us as enemies of democracy and human rights and serve as symbolic anchors in the narratives we present in favor of our own ideas of democratic liberation. The reason is that Ol' Gene and Theodore "The Man" Bilbo were uncreative supporters of stale projects of a uniquely southern form of liberal thinking that took it as axiomatic that black people were incapable of participating as full partners in democratic civilization. But there were other, more creative thinkers who rose to defend the old caste structure as well. They presented upgraded exclusive visions with a logic that made it respectable to support the Jim Crow system openly and even courageously. Their logic was tight and popular enough that these figures explored it at length on air in the era up to and immediately following the transformative school integration case in 1954.

One might wonder how it was that these overtly racist senators, dedicated as they were to "delaying the dream," in Keith Finley's phrase, went about defending what appears now to be the indefensible.[9] Was there really a vision of the overall public good that today lies obscured beneath the cruel cadences of white supremacy? Indeed there was, and the vision was ingeniously linked to the American liberal tradition, broadly understood, in a way that defined the true enemies of freedom as the race mixers and northern interlopers who refused to accept the principles of states' rights and ethnic self-determination.[10] Senator Richard Russell of Georgia, Ol' Gene's son, Herman Talmadge, and others like James Eastland,

senator from Mississippi, would defend the South in this way. Their philosophy was a variant of social Darwinism that mixed in a narrow reading
of Alexis de Tocqueville. The idea was that modern life can be thought of
as a contest between civilizations in which the progress of civilization as
a whole could be promoted by those who struggled in the spirit of community. In this struggle, some communities would rise and others would
fall, but the driving force was a sense of pride in one's own community
(defined in narrow ascriptive and ultimately biological terms). Because
democracy itself was carried in the social mores of the Anglo-Americans,
as Tocqueville had argued, southern apologists, as the bearers of that tradition, had a right to be proud of their accomplishments and to dominate
those who fell outside it. In this way, freedom was advanced even as the
"weaker races" were condemned like dodo birds to fall into oblivion—
either physically or culturally, as the case may be.

Senator Richard Russell proved most capable of defending this
ideal of cultural selection in a way presentable enough that he has
evaded the condemnation of history. Unlike Senator Bilbo, who left
the Senate as a national disgrace (if still a local hero), and even Strom
Thurmond (who at the age of one hundred would be remembered as
the very symbol of midcentury racial division), Senator Russell survived
this inglorious period of his public life to serve in the Senate until his
death in 1971, only to have a Senate office building named after him the
following year.[11]

In a radio episode of *Meet the Press* on July 30, 1948, in the midst of
the divisive Dixiecrat rebellion against Harry Truman's Progressive civil
rights plank, Russell engaged in the following philosophical debate with
James Reston, Washington correspondent for the *New York Times*, in a
stunning elaboration of his Darwinian reading of Tocqueville.

James Reston: Senator, the philosophy you've just described here about the white
race being as you've called the greatest race . . .

Larry Spivak: Yes! [*indicating interest in the subject*]

Reston: What effect do you think that philosophy has on, eh, our policy all over
the world when you express a—a view such as that, a view like that going out
from a United States senator.

Richard Russell: Well, I can't see that it would have any adverse effect on anyone
so long as we do not undertake to deny the people of any other race the right
to believe that they are the greatest people on earth. Why, this business that

you shouldn't have any pride of race, or any pride of state, if you boil it all down it means you shouldn't have any pride of country, or any desire to defend your country. . . . What's built this country? It's been the competition between the small towns within the state. It's been the competition between the states of the union, and, uh, if it's un-American, and it can't be in any degree un-American, to have pride of race so long as you don't impose on anyone else. . . . I want to show the absolute fallacy of complaining that there is anything of the Hitlerian philosophy in a man being proud of his race. Hitler took away all the rights of those who were members of the minority race; I would not deny them one right. He fixed where they could not be proud of their race; I am hoping and praying that the Negroes will develop a substantial pride of race.

Albert Warner (moderator): To keep on this philosophical line for just one question, Senator, hasn't it been the cooperation of the states under the Constitution rather than competition which has made for the greatness of this country?

Russell: Yes, but you've got to have some incentive to cooperation, and the belief that your state is the best, eh, and that your community is the best and your effort to make it the best and your effort to make your state the best, is the things that's built America.

To southerners like Russell, the struggle for and future of democratic civilization depended on the variability and autonomy of local groups whose sense of local pride would extend outward to larger associations. In this way, an exclusive struggle for recognition would guarantee that the appropriate reward be assigned to groups. It is as if history could be thought of as a kind of giant football league in which teams would compete in desperate games to demonstrate their relative superiority to posterity.[12] Russell and those who followed in his wake imagined that the races had always been free to compete with one another and that they continued to stand in relation to one another as foreigners who occupied what were ultimately separate nations, celebrated in the degree of their contribution to world history.

From his eminent position, Russell had many occasions to appear on *Meet the Press*. In February 1950 on national television, Russell clarified his defense of segregated streetcars to Ruth Montgomery of the *New York Daily News*. His choice of reference highlights both the indelibly alien quality of the former slaves in his vision of democratic society and his callousness to the damaging loss of dignity that might result from falling behind in the historical "clash of civilizations" that so many southerners identified with their brand of Republican constitutionalism. As Russell told the story, a democratic citizen should be a good sport in the cultural war to win the future world civilization.

Ruth Montgomery: But, Senator, I just want to say, think how humiliating it must be to a person to be treated as second-class citizen who is told that he can't sleep in a hotel where you do or sit next to you.

Richard Russell: Well, that term "second-class citizen" is one of those euphemistic labels that I'm talking about that is applied to these circumstances. There is nothing under the law that is any second-class citizenship, and I think it is only an inferiority complex that causes them to feel that way. Now, when the British go to India or to China, do they insist on breaking into the Chinese homes and into the Chinese private establishments? They establish their own homes and their own clubs, and even though they are a minority race, infinitely more than the Negro in the United States, they don't have an inferiority complex that makes them feel like they are being discriminated against.

What this philosophy made clear to Russell and to other prominent partisans in this mold was a profound idea that was developed contemporaneously in England by sociologist T. H. Marshall. Marshall promoted a concept of social rights to an audience in Cambridge, while Senator Russell had been arguing against the same to a national audience of influential Americans. The core of the social rights idea was that liberal societies had developed to the point that they were now providing guarantees for all of their citizens that they should not become second-class members of their own civilizations. Marshall's social rights were developed in reference to the class structure, but the concept could be extended to considerations of cultural intolerance and exclusion as well. While African Americans might have been suffering under the pressures of capitalism, the immediate problems they faced came in the form of cultural discrimination. What they needed were new rights of first-class citizenship that protected them more from bigotry than from bigwigs in the short run. Russell dismissed these claims for new rights—group rights—in any of their forms as beyond the mandate of a government of a free people. Russell was a thinker firmly committed to Berlin's principle of negative liberty and, in his use of it, placed the adjective *negative* in a new light.

Larry Spivak: Well, Senator, do you believe that in a democracy that there should be anything like first- and second-degree citizenship?

Richard Russell: . . . I know of no place there is second-class citizenship, eh, ah, that is imposed by law. Ah, the idea now seems to be that you're going, by this legislation that's pending today, that you will take away the rights of a man because he happens to belong to the 90 percent of the people of this nation who are white, at the behest of the 10 percent who happen to be Negro, ah, eh, under guise of a civil right, but you are really creating a new right, and most of these bills, at the expense of the rights that have long been considered sacred and, ah, elementary.

We can see how Russell cleverly invokes the Jeffersonian legacy, much like Ol' Gene Talmadge had with Jackson, but this time with flair. By referring to "sacred and elementary rights" as opposed to those that were self-evident,[13] he positions himself with Jefferson's original draft of the Declaration of Independence against northern secular icons like Benjamin Franklin and John Adams, who helped edit the founding document. Russell is engaged in a struggle for civil position. He is looking for creative ways to develop a path to the future that builds on the classical and southern tradition of American liberalism. He will not concede the moral high ground of his segregationist impulses to grant the northerners a political victory. He plans to fight them much like Lee did at Fredericksburg and Chancellorsville. In this, he shared his view of the sacred and elementary rights with Strom Thurmond, who on October 29, 1948, defended his candidacy for president in terms of a view of democracy that explicitly denied the legitimacy of what T. H. Marshall described as the social element of citizenship.[14]

Larry Spivak: Governor, you've been preaching the importance of saving our democratic form of government. What exactly does democracy mean to you?

Strom Thurmond: It means preservation of personal liberty and constitutional government. It means maintaining the freedom and the liberty that the people of America now enjoy, and which they would not enjoy if President Truman's so-called civil rights program went into effect—when a man couldn't hire whom he wanted to, he couldn't fire whom he wanted to, and when a man had to work beside people he didn't want to, and other things I could mention under these laws.

The crucial point in all of this is that the southerners had correctly recognized that, under the banner of intergroup tolerance, otherwise known as equal protection of groups, civil rights advocates were struggling to establish new rights—group rights—that they demanded ought to be protected under the Constitution. These new rights were not the sort that protected the individual citizen from abuses committed by the government but from abuses committed by fellow citizens. The villain in this story was not the bureaucrat but the bigot. Free exchange on the market was reframed as coercive and discriminatory, because discriminatory employers and shopkeepers could safeguard their cultural privilege by abusing their market power to shame and humiliate African Americans as a group. In this, they were supported by the white majority. As Russell argued, under the Roosevelt and Truman initiatives to protect minorities against discrimination (the FEPC bill), "an entirely new so-called civil right is established. That bill declares in its preamble, that 'the right of one citizen to give another a job is the right of the man that looks for a job, and that he cannot be discriminated against on account of race, creed, or color.'" What Russell, Thurmond, and not a few northern industrialists recognized was that this new interpretation of the Fourteenth Amendment opened the door to the regulation of commerce and free exchange with respect to cultural difference in ways that even the social democrats of the New Deal had not imagined. What were once thought of as private decisions on the free market would now be subject to inspection for signs of racial bigotry. The challenge to regnant conceptions of freedom as private enterprise was undeniable, however justified these initiatives might be.

In Russell's world, it was outside the scope of legitimate government to get into the business of regulating recognition. He saw such pride as something that had to be struggled over and won, not something that could be guaranteed by "the police power" of the federal government. The future of democratic civilization itself depended on a kind of marketplace of group dignity that would reward virtuous behavior and punish vice. Bigotry was enlisted by the spirit of democracy through a natural sequence of cause and effect. The democratic problem for southern whites was not white racism but the civil immaturity of black people, whom they saw as incapable of supporting the norms of democratic civilization. If "the Negro" had a future in this complex world, he would need to be liberated from his tutelage by the stronger race. As Ol' Gene Talmadge put it back in 1946, "Well, I propose to help in every way we can. He's a weaker race, he, ah, we can help him in education, in his line, and his environment and his future opportunities of life. He has only an artificial civilization of about 150 years."

With leaders like these, African Americans of talent had little hope of realizing their dreams, but the stakes in the confrontation between the freedom argument proposed by the advocates of private enterprise and the tolerance argument posed by adversaries of discrimination was difficult to parse in the heat and drama of the civil rights movement. However it sat in political discourse, the emerging fight against discrimination intended to limit the competitive advantages that whites enjoyed in education and employment. Its real target, however, was the invidious cultural basis of claims to deference that whites had enjoyed in the South as long as they had lived there. When Theodore Bilbo's successor in the Mississippi Senate, John Stennis, appeared on the program in 1949 to defend the right of unlimited debate (that is, filibuster), he named this tidal force quite clearly:

Larry Spivak: Well, Senator, what useful purpose do you hope to serve by talking indefinitely?

John Stennis: Well [*exasperated*], it's mainly a negative purpose, frankly, so far as the civil rights program is concerned. Mr. Reynolds mentioned that a great part of the civil rights program, if applied in the laws as they are written, will absolutely destroy a great deal of the social order in the South in my opinion. And it will be very, very injurious to all races there. Because it's bringing change in the wrong method—

Spivak: Well, now, Senator—

Stennis: Too fast! By coercion!

The moral order itself was at stake. The social standing, dignity, and pride of its citizens were in play in an elementary way. It is not clear that Stennis, Russell, and others ever thought that American blacks could rise to the status of civil maturity, but it is clear that they feared that they would not do so anytime soon. This invidious contrast of civilizations assured their commitment to a repressive project of cultural supremacy in the name of liberal egalitarianism. Northern libertarians and opportunistic fractions of the business classes opposed these reforms because they presented challenges to Lockean property rights, but southerners saw in them the substance of the civil rights movement; they saw the makings of a status revolution that they opposed as bitterly as they would a Bourbon king.

This struggle for a democracy of dignity was revealed in the comments of the leader of the civil rights struggle in Albany, Georgia, Dr. William G. Anderson, when he reflected on the otherwise disappointing results of the movement in that city on July 28, 1962.

Larry Spivak: Dr. Anderson, you have made very little progress toward desegregation in Albany with these demonstrations. Have you accomplished anything at all, in your judgment?

William Anderson: I certainly think we have accomplished a good deal. Not so much materially, but we have accomplished a good deal so far as the individual Negro is concerned. He has a new sense of dignity and respect that heretofore has not been demonstrated or made manifest, and this I believe will be the ultimate salvation of the Negro in the South.

This new right "of the man who looks for a job," a once private matter now made public, would help provide the material opportunities toward the realization of the ultimate goal, identity: "a new sense of dignity and respect." Access to a job, a college dorm, a bus seat, or a hotel room were all valuable in themselves but were rendered sacred only insofar as they served as vehicles for identity formation. The fight against discrimination was about education and jobs on the surface, but at root it was about human dignity and the antibigotry sections of the democratic storybook. On the face of the movement was a kind of modified class politics, but at its heart was a struggle for cultural diversity. By treating the secondary infections, one got closer to curing the disease of racism itself. Having demonstrated its success, the civil rights movement would come to serve as a model for democratic practice worldwide (perhaps another form of American hegemony) as problems of ethnic and cultural difference exploded with the collapse of the colonial empires.

In the 1940s, the tolerance agenda had been carried primarily by the president through executive orders like the FEPC, but it found explosive confirmation in the decision of the judicial branch in 1954 concerning integration of schools. When the Warren Court invalidated the practice of discrimination in the school system with the *Brown v. Board of Education* decision, the stage was set for the newly empowered social/cultural rights activists to "wash away the customs of centuries." How this played out on *Meet the Press* is well captured in this exchange between May Craig (who might be thought of as an indicator of the conscience of mainstream America in the period) and Herman Talmadge, appearing twenty days after the decision.

May Craig: The Supreme Court is set up by the Constitution to interpret law [*emphasis*]. Do you set yourself above the Supreme Court?

Herman Talmadge: I might give you better authority than myself, Mrs. Craig. The preceding Supreme Courts held that separate but equal facilities were valid under our Constitution.

[He then lists a number of revered judges as a kind of distraction.]

Craig: But, Governor, what's that got to do with it? They're dead and gone now. You're dealing with a present Supreme Court and a present decision, and can you set yourself above it?

[He perseverates with a quote from Justice Cardozo.]

Craig: But, Governor, again I feel you are evading me. Justice Cardozo did not participate in this decision. This was a unanimous decision of all the nine justices, only two of them appointed by a Republican, and they have said segregation must go. Now I ask you, how can you set yourself above the Supreme Court?

Talmadge: Let me answer that question in this way. I admit that the Supreme Court has ruled and under the Constitution of our United States, having made that decision, it becomes the supreme law of our land. But I must recite to you, there are many precedents in history where tyranny has been resisted by the people, and when you by simple judicial decree, try to wash away the customs of centuries, the people will not accept it.

Craig: Well, sir—

Talmadge: And the people will not accept it in Georgia!

Craig: One more question. You have said that you would fight for your way of life. You don't mean armed rebellion against the United States, do you?

Talmadge: Now, I hope it will not come to that.

Racial conflict in the South was fought over the issues of lynching, poll taxes, school integration, and eventually busing, but its root causes were deeper. Southern whites were defending their social identity, but they did so emboldened by the fiction of a superior civil identity to which they had special access. The logic can be expressed in a syllogism: liberal values are civilized values; western values are liberal values; western values are civilized values. Southerners fought against the encroaching group rights of the integrationists on the faith that theirs was the only civil society that could preserve freedom and democracy in the world against an array of savage and corrosive forces. They saw themselves as the repository of what Ronald Reagan would later describe as the "last best hope of man on earth." Freedom followed the white man as the course of empire took its way. Like the western frontier hero who was emerging as a stock type of film star, theirs was a fight against barbarism that could not be resolved by do-gooders with noble intentions. It is this feature of the lost persuasion of Senator Russell and his colleagues that we least understand today, and it was a feature that less bigoted leaders later exploited to maximum effect against egalitarian reformers. In the South, the tenuous commitment to equality secured by Roosevelt and the Populists was sacrificed in favor of a focused defense of freedom against the bogeyman of Negro incivility. This clash of liberal principles formed the philosophical basis of "the southern strategy" of Goldwater and Nixon and became a model for ideological conversion for the entire country to a new neoliberal common sense.

Before the Conscience of the Nation

This is a state [Alabama] that continues to do all of the things that are contrary to our democratic creed, at least the political power structure of that state. . . . As long as the conditions of injustice and man's inhumanity to man infiltrate that state, it will be necessary to demonstrate in order to bring these issues to the surface and lay them squarely before the conscience of the nation.

—Martin Luther King Jr., March 28, 1965

There is nothing that so clearly reveals the magic of immersing oneself in the smooth weekly rhythm of the *Meet the Press* archive than the opportunity it presents the viewer to meet Martin Luther King for the first time. The magic derives from the fact that when he first appears on the program, he is not yet really Martin Luther King. He is himself in the first person, but not the third—the towering figure whom we celebrate today. When King first appeared on the program on April 17, 1960, he did so as a young (just thirty-one) and radical social movement leader whose tactics and perhaps even motives pushed the boundaries of American legitimacy. When King began the interview that day, he stood out for his blackness (he was only the third black guest to have appeared on the show after Roy Wilkins and Jackie

Robinson) but also for his seeming naïveté. By the time the show had ended, it was clear that something new was afoot in the field of political culture.

Dr. King's appearance that day marks the first time that arguments of this kind had breached the threshold of respectability that a program like *Meet the Press* could offer. The fact that King was as successful as he was and would one day be ranked among the first echelon of American leaders is almost impossible to imagine from within the purview of this 1960 television program. King made his first appearance on *Meet the Press* as an outsider, but even in his very first opportunity to speak to the nation through this venue, he developed a case that presented the country with the full moral context of the civil rights movement: its politics of conscience, its contempt for formal but nonsubstantive promises, its strategic focus on social drama, its revolutionary ambitions, and its recognition of the threat to democracy posed by intolerance and disrespect. In 1966, in a *Meet the Press* program that perhaps marked the close of this golden period of the politics of difference in America, Roy Wilkins, executive director of the NAACP, snipped that many people believe that "the civil rights movement began in 1960." In this performance by King, one can see why this misconception might have taken hold. Before King's first *Meet the Press* appearance, the civil rights movement was a steady and salient concern of the Washington establishment; afterward, it was part of the central problematic of democratic civilization.

It is instructive to note that the 1960 interview with King began with a challenge. Sometime before the interview, former president Harry Truman had dismissed the sit-in strategy that was the occasion for the interview; Larry Spivak confronted King directly with Truman's statement. King's reaction to President Truman in the opening was powerful and introduces a separation in the spirit of the civil rights movement of 1960 from the visions of those like Truman, who had publicly supported it before. While we might rightly remember Senator Hubert Humphrey for his efforts to promote human rights in race relations, for most Americans in this period Truman remained the symbol of a Democratic Party committed to cultural justice and racial reconciliation. In his response to Truman, King demonstrated confidently in an example of breathtaking self-possession that being "an old friend of the Negro" was no longer enough.

Larry Spivak: Dr. King, former president Harry Truman recently said this: "If anyone came to my store and sat down, I would throw him out. Private business has its own rights and can do what it wants." Former president Truman is an old friend of the Negro, I believe. Isn't this an indication that the sit-in strikes are doing the Negro more harm than good?

Martin Luther King: No, I don't think so. First, I should say that this was an unfortunate statement, and we were very disappointed to hear the former president of the United States make such a statement. In a sense, a statement like this serves to aid and abet the violent forces in the South. Even if Mr. Truman disagreed with the sit-ins, he should certainly disagree with them on a higher level.

This break with Harry Truman and King's resort to a morality and a "higher level" (reminiscent of William Seward's "higher law" abolitionist sentiments in the debate of 1850) pointed out that the sit-ins revealed that the political struggle for human dignity would demand new and uncomfortable solutions and that the symbolic terrain was shifting in revolutionary directions. It was on this broadcast that King made the first of his provocative links between his own acts of civil disobedience and the Boston Tea Party.[15]

Martin Luther King: We feel that there are moral laws in the universe just as valid and as basic as man-made laws, and whenever a man-made law is in conflict with what we consider the law of God, or the moral law of the universe, then we feel that we have a moral obligation to protect. And this is in our American tradition all the way from the Boston Tea Party on down. . . . So that this is all we're doing. In our institutions we give the Boston Tea Party as an example of the initiative of Americans, and I think this is an example of the initiative and the great creative move of the young people of our nation.

Although by this point Dr. King's star was rising so fast and his schedule was so packed that one might easily overlook the importance of his appearance on *Meet the Press*, the capacity of the program to propel a conversation from the intellectual to the popular is demonstrated by Truman's reaction. The next day Truman held his own press conference in Ithaca, New York, which was reported in the *New York Times* under the headline "Truman Believes Reds Lead Sit-ins." In turn, this produced a letter of rebuke from Dr. King to Truman in which he condemned Truman for "an abysmal lack of understanding of what is taking place," which coming from a former "custodian of the nation's destiny" rose to "shocking and dangerous proportions."[16] King had received personal letters from President Eisenhower before, but prior to his appearance on *Meet the Press*, he had yet to become a rhetorical sparring partner for a president. For

Truman, as for many Americans, it was difficult to separate the revolution that Dr. King and others promoted during the sit-in movement from that which Lenin had promoted in 1902. The difference was that Dr. King's movement was based on "the inner longing for freedom and self respect," not on a fundamental contradiction between the interests of capital and the proletariat. This led to problems for those who favored what Senator Russell thought of as protections that were out of step with those Lockean rights long considered "sacred and elementary."

Apart from the concrete details of how the national debate developed during this period, the implications of what was taking place for the development of popular political thought were clear. What was developing on this level was the popular reception of a democratic theory that we would now call the politics of recognition.[17] This developing liberal concept was built on the premise that the state had a role in protecting the dignity of a group of individuals from the actions of another group, even from actions that were not directly violent. In essence, it brought a certain frame of mind under the domain of law if it led to discriminatory behavior. Dr. King had embraced this transformation. He envisioned a revolutionary campaign against "a basic problem in human relations" represented by systematic humiliation. What was novel in this approach was that humiliation itself was the problem, not simply the material consequences that issued from it. Lynching, disenfranchisement, and even concentration camps were material extensions of misrecognition, but they were not the root cause of the problem. The goal was to create what Dr. King called "the beloved community," in which a change of heart would transform not only patterns of behavior but also hearts and souls. Bitterness would, in time, melt into mutual respect. It would be difficult to articulate a more explicit formulation of Isaiah Berlin's concept of positive liberty than this.

Larry Spivak: Well, now you have yourself said that the aim of your method of nonviolent resistance is not to defeat or to humiliate the white man but to win his friendship and understanding. How successful do you think you have been, or are being, in winning the friendship and understanding of the white men of the South?

Martin Luther King: Well, I should say that this doesn't come overnight. The nonviolent way does not bring about miracles, in a few hours, or in a few days, or in a few years, for that matter. . . . Of course, I can't estimate how many people we have touched so far. That is impossible because it is an inner process, but I am sure something is stirring in the minds and souls of people, and I am sure that many people are thinking anew on this basic problem of human relations.

This "inner process . . . stirring in the minds and souls" of the people was promoted through a conscientious politics that broke with conventions of protest and therefore gained the attention of an apathetic community. It required techniques that dramatized situations that could not be disregarded and confronted the public with the moral implications of inaction. Direct action was the key. For King, the politics of social drama did not justify demonization, but they did require a kind of vilification process so that the adversaries of liberty like Senator Bilbo and later, Bull Conner, could be targeted by the aroused masses. His approach might be called redemptive vilification: the former oppressor was a villain in the drama but could be redeemed when he was encouraged to think anew.

Spivak: Wouldn't you be on stronger grounds, though, if you refused to buy at
    those stores, and if you called upon the white people of the country to follow
    you because of both your moral and your legal right not to buy?
King: I think sometimes it is necessary to dramatize an issue because many people
    are not aware of what is happening. I think the sit-ins serve to dramatize
    the indignities and the injustices which Negro people are facing all over the
    nation.

This otherwise routine political broadcast in April 1960 was the moment when the status revolution in American politics reached a new level of maturity and self-confidence. The active social recognition of one's human dignity, even beyond the toleration of difference, was soon to be established as an embattled cultural right that could be overtly defended rather than a merely abstract characteristic that came along with formal citizenship. King demonstrated that the goals of the civil rights movement did not lie only in fighting discrimination or overcoming disparities in socioeconomic standing but also in what we would now call celebrating diversity. Political techniques were validated for their dramatic potential to appeal to the morality of the mass conscience to overcome abusive interpersonal behavior. The threat to democratic civilization was in our hearts, not only in our laws. Cruelty had been marked as an undemocratic and even un-American attitude. The revolution had been televised.

The next few years in the history of the civil rights movement proved to be as revolutionary as many of the movement's leader's suspected they might be. Not only was King leading what he might have

called his own version of the Tea Party, but in the height of the transformation, the language of revolution was commonly employed and
continues in the folklore of African American politics. To underscore
this point, NBC broadcast a three-hour special on September 2, 1963,
entitled "The American Revolution of '63." It was announced at the conclusion of the *Meet the Press* episode in which King appears with Roy
Wilkins to discuss the upcoming March on Washington, which brought
King political immortality with his "I Have a Dream" speech.[18] Deeply
American in character, this was not the kind of revolution that would
erect guillotines on the National Mall, but it would project its revolutionary consequences in how we think about and portray minorities,
women, gay people and others across the decades.

In that 1963 performance on August 25, the reporter Robert Mac-
Neil pursued a fascinating line of analysis that allowed him to explore
the dramaturgical strategy that King had outlined in his 1960 appearance. MacNeil was, of course, not the first to pick up the unintended
consequences of how this transformative politics of conscience played
out,[19] but his questions bring out a problem that may be endemic to
transformative political movements. To promote changes through civil
and nonviolent means, it is necessary to appeal to the mass conscience
with dramatic demonstrations that provide a clear and confrontational
story line. What had distinguished King's cultural rights revolution
from earlier examples was his sense that nonviolence had to play a central part; for, as he would say in an appearance dated August 21, 1966,
"The minute the nomenclature of violence gets into the atmosphere,
people begin to respond violently, and in their unsophisticated minds
they cannot quite make the distinction between defensive and aggressive
violence." Even so, a nonviolent movement had to raise the volume of
social unrest, which had the potential to lead to dashed expectations and
broken hopes.

Robert MacNeil: Mr. Wilkins, the march on Wednesday [August 28, 1963] is the
  psychological climax of a movement that has been crescendoing for many
  months. What do you plan after Wednesday?

Roy Wilkins: After Wednesday, of course, will be the follow-up on the crescendo, as you say, that has been developing. It will be immediately
  addressed to the task of getting legislation through the Congress, and
  then it will proceed, as it must proceed, on all local and state levels,
  to the elimination step by step, or sweepingly as the case might be, of

remaining pockets of discrimination, even while we wait for legislation from the Congress. . . .

MacNeil: I was wondering how you were going to maintain the militancy of your followers after having brought them to such a pitch as this march will achieve, without making it difficult to keep them nonviolent.

Wilkins: Mr. MacNeil, our people are coming to Washington to show their government how deeply they feel about this matter, and they are not coming here to stage violence or to put on any stunts. They intend to go back from this place, which is as you say a peak, but only a notification of their national government. They continue to go back to their home communities and continue in the same tempo, on the same goals that are there in each of the states and the cities and localities in which they live.

That movement tempo was maintained, and it swept before it opposition to the landmark civil rights and voting rights bills of 1964 and 1965, respectively. But concerns about the aftermath of the "psychological climax" of the movement lingered and were increasingly voiced from friendly sources as well.

Richard Wilson (Cowles Publications): Dr. King, in that connection, an advertisement was published today in the *New York Times* by Freedom House. . . . I interpret the text of this advertisement to reflect a feeling among those thoughtful people that moderation now is required more than it has been in the recent past. Would you interpret this statement in that light?

Martin Luther King: I would be the first to say that if moderation means moving on toward the goal of justice with wise restraint and calm reasonableness, then we must pursue this path, but if moderation means slowing up at any point and capitulating to the undemocratic practices of many of the forces that are against democracy, then it would be tragic and certainly immoral to slow up at this point.

As even the most prudent of the civil rights leaders must have expected, the appeal of more confrontational, threatening, separatist, and even violent elements within the movement did prove to be irresistible in the cultural rights revolution. The rise of these tendencies can be clearly seen in the pivotal congressional election year of 1966. The increasing diversity of leadership in the movement and the strategic decisions to expand the dramatic struggle from the South to the North had opened new possibilities for the discipline King had spoken about to break down.

Unsurprisingly, Mississippi provided the setting. The first student to enroll at the University of Mississippi, James Meredith, had been shot on June 6, 1966, the first day of his march across the state to remove fear of transit among blacks who lived there. After the shooting, fear quickly transitioned to anger. That day, the new leader of the Student Nonviolent Coordinating Committee, the volatile Stokely Carmichael, gave a famous speech from which the term "black power" derived. The salacious appeal of this phrase is difficult to overemphasize. On June 19, 1966, James Meredith appeared on *Meet the Press* in response to claims that he would resume his march and this time he would go armed. This did not provide comfort to the unsettled white community that was on the path to Independent Party status.

Haynes Johnson (*Washington Evening Star*): I don't want to belabor this point about being armed or not, but it seems to me that an awful lot of people in this country are very concerned about this, Mr. Meredith. . . . I am not clear from your answer to Mr. Sitton whether you in fact do intend to carry a weapon with you or whether you urge other Negroes around this country to be prepared to defend themselves.

James Meredith: Well, I think that the responsibility for the maintenance of peace and order is with the government. . . . When these people fail, then the ones who are affected have responsibility, and I never will relinquish that responsibility.

Johnson: Are you suggesting that you should then be prepared to take things into your own hands, the Negroes?

Meredith: Certainly, if all the other responsible agencies fail to do so, there is no choice.

Later that summer, the Chicago Freedom Movement experienced its own psychological climax in an attempt to provide a dramatic backdrop for a housing bill that was pending before Congress. On August 21, *Meet the Press* aired a special triple-length, ninety-minute episode on what was described as "the greatest domestic problem facing the United States: race." The episode was truly one of a kind and has not been successfully reproduced. The unique mix of views presented on the program and the specific timing of the program to air in that week demonstrates why the *Meet the Press* record is so revealing of central tendencies of established American opinion. The summer of 1966 is easy to forget in our Whiggish memories of the movement because less was gained then than at other times, but it is here that the current pattern of the clash of liberal traditions first developed.[20]

Appearing that day on the same stage were Roy Wilkins, Whitney Young of the Urban League, Floyd McKissick of the once nonviolent Congress of Racial Equality, Stokely Carmichael, and James Meredith. Dr. King was unable to attend in person because of the demands of the demonstrations in Chicago and could only appear in a remote Chicago studio for the first half hour. The implicit drama of the situation was tapped into by James J. Kilpatrick.

James J. Kilpatrick (*Richmond News Leader*): Dr. King, you have been quoted as saying that you have encountered more hatred among white opponents in Chicago than you have encountered in the Deep South. How do you account for this?

Martin Luther King: I think for years the hatred existed beneath the surface in northern communities, and as I said earlier, it is coming out now. I think also we have to see that this is something of a dislike for the unlike. You see it a great deal among the lower-income ethnic enclaves who have their basic fears about Negroes.

Dr. King had been injured by a thrown brick two weeks earlier as he had marched in Marquette Park, one of these ethnic enclaves, and would be marching in another called South Deering on the South Side after he left the studio. He demonstrated his conviction that the struggle against what was called de facto segregation in the North was just as important as was the effort against de jure segregation in the South and that it would proceed according to the same playbook. The skepticism of political leadership toward the strategy was pronounced and included a reaction from President Johnson:

Larry Spivak: Johnson just gave a speech yesterday where he warned that violence and discord would destroy Negroes' hopes for racial progress. Now, isn't it time to stop demonstrations that create violence and discord?

King: Well, I absolutely disagree with that, and I hope that the president didn't mean to equate nonviolent demonstrations with a riot, and I think it is time for this country to see the distinction between the two. . . . I think demonstrations must continue, but I think riots must end.

Dr. King's faith in democracy and its civil dramas never waivered. He demanded to push on through the panic of white liberals who began to fear that bright lines between civil progress and civil unrest were fading as the movement moved north.

Richard Valeriani (NBC News): Dr. King, to follow up Mr. Spivak's question, recent polls suggest that in terms of national reaction, demonstrations are now counterproductive. By continuing them, don't you run the risk of doing more harm than good?

King: Again, I contend that we are not doing more harm than good in demonstrations, because I think demonstrations serve the purpose of bringing the issues out in the open. I have never felt that demonstrations could actually solve the problem. They dramatize the existence of certain social ills that could easily be ignored if you did not have demonstrations. I think the initial reaction to demonstrations is always negative . . . and I am still convinced that there is nothing more powerful to dramatize a social evil than the tramp, tramp of marching feet.

On that August day in 1966, Dr. King looked tired as he appeared on-screen, separate from the other leaders, almost hinting at things to come. After he left the program, the perspectives of black leaders who were less committed to King's "calm reasonableness" remained in the spotlight. As an example of how things had changed, Floyd McKissick discussed why he had lost his commitment to the nonviolent ideal. August 1966 was the moment of truth for the revolution.

Floyd McKissick: First of all, I believe that the moment of truth is here for the simple reason that, one, nonviolence is something of the past. . . . I think it is difficult now to harness and have the control over demonstrations at many points for the simple reason that most of the black people in the communities do not and will not agree to be nonviolent. . . . We say that we can march down the street and if nobody hits us, okay, you have got nonviolence. But if somebody hits us, then you better have an ambulance on the side to pick up whoever hits somebody.

Whitney Young and Roy Wilkins expressed their concerns with what they saw as overreactions on the other side of the debate. Young shared his frustration about the flack over black power over the summer: "We deplored the country's obsession and preoccupation with a debate about a slogan which we felt deterred the country from concentrating on the problems of poverty and discrimination." Wilkins attempted repeatedly to set the genre of their performances in the context of law and regular progress: "We are having some manifestations of abrasive resistance, but actually progress is being made and we are going forward," and "we all come to the courtroom and to the law eventually. We find we can't solve it with rhetoric." But the excited voices carried farther in this environment.

James Meredith responded to a question about his march in Mississippi wryly. "As you recall, I didn't march through Mississippi. I was shot the first day, and of course, all of the other gentlemen carried on the march in Mississippi." At one point Larry Spivak drew him out as only Spivak could draw out his guests:

Spivak: Are you suggesting then that if several Negroes are killed or any white men are killed and the law does not punish them, as happens very often in the case of white men too, that people ought to organize as vigilantes and go out and take the law into their own hands and commit violence? You are not saying that are you, Mr. Meredith?

Meredith: That is exactly what I am saying: exactly.

Not long afterward, Stokely Carmichael responded in the way that made him, at the same time, one of the most infamous and celebrated characters of the period.[21]

Carl T. Rowan (*Chicago Daily News*): Mr. Carmichael, do I detect that you agree with Mr. Meredith that the Negro may take to arms?

Stokely Carmichael: I am here to answer Mr. Spivak directly that if in fact the law— and let it remain crystal clear that in this country we are the only people who have to protect ourselves from the protection. . . . And I agree 150 percent that black people have to move to the position where they organize themselves, and they are in fact a protection for each other and in fact of that 180 million people, because I am a little bit tired of that 90 percent theory. . . . While we may be 10 percent inside the country, continental borders of the United States, we want to make it crystal clear that we are well located in cities across this country and that if in fact 180 million people just think they are going to turn on us and we are going to sit there, like the Nazis did to the Jews, they are wrong. We are going to go down together, all of us.

In this way, the summer of 1966, the golden era of the American status revolution, settled into uncivil channels. On the one hand, the outline of a politics that placed the "basic problem in human relations" of status, social standing, and respect at the heart of the democratic project was established. On the other, the movement had reached its "moment of truth" with key parts of its leadership forswearing action in the civil sphere. Whitney Young countered Carmichael with the practical view that one does not get pride or dignity or power "simply by being white or being black, but by mobilizing into various groups who have similar ideas and working toward those ends." There would be always be a place for cooler heads like King, Wilkins, and Young in the civil rights movement, but the national conversation about the cultural rights revolution had turned. As the neoliberal counterreformation played out, the hotter heads like Stokely Carmichael would prove to be great casting material. The stage was set for the backlash.

The Individual Predatory Criminal

Perhaps we haven't been as articulate as we should in an effort to define the ravages that the individual predatory criminal is inflicting upon the society he invades. . . . But I do say that we ought not in the process be making a sacrifice of the bulk of our law-abiding society in order to favor the comfort and caprice of someone who has indicated his inability to function in a free and democratic context.

—Stanley Schrotel, president of the International Association of Chiefs of Police, May 5, 1963

The ideological reaction of the white majority to the cultural rights revolution of the civil rights movement had begun long before the movement's nonviolent discipline began to falter. The most common way to portray majoritarian political developments in this period is to label them collectively as the "white backlash," but it is more descriptive to label them as the "counterrevolutionary panic." Much of the panic played out through the recycling and revival of old uncivil stereotypes about African Americans, but the panic was evident even in those white leaders who were considered "old friend[s] of the Negro." In the *Meet the Press* episode of March 28, 1965, which followed the Selma march across the Edmund Pettus bridge and President Johnson's "we shall overcome" address to Congress, Dr. King was again confronted with Truman's disapproval, through Larry Spivak, after King dropped out of the march to Montgomery.

Larry Spivak: Dr. King, former president Truman was quoted by the AP as saying that the march from Selma—and this was his word—was "silly" and can't accomplish "a darn thing" except "to attract attention." There have been two beatings and a federal expenditure of troops of about three hundred thousand dollars. Would you say that what the march accomplished was worth that cost?

Martin Luther King: First, I would say that the march was not silly at all. I would think that the march did more to dramatize the indignities and the injustices that Negro people continue to face in the state of Alabama and many other sections of the South more than anything else. I think that it was the most powerful and dramatic civil rights protest that has ever taken place in the South. . . . We go on with the faith that unmerited suffering is redemptive.

That experience of unmerited suffering was about to be more evenly spread throughout the community, and the nations' mayors were to become the frontline witnesses. The 1965 summer riots in Watts, Los Angeles, had been followed two years later with perhaps even more troubling episodes in Newark, New Jersey, and Detroit. The riots in Detroit left that city's Progressive leader, Jerome Cavanagh, flabbergasted, with visions of disaster on the horizon. On July 30, 1967, he spoke in tragic tones on *Meet the Press*: "Let's be frank about it. Underneath the surface, this in fact was a race riot and a race revolution," and he warned of the need for Congress to act. He said, "There is a madness in the country, and the Congress reacts by being indifferent, sometimes not just indifferent, just by being completely negative about it." As Cavanagh put it, "We may pacify every village in Vietnam, over a period of years, but what good does it do if we can't pacify the American cities? And the American cities are not pacified; there is no question about it. . . . Maybe Detroit was a watershed in American history, and it might well be that out of the ashes of this city comes the national resolve to do far more than anything we have done in the past."

In March the following year, Henry Maier, the Socialist mayor of Milwaukee (a city intriguingly referred to as the Selma of the North in a recent history of conflict in the city in this period[22]) appeared with other embattled mayors to discuss how he was reacting to the challenges of the nationalization of the movement. Maier had reason to be concerned. In a 1967 civil rights march through Milwaukee, a favored chant ran as follows: "Before I'll be a slave, I'll put a Polack in his grave."[23] The "basic fears" that King had exposed among the white ethnics in Chicago had now aroused the anger of African American activists. Like Cavanagh, Maier believed that the problem was epic in proportion and that it would take the resources of the federal government to address it. In an episode following the release of the Kerner Commission report on urban riots and civil disorders on March 3, 1968, Maier advocated pulling money from space and agriculture programs to fund programs in the city. Framing his own approach not as a war on poverty but rather as a "war on prejudice," he pivoted from inequality to intolerance as the root challenge to moral order and civil peace. In this, Maier was simply following the prevailing narrative.

As might have been expected after such an intensely symbolic struggle, the politics of recognition was intensifying even as battles for individual and social rights for African Americans were being won. The previous year, on February 19, Whitney Young had described the findings of an earlier commission report on crime as follows: "What I think is probably today even a greater problem than police brutality . . . is, police humiliation, disrespect, the differential in approach and treatment of the minority rather than the physical abuse. I think it is a verbal abuse that is probably more of a problem today." The root causes of the conflict were coming into focus; not so much physical coercion by the police, but systematic misrecognition by the power structure.

Members of that power structure had a perspective on the escalations as well, and they focused on the cocktail of crime, riots, and civil disorder that is now a natural part of our conversations but was then a novelty of symbolic entrepreneurship. Perhaps the most telling instance of how these concerns entered the national spotlight can be found in the May 5, 1963, episode before the backlash and the riots. This was the first time that a *Meet the Press* panel had discussed the problem of violent crime committed by individuals, whatever their race, although the problems associated with organized crime were commonplace.

Appearing that Sunday was Stanley R. Schrotel. The association of blacks with crime was nothing new, but it had never carried the imprimatur of a *Meet the Press* conversation. The idea was progressing in established opinion from a bigoted stereotype to a focus of legitimate civil concern.[24] Chief Schrotel came armed with a new icon of incivility, the "predatory criminal." This episode is so revealing and consequential because it aired the week of the "Children's Crusade" in Birmingham, Alabama, the very moment when dogs and fire hoses became universal symbols of racist oppression. Insofar as we learn something important about America by taking note of how *Meet the Press* booked a guest to react to it, we learn much of what we need to know about racial fear from Schrotel's performance. Here is how the episode began:

Larry Spivak: Chief Schrotel, the FBI figures indicate a 7 percent increase in national crime this year, another all-time high. How alarming do you consider this situation, or is it normal for a country like ours constantly to increase its crime rate?

Stanley Schrotel: In terms of the economic impact which has been calculated at approximately $3 billion and the implication of human suffering in terms of loss of freedom, injury against the victim, I would say that this is a most serious problem.

Spivak: Is there a basic reason for this increase in crime, or are there major reasons for this in your judgment?

Schrotel: It is rather difficult to isolate the reasons, but there is certainly some concerted opinion relative to the effect that in-and-out migration in large urban centers in our nation is having upon the increase in crime incidence, and when we look to the fluctuation in crime volume in the major centers, I think here is where you will find the explanation for the overall national increase.

One can almost smell the fires in Watts beginning to burn. Spivak sets up the social drama that will play out over the next five decades in a relatively innocent way:

Spivak: Chief, in a recent interview in *U.S. News and World Report*, you said, "The bulk of our society takes a rather apathetic attitude toward the enforcement of law and the maintenance of order." That is a pretty serious indictment of our society. Upon what do you base that?

Schrotel: . . . We have not in my judgment employed the authority delegated to us in every way that is calculated to win and hold the confidence of the society that we serve. When we do this—and we are working diligently to accomplish that objective—I think that we then can express intelligently and in a meaningful way to the people who are willing to listen, after we have gained their respect, what in our opinion ought to be done in order to use the enforcement establishments more effectively to insulate our respective jurisdictions against predatory crime.

The term "predatory crime" is the most important innovation in the discourse of this episode; it portrayed the African American in uncivil terms as a member of a group in need of reform. It stigmatized the urban black population in much the same way the organized crime iconography had been used to stigmatize the union movement just a few years before, and both of these ideas had legs. (More than thirty years later on February 19, 1995, Charles Rangel, himself part of the march to Montgomery that Truman had found so silly, said on *Meet the Press*, "All we see on TV are polite white cops arresting black kids. I mean every day they have some program like that. Every problem that we have it appears as though the minority and poor are responsible for it.") Prior to this episode in May 1963, the very notion of predatory crime had yet to become an issue of national importance, let alone one of the most serious problems facing the country as Chief Schrotel had suggested it was. We now take for granted that African Americans are incarcerated at rates unknown anywhere else in the developed world.[25] What we do not remember is that the discursive link between predatory crime and blacks was initiated in respectable conversation in response to an FBI report the very week Bull Connor used dogs and fire hoses on Birmingham schoolchildren. At this crucial moment, and with a single report, the FBI had turned the national conversation on race in a direction it had never taken before. How this innovation was received by the "middle American" whom Richard Nixon would identify and exploit as the silent majority six years later is made clear in an exchange between Schrotel and May Craig:

May Craig: Chief, collective public virtue can certainly only flow from the collective private virtue. In my thirty years on the sidelines watching the American people, I have seen what is a shocking deteriorization, both public and private, in the American character. Now, to what do you lay that, if you agree?

Schrotel: . . . I should say that our police officers, acting in good faith, will find a youngster involved in some misdeed. According to correct and proper procedure, they will advise the parent of the youngster of the involvement of the child. Rather than evoke from the parent a degree of concern about the child's misbehavior, normally this is expressed in a kind of antagonism against the police, who are doing nothing more than discharging their duty.

Craig: . . . People used to be afraid of going to hell. Do you think a part of this is because we have lost God and put nothing in his place in this country? . . . There seems to be so much more sympathy for the criminals than the decent people. It used to be you prosecuted a criminal as against society and now it looks as though you are arraigning society and protecting the criminal. There is so much sympathy for them. This mamby-pamby psychiatry explanation of a rapist who is overcome or something.

And just in case the context surrounding the "shocking deteriorization" in American character that Craig had witnessed and its corresponding "mamby-pamby psychiatry" explanations were not explicit enough, Larry Spivak drew it out in his inimitable way.

Spivak: Chief Schrotel, you and other chiefs of police in the big cities particularly have complained that Negroes have contributed in larger share to crime than their numbers justify. Where do you place most of the blame for this, on the Negro himself or the society which has treated the Negro as a second-class citizen?

Schrotel: Well, Mr. Spivak . . . I am sure that the Negro's involvement is the result perhaps of his substandard relegation in a highly competitive society. . . . I don't think we can suddenly cope with this social malady by hiding it under the rug and providing all kinds of excuses or defenses in terms of the Negro involvement. I think that you can certainly understand why someone who is economically deprived would steal for the necessities of life, but I can't for the life of me understand why someone would engage in predatory crime and resort to all kinds of vicious devices to violate the person of the victim that he is militating against. . . . This is the message that the police are attempting to say when they bring out the dimension of this cultural involvement in the crime complex.

To find a way to break the sectional confrontation between North and South that was going so poorly for them, white southerners had been trying to nationalize the race issue for decades. Senator Russell had once imagined a massive program to promote out-migration of blacks from the South to the North. He had said on *Meet the Press* on February 18, 1950, "The only fair solution to it is to distribute your Negroes equally throughout the country. We've got nearly three-fourths of them in the South, and we'll have an acute problem and the rest of the country will be trying to kick us around as a political football until we do make this a national problem."[26] But this fear of violent crime brought a new way for many white Americans to deal with the fears they had of the civil disorders that had been so dramatically placed before them. They could rally against the "vicious devices" of the internal other with police power.

The FBI's argument that Chief Schrotel was promoting followed the logic of what might be called a "theory of relative depravation." In contrast to the relative deprivation arguments that sociologists developed during World War II to explore the nature of competitions for status in complex organizations,[27] the relative depravation argument suggested that the out-group was corrupted or depraved by virtue of suffering through an extended period of oppression and exclusion from the society of the in-group. This led to criminal behavior that included intention "to violate the person of the victim" as Schrotel suggested, and these were far more terrible to imagine than simple criminal behaviors.

The innovative image of the predatory criminal was directed at a newer interpretation of an old problem, what might be described as the corrigible incivility of the Negro. As Chief Schrotel described it, the predatory criminal had demonstrated "his inability to function in a free and democratic context" as he takes out his aggression "upon the society he invades." Blacks were not irredeemably fallen but were understood to have been unkindly corrupted by the forces of history. They could therefore be introduced to "civilized" society if institutions were designed in a way that promoted the internalization of civil norms in the African American community. This may have been a new form of racism, but it was eminently compatible with the American political tradition. For those seduced by this monocultural appeal, it was easy to imagine that until the problem of relative depravation was remedied, democracy would have to function separately but equally until it was solved. But above all, it was crucial not to yield to the "artificial civilization" of the Negro with an attitude of what would come to be called "permissiveness."

The chief of police in the Los Angeles riots understood this in terms that Richard Nixon would exploit to maximum effect. In a defensive interview on August 29, 1965, in which the infamous and popular Chief William H. Parker appeared to explain why the chaos in Watts had played out the way it did, he borrowed a page from Schrotel's playbook and made a case about the civil virtue of security from barbarism that would prove popular for decades.

William Parker: Unless the people begin to support the rule of law and the men who represent the force that represses crime, why then eventually the permissiveness of this society will overwhelm the police.

Not long afterward, on December 12, 1965, Senator Daniel Patrick Moynihan appeared on *Meet the Press* to discuss and defend his already infamous report *The Negro Family.* The report had been sharply criticized in the months following the Watts riot, an event that had effectively accomplished Russell's objectives of nationalizing the race problem, and Moynihan was on the program to bring the light of reason to the subject.

It is hard to imagine a more confident and compelling figure than the one Moynihan presented to the *Meet the Press* audience that winter evening. Moynihan considered himself, with cause, to be a civil rights activist, but a tough-minded one with the courage to take seriously the kind of "mamby-pamby psychiatry" explanations that May Craig had recently mocked in a way that elucidated rather than excused. In his view, the problem of the "Negro slums of our cities" was the result of "the culture of poverty. It is poverty and discrimination that does this to people. It has nothing to do with the color of their skin or the shape of their eyes. It has everything to do with how they are treated by the society within which they live." In other words, Moynihan subscribed to the theory of relative depravation. No one was better suited to bring this point out than the sardonic Robert Novak.

Robert Novak: Mr. Moynihan, as you well know, there was an undercurrent of criticism of the Moynihan report at the White House Conference on Civil Rights just a month or so ago, and this was all the more startling because your report is facts. But it was nonetheless criticism, was it not?

Daniel Patrick Moynihan: There are a great many people who thought we shouldn't talk about these things, I suppose. There always are people who, understandably, genuinely feel that way. But if you will remember, fifteen years ago it would have been thought a very bad thing indeed to talk about low IQs of Negro children on the grounds that that might give ammunition to racists, to enemies of school integration. Today I think civil rights leaders know that that is not only a good thing to talk about, but it is the best possible argument for showing the schools aren't doing their job, and they bring these matters up and they put them on the table and say, "What are we going to do about that problem?"

To civil rights leaders schooled in the baroque justifications of the Jim Crow system that had been trotted out from the time of the first civil rights bill in 1875, Moynihan's prescient observations about the coming confrontation in the North felt like more of the same. Here was Ol' Gene Talmadge dressed up in new clothes.

An incredulous Simeon Booker of *Ebony* magazine wondered if Moynihan's report was not an indictment of the black family in general. "If this be true, how do you account for the massive Negro revolution with demonstrations involving families of every income level?"

Simeon Booker: Really, Mr. Moynihan, isn't the problem essentially a white problem—discrimination and segregation have shaped the social conditions of
the Negro?

Moynihan: Mr. Booker, it is an American problem.

And this was an American problem that did not yet take well to white criticisms of black roles in it. Just six months after the Moynihan appearance on June 19, 1966, James Meredith of University of Mississippi fame described the nature of the problem of racial cooperation in the process of reconciliation.

Claude Sitton (*New York Times*): Mr. Meredith, if whites and Negroes cannot work
together in the Negro rights movement, the black movement, and the civil
rights movement, is it possible that we can have an integrated society finally?
Do you think it can be achieved?

James Meredith: I thought I said they could work together and not only could
but should. . . . There are two important sides to this racial question in this
country. The one side is what the Negro has to do. The other side is what the
general society has to do. . . . I think the Negro community has to do these
things, and I think only the Negro community can do it. Such things as
building pride in the community, in the family, these types of things. I think
only the Negro can do it.

In such a heated environment, the "old friend of the Negro" could go only so far. Moynihan had traveled across the line of friendship; talking about the other fellow's family and culture amounted to what was called in the black vernacular "playing the dozens." This was a topic that was too hot to handle at that point in the public conversation. There were some things that "only the Negro community" could do and certain places to have frank conversations about culture and trauma. Whites were not yet welcome to the family meeting. Because Moynihan was the best the liberal establishment could do on this topic, and because he was so openly savaged for his earnest engagement, the American problem went underground, where no one could predict how it would develop.

Perhaps the best way to illustrate how controversial the Moynihan report had become in the civil rights community and how defensive the liberal establishment was about it is with an example from the pivotal August 21, 1966, episode of *Meet the Press* during the Chicago Freedom Movement. Moynihan had previously defended his argument against what he called "the disapproval of a few white liberals from Boston who think I shouldn't raise the subject because it is impolite." When confronted by dismissive criticisms of the senator's intentions by black leaders in the special edition on civil rights, moderator Edwin Newman was driven uncharacteristically to cut off debate. His curt reply reveals his opinion of the criticisms he has just heard. "I think I had better cut off the discussion of the Moynihan report since Mr. Moynihan is not here to defend himself. I think—and I know him quite well—that you have mistaken what he said."

Martin Luther King had set the narrative of racial redemption deep in the nation's conscience through the vehicle of the civil drama, the "tramp, tramp of marching feet," which would rouse the conscience of the nation. Now a new story was consolidating on the right in which the villain was an attitude that critics would much later label "political correctness"—where permissive do-gooders looked past glaring problems that might lead to open and violent insurrection against the whole of the body politic. Worse yet, this attitude was based on the standards of politeness set by what Moynihan had labeled an "Eastern elite." Racists and the merely anxious could therefore point to a second new villain, the elitist bigwig who hailed from the big city. He was no longer rich but a snob and a fool.[28] From this unresolved moment of crisis, two incompatible and even contradictory ideas would live unhappily together for the next three decades. The majority of white America would thereafter be committed to the achievements of the status revolution, while many would be concerned about the anticivil qualities that the history of status oppression had itself produced. Unsurprisingly, this led to a situation in which silence and degenerative conflict could thrive together.

It Is Not the Bus; It Is Us

The code word for racism in this campaign has been the bus. It is not
the bus; it is us.

—Jesse Jackson, May 30, 1976

The 1970s (a decade that would metaphorically last well into the
late 1990s) was characterized by a clash of liberal traditions. The first was
represented by the cultural rights philosophy of Martin Luther King, his
story anchored by the conception of villainy now represented by George
Wallace of Alabama. The second was represented by Ronald Reagan, his
story anchored by a more subtle conception of villainy represented by "a
few white liberals from Boston" who believed that they "can plan our lives
for us better than we can plan them ourselves," as he noted in a 1964
speech. King's story relied obliquely on arguments sometimes made by
challenging figures like the radical Algerian separatist Frantz Fanon about
the ties between dignity, freedom, and colonial oppression. Reagan's story
relied on arguments made by classical liberal icons like John Locke and
emerging ones like Friedrich Hayek. They stressed the ties between property, freedom, and feudal oppression. If we place these ideas in terms of
Isaiah Berlin's typology of positive versus negative liberty, Dr. King's project was an exercise in positive liberty with an accent on tolerance, whereas
Reagan's was an exercise in negative liberty with the accent on freedom.[29]
Although these emerged from the same sociopolitical cauldron, their visions were not readily compatible, even as Americans celebrated them both
and dithered on the race issue through the long decade of the 1970s, using
coded language to mischaracterize one another.

Central to this period were the imagery of the school bus and
the shorthand for racial integration: busing. Busing children from
poor and separated districts to more affluent and integrated ones was
only an example of a host of affirmative solutions that newly empowered civil rights advocates were now considering to deeply entrenched
racial problems. Although the voters were divided in their support of
such affirmative measures—affirmative in the sense that they validated
antisupremacist group rights—the courts had played the role that the
legislative and executive branches could not in expanding the scope of
the democratic project to include policies toward cultural inclusion. As
Walter Mondale put it on March 1, 1970, "The single most important
step" to be taken in the field of civil rights was to nominate "judges to

the Supreme Court who are committed to human rights. If the court backs off the enforcement of human rights laws of this country—and they have often saved us from ourselves—then I think the cause of human rights could easily be lost." Translation: Americans would have never voted for this if they had had the chance, but democratic decisions are not always right.

Mondale's concerns were well placed, because despite an explosion of Democratic congressional representation and active court support for the new liberal principles, the argument for cultural over individual rights was turning against the Democratic Party. By 1976, an African American leader like Mayor Jay Cooper of Pritchard, Alabama, could inveigh against eight "plague years for black people in America," and Mondale was derided with effect as "Mr. Busing."

How bad things had gotten for status reformers by mid-decade is demonstrated in an episode from July 2, 1978, that exposes what James J. Kilpatrick had earlier described as "one of those areas of monstrous disagreement" on the American problem. The guest that day was Eleanor Holmes Norton, then chair of the federal Equal Employment Opportunity Commission. Her appearance was timed as a response to the Supreme Court decision now known as the *Bakke* case that dealt directly with charges of "reverse discrimination" and quotas in higher education. She is the last guest to appear in this cause with the kind of confidence and resolve that can only derive from a clear sense of riding that arc of history toward justice.

Alan Otten (*Wall Street Journal*): Mrs. Norton, it has been twenty-four years since the Supreme Court ruled on the school desegregation cases. The litigation is still going on, and there is still a lot of uncertainty. How long do you think it will be and how many suits are going to have to be brought through the courts before employers and admissions officers know a little more what they can do in this field of admissions and job hiring?

Elizabeth Holmes Norton: For a long time after the *Brown* decision, the Supreme Court did not reach the point of ordering the kinds of remedies that frankly are at issue in the *Bakke* case. In the late sixties, the Supreme Court began to order race-conscious remedies, including very specific quotas. At that point and that point only did we begin to see wholesale integration of schools in the South, so that schools in the South are today more integrated than in the North. The important things about these remedies, as harsh and painful as they may seem for a short while, is that they take us through an inevitable transition period and get us through it, so that finally we may get out of it. The inevitable postponement that has taken place has only increased the necessity for harsher and harsher remedies.

Nor was Norton's confidence in the inevitability of harsher remedies to follow noncompliance with the new rights regime in any way shaken by the shifting political winds. She did not doubt the durability of these newly won cultural rights.

Carol Simpson (NBC News): But you do agree that the climate may change?

Norton: Yes, there may be employers who are foolish enough to regard the *Bakke* case as allowing some slowdown. I think their own house counsels, to the extent that they are competent, would advise them otherwise.

Norton's tone must have been received as imperious and threatening, sending chills down the spines of those committed classical liberals who had cheered on Bakke in his efforts to struggle for race-blind justice. One imagines the ranks of the Reagan Democrats surging with each sentence Norton uttered. In moments like these the fragile group rights attached to abstract categories like occupational structure were conflated with group rights attached to more visible categories like race and gender, jeopardizing support for both in the process.

To highlight the turn against the cultural rights agenda, a number of advocates of strictly individual rights came forward as heralds of President Ronald Reagan on his path to political transformation. A representative example is the appearance on June 18, 1978, by Howard Jarvis, the leader of the tax revolt.

Bill Monroe (moderator): Mr. Jarvis, Jesse Jackson and Senator McGovern, among others, have suggested that there is an element of racism in the campaign for Proposition 13, and one poll showed that supporters of Proposition 13 were particularly critical of welfare. What is your response to that?

Howard Jarvis: The answer to that—I heard McGovern when I got here yesterday—it is probably asinine and inept. He has never been in touch, I don't think. He is totally unrealistic. As a matter of fact, we had major support from minorities for this amendment. . . . Anyone who knows anything about the subject wouldn't make asinine statements like that, and we had major support in both the brown and black communities, and they understand it.

It took a few years, but conservatives had cracked the race code. One no longer needed to be critical of blacks to oppose civil rights law; one needed only to be a lover of liberty—classical liberty under a strict construction of the Constitution—and an opponent of group rights in any form. By 1978, it was easy enough for opponents of the civil rights legislation to promote civil rights values. The Reagan freedom script from his time running for governor during the great housing dispute of 1966 had worked. As Reagan demonstrated, one could embrace antiracist ends and deplore antiracist means at the same time. Classical liberals fought multiculturalism in the late twentieth century much the same way they had fought Socialism in the late nineteenth; individual rights did not imply group rights.

After Reagan, this sensibility began to take hold more generally, and only one champion of the cultural rights agenda had both the stature and the stamina to stay in the fight for the long haul. From the late 1970s to the early 1990s, when it came to the topic of race, *Meet the Press* became the Jesse Jackson show. In his early days, Jackson was a sprightly agent of the counterculture; over time, he came off more like a defending heavyweight champion appearing opposite ever-more-energized followers of Ronald Reagan's liberal vision of a race-blind community. Jackson often debated William Bennett, including debates on the infamous book *The Bell Curve* ("ancient garbage"); debated conservative black leaders on occasions, like Louis Farrakhan's Million Man March ("the sense of urgency is driven by pain, not driven by one personality)"; and attacked Ward Connerly and his California Civil Rights Initiative, which he described as a kind of "ethnic cleansing." Jackson made the case for organizations like his People United to Save Humanity and for his presidential campaigns in 1984 and 1988. He made the case for Palestinian rights and against drugs and explained the importance of Nelson Mandela's efforts in South Africa. He consistently advocated closing the gender gap and criticized corporate power in a way that perhaps only Ralph Nader would do as vehemently.

Jackson fought for the legacy of Martin Luther King. His opponents fought for the legacy of Ronald Reagan. King was dead, but Reagan was alive, and so was the fire of his conservative movement opponents. But Jackson's efforts, easy as they were to tie directly back to the civil rights vision of Dr. King, parted with him in a single stylistic way. King had managed to disarm his opponents with unanticipated expressions of civil affection. On air, Jackson seemed incapable of showing the love of one's enemies that had insulated Dr. King's efforts to "transform the whole of

American society" from charges of selfishness and factionalism. The threat of being cast as a narrow partisan and power politician is a constant risk in civil competitions. If a leader's ideas can be portrayed as benefiting only a special interest or as relying on means that are incompatible with the leader's stated ends, it is easy to deconsecrate his message and moral appeal.[30]

This was precisely Jackson's weakness, and it was a big one. Jackson preached a message of love and forgiveness, but he had cut his teeth in the days when the civil rights fight had come North and Martin Luther King had "revealed in Chicago" the "blatant social hate-filled cancer" he found there as he described it in his fateful August 21, 1966, interview. Perhaps as a result, Jackson often fell prey in his zeal to the appearance of special-interest advocacy and the apologetics of power politics.

There are times when it is necessary to break with one's allies in order to clarify one's larger moral vision. This Jackson would not do. His approach was to "Testify! Be Witnessin'" about the evils he had seen,[31] and when he was good, he was like no other. This single-geared approach to politics conspired with his penchant for colorful language in such a way that he was always cast as a black leader, never simply an American leader who happened to be black.[32]

His forgiveness of former racial oppressors appeared conditional on a kind of assimilation to his particular vision and standpoint. He was left to perform the project of liberation by himself and became, from the standpoint of the median voter (that person in the middle of the ideological spectrum), little more than a voice calling in the wilderness as America's racial politics devolved into what was called in the title of one episode, "black, white, and angry." In part because he promoted solutions that had been precoded as illiberal and more detrimental to liberty than the problems they were meant to solve, Jackson was not able to break through the authenticity barrier any better than was anyone else in the period. Consequently, the cultural rights agenda was left without a clear leader.

The introduction to the Million Man March *Meet the Press* episode in October 1995 probably says all that needs to be said of this nadir in our national conversation on race: "Our issues this Sunday morning: the future of black America—jobs, poverty, crime, welfare, out-of-wedlock births, the racial divide after the O. J. Simpson verdict, and more." With its champion, Jesse Jackson, positioned as a well-meaning but incorrigibly factional leader of an occasionally intolerant and power-hungry coalition, the conservative forces were in a commanding position to promote freedom arguments in the classical mold to promote wrenching changes in the larger system of social security that had been established in the New Deal.

If Jackson was the leading bridge figure on the race issue in this period on the left, Newt Gingrich was his partner on the right. Gingrich's contribution would come later, but the Gingrich revolution of 1994 that carried the Republican Party to power in the House for the next twelve years is impossible to understand outside the context of racial tension that continued to fester through the long 1970s. This is not to say that Newt Gingrich was a racist but that he was one of the leading intellectual forces behind the race-coded ideological dismantling of the master synthesis of private enterprise and social protection that defined the exceptional political economy of the United States in the twentieth century.

Gingrich could see as few others since Reagan how the value of freedom could be used to attack the institutional supports of the New Deal equality agenda by exploiting middle American concerns about the newer Democratic commitment to rebalancing divisive cultural forces. Much as Goldwater and Reagan had done before him, Gingrich recognized that control over civil power was a function of identifying the most salient threat to democracy and consecrating one's policies in its terms. Where once Depression and spiraling economic inequality had convinced the majority that corporate power was the central threat to American liberty, after John Kennedy and Jimmy Carter had backed off the class rhetoric of the New Deal, the persuadable Americans could now be led by the threat of do-gooder government to disengineer the culture that many thought made possible the roaring mixed economy. When Gingrich hit the stage, he knew that the case for multiculturalism had never been made. Accordingly, he had a weapon he could use to unmake the welfare state itself.

Gingrich also knew that after Martin Luther King's shaming triumph, it was not the minority groups themselves that were seen as a threat to American civility but rather the government's efforts to transform traditional American culture with a permissive attitude toward social problems. He gambled that swing voters were not yet ready to consider all lifestyles equal, a condition he could use to his advantage. He could exploit the lingering air of suspicion about the reticence of African American leaders to confront distorted African American folkways to promote his libertarian agenda in antiracist and inclusive terms. In this, the post-Moynihan silences of the race-coded epoch only abetted his plans.

Like John Tower before him, Gingrich understood that the path back to McKinley-era America required that he break the faith of Americans in what government could do for them. The goal was to heighten concerns about what government could do *to* them. If middle Americans could be convinced that the imposed silences on race and behavior that followed Moynihan's appearance on *Meet the Press* were simply intended to conceal the structurally induced pathologies in the African American community that many suspected were there, then the private-enterprise conservatives could shatter majority support for the New Deal social rights agenda by peeling off the remaining cohorts of the white working class.

Because his approach was formally inclusive and patterned on classical conceptions of tolerance, even those whose hearts had been changed by the civil rights movement could get behind his efforts. Moreover, by emphasizing Alexis de Tocqueville's more conservative tones, Gingrich could promote his libertarian vision through an honest celebration of traditional democratic folkways—triggering the moral taste buds of the culturally orthodox. In this way, Gingrich and his colleagues used the quiet of the race codes to transform the class struggle into a culture war that they could easily win. Just as busing and affirmative-action programs, modest in implementation as they often were, had been civilly desecrated as adverse to the philosophy of a free people, by association, this trick could be used to break off support for all of the social rights programs of the New Deal welfare state.

The rollback began at its weakest point of the social security agenda with the relief programs that had themselves been associated uniquely with the term "welfare."[33] As the *Meet the Press* record demonstrates, when neoliberal thinkers launched their offenses on social protections programs, they often did so in the context of otherwise-distracting debates like those on affirmative action. The playbook was clear; liberals defended the limited steps they had taken toward implementation of racial balancing in terms drawn from the language of tolerance, inclusion, and diversity, while conservatives bludgeoned them with formulaic invocations of freedom and individual rights. It is as if the Republicans had learned to outflank their class enemy with vilifying arguments about the intolerance of race-conscious policies and then run down his ranks with little opposition.[34]

This kind of thing was touchy in its early phases when Ronald Reagan made ham-fisted references to welfare queens and began his 1980 presidential campaign in a town that was the site of a well known, civil rights–era lynching. But by the early 1990s, the core values of the pri-vate-enterprise model could be promoted both by aggressive ideological entrepreneurs like Newt Gingrich and by vouched racial progressives like Jack Kemp, without resort to polarizing implications.

In the *Meet the Press* program that aired on October 8, 1995, Jack Kemp appeared to discuss the dramatic showdown between Newt Gin-grich and Bill Clinton over Medicare, support for dependents, budget deficits, and taxes. Important as these issues were, they carried none of the dramatic potential of the major story of the week, which was the O. J. Simpson verdict. Although the topic was the role of government in the economy and the impending shutdown, the focus at the time of the government shutdown was black-on-white murder. Racial anxiety pro-vided the imagery of the moment, but true to script, Kemp did not fail to capitalize on the opportunity to promote the private-enterprise system.

Tim Russert: Jack Kemp, should the president of the United States find an opportunity to address the nation on the subject of race?

Jack Kemp: Well, I would say yes. Because I believe this is, without a doubt, as
David Broder just mentioned, the single most important issue among our
national family. . . . The problem is we have a welfare system that traps people in dependency, that punishes work, that doesn't allow people to save, that
breaks up the family, and that is eroding the very basis of our democratic,
liberal, small *l*, society. And I think there's the two Americas. One is mac-
rodemocratic and capitalist and private property based. The other one is an
economy that is almost a Third World Socialist model, and we should be
reforming it, make more people able to climb up that ladder and get into the
black or white middle class.

Kemp's story line was new, but it came directly from the playbook of Eric Johnston. In Kemp's story, the Democrats had not only failed to spread democracy around the world; they had also created conditions at home that invited domestic tyranny through racialization of conflict.

An earlier episode from February 19, 1995, is even more explicit and shows how the affirmative-action hook could be used as a trigger for a discussion about the benefits of liberalizing economic policy. In the 1990s, a cultural conflict provided a great opportunity to play out one's class politics. Taking second place only to the 1946 Theodore Bilbo affair, the following episode presented racial conflict at its highest fever pitch. It is worth quoting at some length.

Tim Russert: Welcome again to *Meet the Press*. Our issues this Sunday morning, the most divisive and potentially explosive problem confronting our nation: race in America. What should be done about welfare, poverty, crime, jobs, affirmative action, teenage pregnancy, and more? Our guests, former Republican congressman and housing secretary Jack Kemp; University of Chicago professor of public policy William Julius Wilson; Democratic congressman Charles Rangel of New York; and author of the bestselling but controversial book *The Bell Curve: Intelligence and Class Structure in American Life*, from the American Enterprise Institute, Charles Murray.

The otherwise unflappable Charlie Rangel used the occasion to channel his inner Stokely Carmichael, while Murray flirted with ideas that had more in common with the theory of eugenics than with mainstream social science.

Rangel: . . . I truly believe that the assault on affirmative action is a part of a political strategy to attack minorities, the poor, and to allow those people who are frustrated . . . to scapegoat minorities, immigrants, and poor folks. . . . This happened in Europe . . . all of these things, when you start looking at it, fits into a pattern that people who are just frustrated with their lack of security can now find a scapegoat . . . whether it's California with Mexicans coming across the country, whether it's people wanting to feel better about themselves and writing books [*points to Murray*] and doing things to allow people to feel superior about themselves—it's a terrible thing that's happening. . . . It's a tragedy because of the silence of good people.

. . .

Murray: Well, I think affirmative action, as it's currently practiced, is poisonous. Not because it's depriving white people of jobs but rather because . . . it systematically puts into the same place people of different ethnic groups of radically different levels of ability.

. . .

Rangel: Affirmative action is nothing; it is nothing to upset anybody. It's good for talk shows. It is not an issue.

After the Rangel and Murray exchange, the opportunity to hear from the esteemed professor of sociology, William Julius Wilson, was welcomed. In his comments, Wilson was forceful and came across on air stronger than even his words implied, often pointing downward with his hand for emphasis in a way that evoked concerned looks from both Tim Russert and Gwen Ifill.

Wilson: You know, let me just say that I think that there is a broader issue in
which affirmative action should be discussed, and that is the growing racial
divisions in this country and the growing hostility between groups. . . . It's
getting ugly. . . . We've got to change our rhetoric. When—people are expe-
riencing economic difficulty right now, so they're vulnerable to demagogic
messages to divide the races. Instead of associating their economic insecuri-
ties and pessimism about their future with economic changes . . . they blame
each other. . . . That's what we should be talking about.

Undaunted, Charles Murray used his *Meet the Press* moment to complete a
thirty-year cycle by returning to the field that had lain largely fallow since
the Moynihan affair.

Murray: So insofar as we aren't willing to recognize the underlying reason for some
of this hostility, I think what we've done is we have created an underground
dialogue which is just as poisonous as you say and at the surface, in the kinds
of shows like this, for example, or in the newspapers and so forth, it's all
excruciatingly correct. I think there's just got to be a lot more candor.

Affronted, Gwen Ifill confronted Murray with statistics about the relative
success of white males. She meant to catch him off guard, but his response
came across as a defiant apology to the system of status quo and racial
privilege.

Murray: How do you measure the success of the American ideal? . . . [*laughing sigh*]
I think an awful lot of white people are real tired of being talked about as if
given the least opportunity, they're going to go out and behave in racist ways.
I think they are tired of being treated as if they have to be constrained and
confined and have laws made in order to keep them from being bigots. And
if we're going to have a more productive dialogue about race in this country,
I think that kind of underlying feeling among whites has to be recognized.

With this open exploration of racial anxiety, the floor was open to Jack
Kemp to play Ronald Reagan; if the problem was racism, the answer was
private enterprise, and he advocated for the elimination of the social relief
programs that would in fact be significantly cut back the following year.
His neoliberal agenda seemed perfectly politically correct in the context
of Murray's bad-cop routine.

Kemp: Could I just make a quick point about what Professor Wilson said? I
couldn't agree more. . . . Notwithstanding the terrible burden that is placed

upon people who are today in a welfare system that is a disgrace to this country and a cancer eating at the relations that Professor Wilson talked about, if
we changed that and provide positive incentives and a positive growth-ori-
ented opportunity society, in my view it will make it a lot easier for black and
white dialogue [*Wilson nodding his head*] to take place in this country and
remove some of this ugly racism in our nation.

Martin Luther King had remarked upon a "hate-filled cancer" in Chicago
when he unsuccessfully took his movement north to fight de facto segregation. Jack Kemp saw the cancer as well, but he located it in the social
support programs that were the fruit of the New Deal, and much of the
persuadable population followed his lead. The period of implementing the
new cultural rights gained with the race-based legislation of the 1960s had
resulted in something unforeseen, the elimination of welfare as we know
it. Over time the same tactics would be used to attempt to reform the
more popular programs like Social Security and Medicare by replacing
them with private alternatives. The tolerance debate had opened a gap
through which the advocates of freedom could attack at will the programs
designed to reduce inequality.

When it was time to pass the landmark Civil Rights Act that Hubert
Humphrey described on *Meet the Press* on March 8, 1964, as "the greatest
achievement in the field of human rights since the Emancipation Procla-
mation," free-market liberals like Barry Goldwater and Ronald Reagan
balked for reasons that would become clear only decades later. It was left
to the libertarians like Representative Ron Paul of Texas to explain what
the Goldwater affair was all about, as he did in an episode that aired
December 23, 2007.

Tim Russert: You would vote against the Civil Rights Act if, if it was today?

Ron Paul: If it were written the same way, where the federal government's taken
over property—has nothing to do with race relations. It just happens, Tim,
that I get more support from black people today than any other Republican
candidate, according to some statistics. And I have a great appeal to people
who care about personal liberties and to those individuals who would like to
get us out of wars. So it has nothing to do with racism; it has to do with the
Constitution and private property rights.

Classical liberals and libertarians were opposed to the cultural rights agenda of the civil rights movement for the same reason they were opposed to

the social rights agenda of the New Deal: it violated the bedrock principles of personal freedom and individual rights. As strategic silence fell upon the country in the era of coded race talk, the ideological fragility of the cultural rights programs had provided the opening for classical liberals to spread their message of private enterprise and personal responsibility largely without opposition. Open-minded enterprisers like Jack Kemp and Ron Paul could join with enterprising opportunists like Newt Gingrich and Howard Jarvis to promote a truly liberal (that is, individual) solution to the old social rights problem. The answer was to have a capitalist economy managed by executives as diverse as the country it served. It was to be a coalition of freedom and tolerance without the distractions of socialistic concerns about equality. Somewhere the revolution had gone awry.

Redemption on the Cheap

Tim Russert: Bill Raspberry, is the United States of America prepared to elect a black president?

William Raspberry (*Washington Post*): I think almost because of the differences we've been talking about, a Colin Powell would have a shot. It would be, in a way, redemption on the cheap, if you follow me. And I don't mean that the presidency is cheap. What I do mean is that with one vote, whites who are doubtful about this question could purge themselves of any guilt over our racial situation. It would be interesting.

—October 8, 1995

Once a string of facts has been connected by a line of reasoning, it is quite difficult to imagine that the connecting line ever had to be drawn in the first place. The election of an African American president is a narrative like that. Looking back on developments since the Republican revolution in the congressional elections of 1994, it is difficult to believe that the Democratic Party could really resist nominating an African American to run for the office and, once nominated, that the country could resist electing and even reelecting him. The retrospective narrative is only reinforced in that the start of the line of reasoning is Colin Powell, the widely revered Republican general.

As demonstrated in that explosive Rangel-Murray episode described previously, race relations hit a new low point in 1995. It was the year of the O. J. trial, the Million Man March, the publication of *The Bell Curve*, and the first Republican Congress to take power after the major gains of the status revolution. It was a time when moderate and jovial African American leaders like Charles Rangel could attack white intellectuals like Charles Murray with accusations that he had suggested that "too many blacks were being born" and that "they should be put on some type of reservation" amid references to Nazi sympathies. From this point, things could only go up, and up they went. On October 8, 1995, Washington began preparations for electing an African American president.

Tim Russert: We have not talked about the most popular black American in the country today, Colin Powell, according to every survey. Reverend Jackson, do you hope Colin Powell runs for president and becomes the first African American to hold that position?

Jesse Jackson: It would be a good thing. But you know what? One week, it's Powell; next week, it's O. J.; next week, it's Farrakhan. These become kind of fig leaves. We're discussing stuff up there, and . . .

Russert: This is the presidency. This is not a criminal trial.

Jackson: Yeah, yeah, yeah, but it's also media recycling fig leaves. . . . And so my struggle with "you" and other media is something I am going to discuss, the pain of black people, not fig leaves that sell newspapers.

Both Raspberry and Jackson were unimpressed with the urge to achieve "redemption on the cheap" and to "recycle fig leaves." As Jackson had said of Farrakhan, the problems facing black America had to do with pain, not personality, and what applied to Farrakhan applied also to Powell. Yet the topic of a black president dangled out there—intriguingly.

Powell did not run in 1996, but he did appear on *Meet the Press* on April 27, 1997, in relation to the high-profile President's Summit on Responsibility. (If Jackson was right that the code word for racism was "bus" in the 1970s, the code word for racial anxiety in the 1990s was "responsibility.") Powell was introduced as "the general himself," and he was given a platform to outline the goals he had as chairman of the summit and share his ideas about parenting, the social safety net, and immigration policy—a range of issues giving the interview the feel of a *Meet the Press* "Meet the Candidates" feature. The most striking moment of the interview was one in which General Powell turned the issue of race relations by invoking the revolutionary spirit that had characterized the civil rights struggle in the heady days of 1963. The imagery of civil rights as part of the revolutionary experience stood out even for such an establishment figure like Powell. The general's language could come across like that of Thomas Jefferson, but to those with ears to hear, it had echoes of the spirit of the Black Panthers as well.

Colin Powell: We have got to realize that the revolution is not yet over. The wonderful words that were spoken in this marvelous city over two hundred years ago are still not reality to all Americans. . . . Anyone who thinks so is just wrong.

By the end of the interview Powell had that incomparable feel of an aspiring presidential candidate, a fact underscored by former president Jimmy Carter's appearance directly after Powell's, which appeared in context to be almost an afterthought. As a conquering general who already had a doctrine named after him, Powell was the insider's insider. Because of his military background, his love of America was not subject to question, and, for the same reason, he came across as the fruit of Harry Truman's efforts to integrate the military, efforts that began the realignment of the Democratic Party nearly a half century earlier. Powell's decision not to run and his misleading performance in the run-up to the war in Iraq in front of the United Nations as secretary of state, displaced the hope that Powell could become the first black president, but it had signaled a symbolic hunger in the country for redemption.

Where this hunger would lead had been foreshadowed in the Democratic presidential nomination contest of 1976. At that point of the primary campaign, George Wallace was still somehow running, even after having become the latest high-profile victim of gun violence when Birch Bayh, a Democratic senator from Indiana with a profile large enough to warrant presidential speculations, had this to say on January 11, 1976, about the man who had stood in the schoolhouse door:

Birch Bayh: One of the real problems we have had in the last seven or eight years is the politics of division. We have had Jerry Ford running against New York City; we have had Richard Nixon and Spiro Agnew running against "Radiclibs" and "pusillanimous pussyfooters" and "nattering nabobs of negativism." We have really had the politics of polarization, the politics of hatred and division; it's been very divisive, very costly to this country. I want to conduct a campaign, and I want to see whoever is president run a government that really pulls us together, that weaves together the common threads that exist in most all of our hearts. Unfortunately, Governor Wallace is a symbol of division, not a symbol of unity.

Shockingly, such a figure would appear on the scene in the fall of 2004 who sounded like Birch Bayh but didn't "look like all those other presidents on the dollar bills." In a story now too familiar to retell, Barack Obama gave the keynote speech at the Democratic National Convention wondering if "America had a place for a skinny kid with a funny name like him." Essential to his appeal was the total absence of the sense of factionalism and power politics that had always tainted African American leaders since the loss of Martin Luther King. Obama's civil vision was that which Birch Bayh had articulated, with the bonus that Obama himself could serve as the very symbol of unity—a kind of anti-Wallace—that had long been missing.

In his book *The Bridge*, David Remnick has an excellent discussion of the speech that Obama delivered in 2007 in Selma, Alabama, that established his civil rights credentials as a member of the Joshua generation who would reach the promised land that King had dreamed of forty years before.[35] As the story went, just as Joshua was able to realize the dream of Moses, so too would Obama realize the dream of King. After two terms of George W. Bush, a kind of white man's white man, the hunger for redemption through symbolic barrier breaking had become more intense than ever.

The hunger for transformation only becomes easier to see in retrospect when we consider events like the Jeremiah Wright affair. A package of video clips from the pastor of the church where Obama had chosen to express his African American identity was widely circulating in all media channels. They arrived on *Meet the Press* on March 16, 2008.

Jeremiah Wright: See, government gives them the drugs, builds bigger prisons, passes a three-strike law, and then wants us to sing "God Bless America"? No, no, no. Not God bless America. God damn America—that's in the Bible—for killing innocent people. God damn America for treating your citizens as less than human.

Playing out in the mold of the video storm that sank Howard Dean's presidential ambitions in 2004—the "Dean Scream"—Wright's rants invoked all the painful memories of African American separatist resentment that had so panicked the country beginning in 1966. Back then in an episode dated July 14, 1968, Howard Innis, incoming director of the Congress on Racial Equality, had spoken about black nationalism by analogy to France and its relationship to Germany, claiming, "It appears to me that throughout the history of mankind, mankind has always organized himself in cohesive units of self-interest." Forty years later, here was Obama's spiritual mentor giving vent to these all too familiar sentiments of black nationalism and racial resentment that had emboldened the backlash for which Obama presented himself as the solution. He was finally prodded out of silence on racial politics. He decided to crack the code in public.

Two days later, Obama satisfied the country's longing for redemption in his March 18 speech on race in Philadelphia. Among the many remarkable lines he delivered was the following claim from its early moments: "I will never forget that in no other country on earth is my story even possible." Why this was so powerful requires the eye of a psychoanalyst. America was on the couch, and here was its therapist directing the country's id from repression to sublimation.

At the height of the era of civil disobedience in 1950, Senator Russell had defended the South as follows: "We have contributed a great deal to the advancement of the Negro; he is better off in the United States than he is anywhere in the world today."[36] Here was a candidate for office who now seemed poised to take the Democratic nomination to run for the most celebrated position in the world, coming close to validating, and perhaps even vindicating, Senator Russell's once seemingly preposterous claim. At the same time Obama explained that for African Americans of Wright's generation, "The memories of humiliation and doubt and fear have not gone away," thus redeeming black separatist anger and the spirit of factionalism and cynical power politics that animated it. "The anger is real; it is powerful; and to simply wish it away, to condemn it without understanding its roots, only serves to widen the chasm of misunderstanding that exists between the races." In 1965, Martin Luther King had claimed that "unmerited suffering is redemptive." Obama banished the silence and in so doing, validated the merit of centuries of complex suffering and guilt that all Americans had experienced with respect to racial division: redemption was at hand.

But redemption would certainly not come on the cheap. Even in the wake of Obama's transformative Philadelphia speech on race, Jeremiah Wright appeared at the National Press Club to defend his honor and his church. Six days later, on May 4, 2008, Obama was on *Meet the Press* to defend his decision to break with his former pastor. At that moment, Obama was facing a tough primary contest with Senator Hillary Clinton in, of all places, Indiana, a state that had once emphatically embraced the Ku Klux Klan and given Governor Wallace's campaign a boost at the height of the white backlash. Obama's riveting conversation with Tim Russert again reveals the continuities of the political culture and the fact that no matter how inclusive and reasonable an African American aspirant to the presidency might be, he would be held responsible for the gamut of black reactions to the tragic history of race relations, even while reaffirming the American creed as only an African American could do in such circumstances.

Barack Obama: The fact that I'm running for president right now is an indication
of how much I love this country, because it has given everything to me. This
country has been a great source of good. I've lived overseas and seen the
difference between America and what it stands for and what other countries
oftentimes stand for and where they fall short. I've, I've said before, my story's not possible in any other country on earth.[37]

On August 13, 1967, Martin Luther King had warned in what would be his last appearance on *Meet the Press* that "the president should always respond to the legitimate and just aspirations of the Negro community . . . but the leaders of the civil rights movement are Negroes themselves." Now with the election of Barack Obama, these two roles were unified in the same person. In the election of a black president, a symbolic barrier had been crossed, and redemption did feel dearer than many might have imagined it would be. In the future, it would be far more difficult to claim that blacks were consigned to second-class citizenship. The challenge of promoting economic equality among the races in an America whose commitment to an activist state was faltering would be great, but as Mayor Adrian Fenty of Washington, D.C., put it on the inaugural episode of January 11, 2009, "That cap of the African American never being a president will never exist for [young black people]. And I think that will have more of an impact on being a role model or anything else than anything we've ever seen in our community."[38]

The American problem was not solved by electing Barack Obama; indeed, there was reason to suspect that economic disparities by race would expand as a result of the conservative backlash against him, but over the long run, by definitively expanding the portfolio of abusive powers against which democratic forces could rally, he proved that in the confrontation between racism and the American creed, the creed had won out just as Gunnar Myrdal had suspected it would.

After Moynihan, open conversation about culture, opportunity, and institutional structure would go underground, but a new sort of villainy had been indelibly written into the political storybook. Bigotry or the abuse of cultural status was now broadly considered to fall within the scope of state interest as well as democratic theory. On the left, both at home and abroad, cultural recognition was recognized as a right subject to a kind of loose regulation (however contested and tenuous its enforcement might be). The challenges of economic equality across the occupational structure were as stark as they had ever been, but after Obama's inauguration, at least the triumph of tolerance was complete.

6

THE GRAVEST PROBLEM
Reds, Rackets, and the Unmaking
of the Democratic Class Struggle

I think Mr. [Eric] Johnston will agree that the gravest problem facing
the United States is the strife between labor and management. It is
affecting the daily life of millions of Americans.

—Albert Warner, October 5, 1945

YOU CAN IMAGINE THE *MEET THE PRESS* ARCHIVE as the recorded
movements of a tuning fork that responds to the resonance of the week's
social dramas as they arise among the political classes of the Washington
establishment. If you were to pick up that record and follow it forward for
a few years from its beginning in 1945, you would conclude that America
had a big problem with class conflict. In fact, you might conclude that this
was *the* big problem that Americans faced as they headed into a period of
global dominance and domestic prosperity that few other nations have
ever enjoyed. It was the problem of class struggle that troubled the descen-
dant American cognoscenti, and given the state of the world's problems in
late 1945, this is really saying something. The Axis powers had just been
defeated. There was a mad rush to fill the power vacuum in Europe that
would soon precipitate the Cold War. Millions of soldiers were returning
home from the front, and they demanded housing, education, and jobs on
a scale as yet unimagined. But in the first dozen regularly scheduled *Meet
the Press* radio broadcasts, it was the labor problem that dominated the
agenda. And apart from the admission of a Ku Klux Klan membership
and the exposure of the Alger Hiss affair, there is nothing that carries the
feeling of having stepped into another world more than these early shows
on labor unions and collective bargaining.

Ideas were in the air in that crucial decade after the war that we
can scarcely imagine today. We are accustomed to watching unions lose

membership and accept the blame for ballooning deficits and educational mediocrity. After the war, labor was either respected as a vehicle through which we would create a very different society or as a force to be feared as much as the Communist menace. The victory of the latter narrative and the failure of the movement to realize its goals constitute perhaps the most important story in one of the most important half centuries in history. Liberals-known-as-conservatives largely won that war on labor, and how they did so is a story worth telling.

Although the specter of Communism always haunted the American union movement, it was Jimmy Hoffa who would be central to the transformation of Washington's worldview. Rising in national attention, Hoffa played the role of a scandalous figure involved in terrifying schemes to secure illegitimate power. Hoffa dominated the conversation about unions during a crucial period of economic reform during the Eisenhower and Kennedy administrations when class struggle still seemed to pose an existential threat for the nation. Thereafter he served as an iconic embodiment of the anticivil qualities of the labor movement as a whole. He was presented as being opposed to the responsible management of economic organizations in a free society. His tactics were coded as contrary to the open give and take of the American tradition. Even his concerns and favored problems—collective bargaining, the common man, the empowered worker—were represented as fictions and mirages.

Once defiled, Jimmy Hoffa and the imagery of a big, white, tough male, a bully with selfish and narrow goals and an outsized contempt for the well-being of the nation as a whole, became the default mental image of the union member. When the images of racist behavior during a hard-hat riot in New York spread throughout the nation in 1969 in response to a student protest of the Vietnam War, it was the archetype of the Teamster that many people had in mind, and these bigoted displays only hardened previous interpretations. As is the case with most iconic representations of villainy, the model was commonly applied even in cases where it clearly did not fit. In the week of the *Sputnik* launch, the president of Harvard praised the role that teachers and education would play in the eventual victory over the enemies of liberty. When public service unions like those representing schoolteachers became central to the political discussion beginning in the early 1970s, the old union scripts from the 1940s and 1950s reappear in *Meet the Press* data. With China rising in the twenty-first century, teachers came to represent the forces of economic backwardness and even oppression in places like Wisconsin and in urban pockets of concentrated poverty. As the record makes clear, the larger story of the union movement in the postwar period is one of cumulative stigmatization of the broader program of social rights that union leaders and economic progressives had supported in the postwar political economy. Despite the victory of Harry Truman and the promotion of the proto-corporatist Fair Deal agenda, the union as the institutional seat for the advocacy of economic equality in the country was short lived, even as the frightening power of the union boss became little more than a chilling memory.

Over the course of the *Meet the Press* history, labor was first labeled as a threat to domestic peace and gateway institution to Communist infiltration, then as a hotbed of corruption and a front for organized crime, and finally as a counterproductive nuisance. Even when unions cleaned their houses and scaled back their goals, they were never fully accepted as reasonable and legitimate organizations with a specialized role in the overall system of economic management. They were seen only to support the narrow interests of their members in certain industries. The vision of a 1940s labor organizer like Walter Reuther and potential of the movement's role in the era of the New Deal were far from realized. After having fallen afoul of the leadership cadres of the Democratic Party, by the 1960s, unions were most commonly presented on *Meet the Press* with a grudging acceptance that only served to signal how unstable and exotic the idea of collective bargaining was as part of the country's democratic imagination.

In the fight to make the world safe for private enterprise worldwide, it was deemed necessary to defeat the Red menace of the Soviet Union. To make it safe at home, it was deemed necessary to destroy the union movement. Washington got both of these jobs done in its century of eminence.

Pinks, Punks, and Parasites

May Craig: I understand at one convention you looked at the Reds, including [Harry] Bridges, and called them pinks, punks, and parasites. Were you ever a little pink yourself?

Michael Quill (Transport Workers Union): No, never pink.

—August 27, 1950

The first *Meet the Press* radio broadcast was on the Mutual Network on June 24, 1945. There was no regular television version of the program until the end of 1947, but the most reliable beginning date for the regular program may be set at October 5, 1945, when Eric Johnston appeared to discuss "the nationwide struggle between labor and management." It is appropriate that the program began in this way and that the tone was so dire, because it gives us some clue about why American political culture seems so hostile to entertaining solutions common elsewhere to the problems of economic inequality and material insecurity. All Americans supposedly have a right to join a union, but if they attempt to exercise this right in practice, they often find that the gap between de jure and de facto rights applies beyond the field of race relations.

At the end of the New Deal and the birth of the American welfare state, the mainstream of the Washington elite was deeply uncomfortable about the power and intentions of unions and their leadership. This comes through not only in the selection of guests but also in the nature of the questions asked and in the framing of the problems that brought about the appearances in the first place. In these early days, it might be fair to suggest that the show's producers, Larry Spivak and Martha Rountree, settled on a pattern that demonstrated the kind of consistency in the selection of guests that would later mark the show, but the biases and concerns about labor that Spivak and Rountree brought with them seem quite typical of many of the leading thinkers of the time. After all, a Red Scare was on, and the Reds favored class warfare against the American way of life.

The first interview with Eric Johnston was obviously a big affair for the *Meet the Press* crew. The archival materials are especially rich for this episode, and we can see there the letters and telegrams between Spivak, Johnston, and the four "ace" reporters who interviewed him. We also have records of the draft scripts for the show and evidence about the kinds of negotiations undertaken to establish what would happen during the interview. One paragraph from the invitation letters sent to reporters provides a sense of the conciliatory mood that Larry Spivak had in mind for the interview and how the producers recognized a kind of parity between the two sides of the labor troubles. "Thanks for your telegram of acceptance. . . . The subject will probably be 'Labor and Capital in a Free Society,' and the discussion will hinge more or less on whether Labor and Capital can prosper at the expense of one another, or whether their interests are much closer than either side has ever believed."[1]

The actual introduction to this important episode provides some insight into how central this discussion was at the time, as well as how provocative it could be.

Announcer: The Mutual Broadcasting System in cooperation with the editors of the
American Mercury, America's distinguished magazine of opinion, brings you
all the excitement and drama of a newspaper press conference. This evening
we have invited to Mutual's Washington studios four of the country's ace
newspaper reporters to get the story on the most important subject today: the
nationwide struggle between labor and management. Since the secretary of
the navy took over the striking oil industry by presidential order last night,
the whole country is asking, "What's next?"

The social drama of the social rights agenda was only to build from here.
In the week following the opening appearance by Johnston, *Meet the Press*
hosted the former vice president and current secretary of commerce, Henry Wallace, who was advocating a proposal for guaranteed jobs and full
employment, one that had been published under Wallace's name under
the title *Sixty Million Jobs* by Simon and Schuster that same year. The
stir caused by Wallace's activist political economy was part of what had
motivated the sense of alarm in key sectors of the business community in
the postwar context. Calmer heads among the captains of industry were
concerned that the traditional free-enterprise system that America had
long enjoyed, the bulwark of democracy, was at risk. To get a sense of what
was so startling about Wallace and why the business community was so
alarmed, consider the inside cover material of *Sixty Million Jobs* and the
work of civil positioning it does to promote a planned labor market as a
central part of the democratic system.

In the book, the Secretary of Commerce demonstrates that our basic American
democracy must be built on sixty million jobs and a $200 billion annual
national income. He does not simply advocate or dreamily yearn for these
eminently desirable objectives. He says that if they are to be attained by
1950—and he shows that they *can* and *must* be reached by then—we are
under an urgent social mandate to plan and build and crusade for them
today.

There must have been quite a bit of trepidation about how to handle this
hot potato. In the script material for this "big get" performance by the infamous Henry Wallace, an editor (presumably Larry Spivak) had marked
the original script as follows:

Mr. Wallace, you said in your new book that [when industry falls down] Government can and ~~should~~ [must help] provide sixty million jobs for the American people. There is a sizable public opinion in the country to the effect that ~~this~~ [any] guarantee by the Government will result [ultimately] in regimentation of industry and ~~private enterprise, which is contrary to the principles for which the war was fought~~ [the American way of life].

The interview with Henry Wallace was a kind of test case for the new program that required delicate framing (the actual introduction softened even this line). Wallace's unrepentant New Dealism might prove to be popular with the American people, but private enterprise, "the principles for which the war was fought," and the American way of life might be at stake if his vision was to come to pass. Even after massive vilification efforts by the business community, the Wallace agenda would eke out passage in highly modified form in 1946, but Wallace-ism would go down in defeat in the presidential election of 1948. Wallace's confident but poorly timed efforts to promote an aggressive social rights agenda in a period of domestic unrest made it possible for many to code his ideas as collectivist and even Communist, which proved to be the kiss of death after the dramatic Communist successes of 1949, when the Soviets got the bomb and China fell to Mao Tse-tung.

Even so, the Henry Wallace episode had both signaled the coming of age of the newest radio program and clarified the contested legitimacy of a guaranteed jobs program in the immediate postwar period. In order to contest it effectively, leading figures in the business community who appeared on *Meet the Press*, like Eric Johnston and the National Association of Manufacturers' Ira Mosher, were pressed to offer an alternative interpretation of such initiatives for fear of their broader acceptance. Amid widespread industry chaos, it did not seem possible to break the union movement entirely, but it was still possible when Mosher appeared on November 30, 1945, to raise fundamental questions about the legitimacy of the decade-long surge in so-called industrial democracy.

Marquis Childs (Press Alliance Newspaper Syndicate): I'd like to ask Mr. Mosher two questions that I think are fundamental to a lot of the talk that is going on around here. First of all, I'd like to ask him whether he believes that trade unions are necessary in our form of society—personally.

Ira Mosher: Well, that's a tough question, Mr. Childs. It's one that I would have to take a long, long time to answer. In the first place you said trade unions. I assume you mean unions in general, and as such I will try to answer your question. Whether they are—you asked if I think they are necessary.

Childs: Yes, to an orderly procedure in our society.

Mosher: No. I don't say they are necessary to an orderly procedure. Now, I don't
dare to leave my answer to your question right there, because someone is
going to say I'm saying that unions are not desirable. Unions have accomplished a great deal for their [*pause*] members. And there are a great deal of
industry men that would actually prefer to do business with unions. By that
I'm not trying to indicate that all industry wants to do business with unions.
Unions have done a job. There is a place for unions in the picture, and in my
own personal opinion, they are here to stay with us.

Childs: Yes, then I would like to ask—this is a supplement in a sense—do you
think that most employers have accepted trade unions as an essential part of
our industrial democracy?

Mosher: There is no question in my mind—industry, management, whatever, by
whatever name we call it—accepts unionism as part of the future of our
country.

Childs: And they wouldn't get rid of it if they [*pause*] could?

Mosher: Well now, I've got to answer that again on a general average. Uh, I've
dealt with unions. I've got a great many friends that deal with unions by
choice. . . . To the extent that they are organized, no forward-looking management expects to do other than to do business with those unions.

But here was the rub: The unions, even under moderate leadership like
that of Walter Reuther of the United Automobile Workers, were demand-
ing that business open up their accounting books to bargain on the basis
of shared profits and the ability to pay. Unions wanted in on the management game to bargain on a more equal footing. For Mosher, perhaps the
leading voice of the business community at that time, this represented a
fundamental challenge to American economic freedom that was nearly
preposterous to consider.

Mosher: In other words, they wouldn't concede to management the right to
manage.

Nathan Robertson (*The Newspaper PM*): Well, Mr. Mosher, that brings up an interesting point. Do you think it's an interference with the rights of management
for labor to bring into collective bargaining the question of profits?

Mosher: I don't see where profits properly come into a collective bargaining procedure. You've got to go back and analyze those things that create profits or
create the lack of profits. The very elements in a business which create profits

are the result of both capital and management, and principally management, and are not the result of labor.

Mosher had appeared on *Meet the Press* to explain why a peak-level labor-management conference had broken down. "The ever-deepening conflict between labor and management," as it was described in that Mosher interview, was a problem that seemed more pressing than all the others facing a nation emerging victorious from war. Buoyed by the social drama of the economic collapse of 1929, the union movement threatened to promote a social agenda that imperiled the traditional rights of corporate management. From a management perspective, the give and take of the democratic class struggle was not producing results that were consistent with a robust conception of liberal democracy. But there was hope on the horizon because the answer to the social democracy threat would arrive draped in the iconography of social radicalism and that haunting specter of Communism.

One of the most colorful exchanges in the history of *Meet the Press* came in the first of fifteen appearances by Senator Robert Taft on January 18, 1946, the congenial guest with a committed liberal philosophy that earned him the title "Mr. Republican." His artful maneuvering in opposition to the Wallace full employment idea demonstrates both how effective the Communist pollution line already was and how clever the Republican messaging apparatus had become. In one of the strangest acts of appropriation in the history of the American national conversation, libertarian-minded Republicans borrowed an idea, "the right to work," that was proposed as the basis of a guaranteed job for those who wanted one—a social entitlement—in the Murray full employment bill that Henry Wallace was promoting. This idea had been enshrined in the Soviet constitution and was as direct a violation of the ethic of strict personal responsibility as one could find at the time. The following year, symbolic entrepreneurs in the Republican Party applied the term to the right of an individual worker not to be forced to join a union if one was organized in his or her workplace. The famous "right to work" line through which classical liberals would combat the unions was, in effect, a Communist slogan that they once decried.

Nathan Robertson (*The Newspaper PM*): Yes, and you also said that the full
    employment bill had originated in the Russian constitution.

Robert Taft: Correct.

Robertson: And in the Communist platform here—

Taft: Correct, and I said so on the floor of the Senate last year when it came up—

Robertson: Well then, why did you vote for the bill?

Taft: It's in the Soviet constitution.

Robertson: Well, Senator—

Taft: Because we modified the right to work, which was there, uh, to a point in which I thought I could properly support it.

Robertson: But isn't that all the president's asking for? Isn't that all the president's asking for is the Senate bill?

Taft: Well, I'll support the Senate bill, but the Senate bill took out, we took out any requirement—we took out the whole business about compensatory spending.

Robertson: But that's all the president's asking for—

Taft: We took out the words "right to work," which come out of the Soviet constitution. We took those out by amendment and then supported the bill.

Robertson: But all the president's asking for, Senator, is the bill that you voted for, and you denounce it as a communistic proposal.

Taft: It was a communistic proposal, which he recommended, and he's willing now to swallow it the way we modified it because that's less than the House modified it. And, uh, I'm, uh, I personally, uh, would prefer to modify it further, although I'm willing to go along [with] this because as we modified it, it is no more than a statement that the president shall submit an economic program every year, which shall take *everything* into consideration, not only the Wallace compensatory spending, but every other consideration, uh, for recommendation for policy, both governmental and affecting private industry, which will tend to bring full employment, which after all is what every government has done, has tried to do since the beginning of time.

It should be said that radicalism in the labor movement in the 1940s was no figment of capital's imagination. Some union firebrands were gambling on the prospect that they had a much stronger hand to extend union power than even moderate visionaries like Walter Reuther had assumed. Not only was there a well-developed Communist presence in many unions but even for non-Communist leaders like Harry Bridges of the International Longshoreman's Association, the labor solutions they were willing to consider demonstrate how far they imagined the political margins could be stretched in the direction of social democracy and economic corporatism. Bridges was brought on the program on November 2, 1945, just days before the scheduled labor-management conference that Eric Johnston was advocating a month earlier on *Meet the Press*. His introduction was markedly different from Johnston's: "A man who has caused more controversy than any other labor leader in the last decade—Mr. Harry Bridges." Bridges's opening premise was simple enough and demonstrates how confident people once were in promoting a social rights agenda with robust democratic discourse.

Victor Riesel (*New York Post*): I understand that the big unions like steel and auto and several million members have filed and called for a strike vote.

Harry Bridges: That's because there is nothing else left to do if the industrialists refuse to bargain collectively, if there is no machinery to settle disputes. The workers must have a wage increase. That is recognized now, not in the interests of the workers or labor but in the interests of all the people of the nation in mass purchasing power. There is nothing left for workers to do except to take a strike vote.

Then Riesel lured him into a discussion of his union's role in using the strike weapon to enter into larger political causes like foreign policy, which seemed a bridge too far even in those more heady days of labor unrest and social imagination.

Riesel: Your union in its publicity releases and statements has been talking about strikes other than those for wages. Some of those involve issues such as shipping GIs home and shipping munitions to put down the Indonesians. Would your union stop working for any other reason than to enforce wages?

Bridges: Well, as a general rule we don't stop working to enforce wage demands. By and large we think and we even believe now that a better case might be made on wage demands through means other than strikes. We have generally followed a policy of not striking except for something more fundamental than wages, although wages are a fundamental issue and even more today.

Riesel: Those are the fundamental issues?

Bridges: Of course, we have struck for other things, and I presume we still will. The Indonesian question is one. Our longshoremen and our warehousemen refused, or tried to refuse—they weren't quite successful—to prevent shipments of airplane engines and parts and scrap iron and oil and other things to Japan years ago. We believe that the same action should be taken with regard to the shipments right now of weapons to suppress the struggle of the

Indonesian people and other people down in the Pacific. I think those things will still occur.

. . .

Robert Glasgow (*New York Herald Tribune*): If the government doesn't do what you ask, does that mean you are not going to handle commercial ships; is that the idea? You are not going to load commercial ships?

Bridges: That is right—after a reasonable length of time.

. . .

Riesel: Mr. Bridges, isn't this a dangerous policy you are following? Doesn't it take the union out of the business, slightly, of wages and hours, and make it a political weapon? What is the difference between saying, "Troops must come home; the Indonesians must not be suppressed," and saying, "The government's foreign policy on the atom bomb must be something or we won't load ships?" Don't you think that politicizing a union that way is a dangerous thing?

Bridges: No, I think it is a very good thing. If a union is not political today, it is not going to live. Our union is constantly political. Not near enough to suit me. It has got to be more political if it is going to live.

Just three weeks later, the labor problem was again the topic of the eighth episode of *Meet the Press*. This time the guest was Walter Reuther, who was there to discuss "the greatest strike to be called against industry this decade." Thus, five of the first eight regular episodes dealt with labor problems and collective bargaining. The terrain of economic justice and social rights seemed open to many far-ranging solutions. Reuther was fighting to get a wage increase predicated on General Motors' ability to pay. General Motors was unwilling to share information about its ability to pay or to admit the principle as valid. Reuther uses the rhetoric of equality deftly and to powerful effect: "Why should there be any secrets?"

Robert Conway (*New York Daily News*): Then I take it you feel the real significance of this strike and this situation is that the entire problem between labor and industry has to be settled more or less along the lines that you have outlined and that this is the beginning of a struggle, that the automobile strike is the front of a struggle for economic justice between labor and capital; is that correct?

Walter Reuther: That's correct, and we don't see how you can come to any intelligent decision unless you have in your possession the facts. This is a

> matter of arithmetic. We have told the corporation all along that this issue should not be settled by arbitrary use of economic power, either by labor or management; let's get the arithmetic on the table, and if we are wrong, we will back down. What is the company trying to hide anyway in their books? Why don't they lay them out on the table so everybody can see the arithmetic?

Reuther's discursive efforts in favor of liberal social rights were the most visionary and well adapted to the setting that one could imagine, but the times were not well matched to the message. Reuther rose in prominence, but war weariness and emerging challenges to business helped Republicans take control of Congress in 1946, where they promoted restrictive labor legislation, the Taft-Hartley Act, named after its cosponsors in the Senate and House, respectively. Opponents of the bill simply referred to it as "the slave labor bill," an effort in civil positioning that needs no further explication.

As international tensions simmered, Communist associations and infiltration in unions became a pressing problem that the unions had to move quickly to resolve. As early as May 17, 1946, Senator James Eastland of Mississippi appeared on the program, claiming, "In my judgment the CIO is the driving force for Communism in America. Southern people will not surrender to Communism. . . . As far as the state of Mississippi is concerned, I think I can say authoritatively that an organization will be set up among real Americans to handle any Communist CIO agitators who invade the state."

While some of the southern leaders were more prone to open demagoguery and reaction than those in the North, the core principles promoted in public debate differed little. Always at the forefront in articulating the antigovernment rhetoric in the postwar period, Taft developed a line in his January 1946 interview that clarified the sentiment that Senator Eastland might have developed if he had wanted to do so: wages could not be raised at the expense of profits whatever the purported facts of the case were because the theory of redistribution was based on both wrongheaded and antiliberal principles.

Nathan Robertson (*The Newspaper PM*): Well, Senator Taft, didn't the fact-finding board in the automobile case find that wages could be increased substantially without increasing prices?

Robert Taft: The fact-finding board adopted Mr. Truman's philosophy of economics with which I wholly disagree. They based their entire, their entire finding on the theory that you can increase prices without increasing wages.

Robertson: But don't you—

Taft: And I wholly disagree with that policy.

. . .

Blair Moody (*Detroit News*): In general I think that anyone would agree with you, that productivity must go up if wages go up, but this happens to be a high-profit company, and uh, and uh—

Taft: Now, Mr. Moody, you [*voice cracking*] [are] advancing an entirely wrong theory. You're saying [*voice surging*] here is a peculiarly efficient company! Therefore, they ought to pay their workers more.

Moody: Well, I didn't say that.

Taft: That's absolu—well that's, that's the logic of your conclusion, and that's absolutely contrary to the entire system of a competitive free economy.

Moody: No, I was merely trying to lead you into talking about the facts, Senator, and you—

Taft: Oh no, no, you were advancing a new theory, and it was a wrong theory.

When the Democrats took back control of Congress after the surprising 1948 elections, the House author of the "slave labor bill," Fred Hartley, appeared to discuss the prospects of a Democratic Congress repealing the act as one of its first decisions, as had been promised. The date was November 26, 1948, and the topic of the first question he was asked was Communism. This was unsurprising because between the appearances of Robert Taft and Fred Hartley, the great Communist scare had begun. The record of this is clear in the *Meet the Press* archive, with appearances by Karl Mundt, Elizabeth Bentley, and Whittaker Chambers through the election summer of 1948, all of whom had titillating things to say about Communist infiltration and Soviet espionage. *Meet the Press* was now an official party to the Red Scare.

Murray Snyder (*New York Herald Tribune*): Mr. Hartley, from Washington, we learned today that two House committees have decided to drop contempt charges against sixty persons who refused to say whether they were Communists. Would you say Congress is already bowing to the election returns?

Fred Hartley: No, I don't believe we're bowing to the election returns in making
that decision at all. We are merely cooperating with the decision taken by the
Department of Justice.

. . .

Inez Robb (International News Service): Mr. Hartley, do you believe that the
November 2 election was a mandate for the immediate and the outright
repeal of the Taft-Hartley Act?

Hartley: It is by no stretch of the imagination a mandate for the repeal of the law.

If there was a clear lesson that critics could draw from the election of 1948,
surely one of the great upsets in presidential history, it came in two steps:
(1) Democrats were somehow implicated in the process of Communist
infiltration; and (2) the Democrats could whip their rivals by champion-
ing the politics of the common man. These features were not joined by
coincidence in the Republican mind.

For those keen leaders who could sense the direction of the winds,
the future appeared bright for those who could exploit this nest of associations. Richard Nixon was among the first to do so, but the era would
be named for the craftiest of the Red baiters. As a new election season
began in 1950, Joseph McCarthy released the famous news of his private
list of fifty-seven card-carrying members of the Communist Party, who
he claimed had positions in the State Department. When the staunch
anticommunist Walter Reuther appeared less than two months afterward, on April 2, 1950, he produced what is probably the most cogent
and far-seeing critique that one can find in this record on the methods of
McCarthyism, which he contrasted with his own efforts to rid his union
of Communist influences.

Walter Reuther: I think the Senator McCarthy episode is really one of the tragic
things that have happened in the past year. Here we are facing the most
aggressive foe in the history of the world—Russian Communism—and this
is a time when America, when every American in any position of responsibility, ought to demonstrate the capacity of leadership and the personal integrity to rise above partisan politics. And I think that Mr. McCarthy's conduct
has been reprehensible, has been irresponsible, and has done exactly what Joe
Stalin would like him to do, because it has played right into the hands of the
Cominform.

Larry Spivak: Mr. Reuther, do you know anything about the charges, the rightness or the wrongness of the charges; have you sat in on any of the hearings?

Reuther: I have not.

Spivak: Have you seen any of the evidence?

Reuther: It seems to me—

Spivak: I am not trying to defend Senator McCarthy—

Reuther: That's true.

Spivak: I'm just wondering about this off-the-cuff statement on an issue—

Reuther: But it seems to me that if a responsible official of the American government—and I say a senator ought to be that kind of responsible official—had information which led him to believe that there were Communist agents in the State Department, that it would be his duty as an American and as a citizen to take that information to the proper authority, to Mr. Hoover, head of the FBI, or Mr. Atchison, head of the State Department—

Spivak: Well, Mr. Reuther—

Reuther: What did Mr. McCarthy do? He goes on a barnstorming tour and starts out with several hundred Communists in Wheeling, West Virginia, and I resented that—you know, that's my hometown—and I kind of resented him using my hometown to start this little a, sort of a carnival barnstorming tour he has. He winds up now, and he's bought himself a microscope; he's trying to find not a couple hundred Communists; he's praying he can find one.

. . .

May Craig: Well, you got shot for trying to clean Communists out of your union, didn't you?

Reuther: I cleaned them out of our union. I don't know whether that is why I was shot; it could be.

Craig: Well, why do you think that they should not be cleaned out of the government if it can be proved that they are there?

Reuther: Oh, I would be the fella making the most noise in America to clean them out of the government if I thought they were there, but if I thought they were there, I would not make a public speech about it. I would go to the responsible head of the government charged with that responsibility and say, "Look this is the information I've got; you check into it, and let's clean the Communists out."

This episode demonstrates two things. First, Walter Reuther was in a good position to defend his union precisely because he had inoculated himself from the potentially polluting association with Communists. Second, at this early date, responsible and savvy journalists like those of the *Meet the Press* pool were easily carried along by the power of the McCarthy line after the social drama of the Alger Hiss case. In general, unions found themselves on the wrong side of the discourse of liberty in the election seasons of the early Cold War, and the best they could hope to do was to hold their positions.

For those union leaders who were more anticommunist in word than in deed, things were much tougher on the public stage. Consider this example with Michael Quill of the Transport Workers Union from August 27, 1950, as the McCarthy machine was picking up steam. The topic is the radical union leader Harry Bridges, who earlier had called for union influence on foreign policy.

Frank McNaughton (*Time* magazine): Mr. Quill, I'd like to ask you about Harry Bridges. You knew him for a couple of years?

Michael Quill: Yes.

McNaughton: Do you think he ought to be deported?

Quill: No, I don't believe so.

McNaughton: Do you believe he's a Communist?

Quill: I don't know.

McNaughton: You testified against him in the executive hearings of the CIO.

Quill: Within the CIO I gave some testimony about the conduct of his union, but I gave no public testimony.

McNaughton: Do you know as a matter of fact that they're going to expel him from the CIO next week, probably Tuesday?

Quill: That will be a matter for the CIO board to take up, and I'm sure it will be decided in a democratic manner.

Martha Rountree: What would your guess be, Mr. Quill?

Quill: I wouldn't guess.

May Craig: Do you think they should have kept Harry Bridges in jail?

Quill: I don't believe they should. If the man was out on bail, I think they should have left him free until the final hearing in his case.

Craig: You don't think he's a menace in a communistic way?

Quill: No.

This interview became even more chilling and prosecutorial as it moved through the allotted thirty minutes.

The public reception of any of the union leaders, whatever their ideological position, through this period was less than sanguine. When Walter Reuther walked out of what was called the War Stabilization Board at the onset of the Korean War and appeared on *Meet the Press* on March 11, 1951, a representative exchange with him went as follows:

Larry Spivak: And you think that in a democracy at a time of war, when some of our sons are in Korea, that when you walk out the way you did, that you are speaking for the plain people of America whose sons are in Korea and who are being drafted?

. . .

Walter Reuther: I say when you fight against profiteering and speculation, when you fight for effective price control, for a fair tax law, for rent control, for these kinds of things, you are fighting to strengthen America, not to weaken it.

John L. Lewis, the towering president of the radical United Mine Workers of America, faced a similar gauntlet in a July 15 appearance in the same year. Two sequences of questioning carry the tone of that interview.

Larry Spivak: Mr. Lewis, the word most frequently used to describe you by our enemies is "dictator." Now, you don't look like a dictator tonight. Are you a dictator?

John L. Lewis: Really, I am soft and peaceful, Mr. Spivak.

Spivak: Is that the answer you are going to let stand, Mr. Lewis?

Lewis: Well, I really don't consider it very important as to whether someone thinks I am a dictator or whether they think I am merely a John Q. Public character.

. . .

Louis Stark (*New York Times*): Mr. Lewis, although you are not a Communist—

Lewis: Do you admit that, Mr. Stark?

Stark: It is labor history, nevertheless, that you did use Communists to help build the CIO.

Lewis: Which one; which one?

Stark: A good many of them.

With the passage of a few years' time, voluntary union purges, and the public humiliation of Senator McCarthy, these Red-baiting attacks on the union movement became a thing of *Meet the Press* past.[2] But no sooner did McCarthy pass from the scene in 1954 than a new category of anticivil iconography took center stage in the public drama in the fight for social rights. In this act, a Communist-fighting, civil Democrat like Walter Reuther played a much smaller role. Instead, new anticivil figures like Jimmy Hoffa came to represent the public face of unionism on this most public of stages. Having weathered the period of populist uprising in which one might have expected the debilitating provisions of the Taft-Hartley Act to have been repealed, the Republican Party found a new source of oppressive associations with which to bludgeon the union movement in the Mafia—an internal other that threatened the civil peace. The union movement had made it through the Red smears of the postwar period on a defensive posture, but once the perceptions of widespread criminal infiltration of the unions became an issue that could benefit triangulating Democratic leaders like the Kennedy brothers, the New Deal coalition that collapsed after 1968 showed its first signs of soon-to-be fatal fractures.

A Giant Wicked Conspiracy

Mr. Beck, you're fighting the mobs on the New York waterfront,
but I have here a statement from the congressional committee
which charges that there's a giant—and I'm quoting—"giant wicked
conspiracy involving extortion, gangsterism and dictatorship" by AFL
Teamster leaders of Detroit.

—Victor Riesel, March 7, 1954

In the sixty-seven years and more than thirty-five hundred episodes of *Meet the Press*, there have been many powerful and even singular moments on the program. As is always true of history, many of the salient events at the time are either forgotten now or are difficult to place in dramatic context. One episode that stands out perhaps more than any other in my exploration of the *Meet the Press* archive was that on June 3, 1956, with Victor Riesel. What made the Riesel appearance so powerful was how strange it was. There was something distracting about Riesel's appearance; he wore thick black sunglasses, and his forehead was shining to a degree that was unnatural even in those early days of television klieg lights. More-over, anyone who had been watching *Meet the Press* would immediately recognize Riesel. This is the same Victor Riesel who had been a regular panelist on the program, but now he was the subject of a news event be-hind the show. It was as if Andrea Mitchell now found herself at the cen-ter of a scandalous conspiracy worthy of Sunday-morning programming. Riesel was a famous labor reporter who had recently been assaulted with sulfuric acid in a garish attack in broad daylight in New York City. No one knew then exactly who had committed the crime (although figures who would be linked to the Teamsters were suspected), but the result was that Riesel was blinded for life. The sheer audacity of the attack and the fact that it was made on a leading and outspoken reporter provided the kind of atrocity story that helped critics of organized labor transform public opinion about the union movement in ways from which it would never fully recover.

Ned Brooks (moderator): Welcome once again to *Meet the Press*. Our guest is Victor
Riesel, the labor columnist who two months ago was the victim of an attack
by an unknown assailant. Acid was thrown into his face, and his eyesight was
permanently lost. The story of the attack has shocked the nation. Rewards of
some forty-five thousand dollars have been offered, but the man who threw
the acid and those who have hired him are still at large. Throughout the
country the case has touched off demands for a thorough investigation of
gangsterism in the labor movement.

In retrospect, it is unsurprising that the Riesel appearance stimulated a major change in a key part of the national conversation. All of the neces-sary elements were there. First, there was a plausible narrative of wrong-doing that lay behind the crime. Riesel had just been on air criticizing a union for its criminal contacts and underworld connections hours before the attack. Second, the public had been primed through a variety of ven-ues and media to see the threat of organized crime wherever it looked. This provided for the necessary sense of symbolic fit— verisimilitude— that is so important for driving media firestorms. For example, Elia Ka-zan's film *On the Waterfront*, itself based on the Pulitzer Prize–winning reporting of Malcolm Johnson, had been released just two years prior to Riesel's appearance, provoking widespread concern about the infiltration of organized crime into the operations on the docks of New York City.[3] And in 1941, the inflammatory right-wing media personality Westbrook

Pegler had won a Pulitzer Prize for exposing racketeering in labor unions and was still plying his trade. The Kefauver Committee of 1952, chaired by the little-known senator Estes Kefauver, held the first widely televised congressional hearings (later to be used to such tragic effect by Joseph McCarthy) on the subject of organized crime. The attention given to this new form of public deliberation had made a hero out of Kefauver, even as it demonstrated the potential of the new medium of television to tell a story.[4]

Apart from these supportive backdrops—the mise-en-scène—for Riesel's argument, one cannot ignore the natural appeal and ideological cogency of the central figure in this drama, Riesel himself, who with his tightly argued rhetorical intervention helped put in motion a chain of events that remains relevant for thinking about class and politics in the United States today.[5] Like any other writer, Riesel was a product of the environment in which he had developed his craft. His columns were sharp witted, timely, and critical. In so many ways he was the natural partner of the show's host, Larry Spivak; he was highly intelligent and driven by a sense of conviction for which he was willing to risk his personal safety. As with many other intellectuals of that era, his experience at City College in New York had produced in him that eccentric blend of fascination with labor, class, and issues of social justice (complete with a militantly anti-communist attitude) that one finds in the later neoconservatives who cut their teeth in debates in that same setting.[6]

Riesel's staccato New York speaking voice and his simple, motivating story made for riveting television drama and still does. On June 3, 1956, the *Meet the Press* questioners led him willingly wherever he chose to take his story, and the moral that he wanted viewers to draw from it was quite clear: There was no question that the attack on him was intended to intimidate him for his writings on corruption in the union movement in general and the waterfront in particular; well-meaning union leaders would be in no position to clean up this mess on their own; the government should become involved in this national crisis, and Congress should take the lead with investigative committees; and the attack would do nothing to stop Riesel in his efforts to reform the labor movement.

Ernest K. Lindley (*Newsweek*): Well, let me ask you this. Is there any possibility in your mind that this attack had a Communist source? That possibility was suggested by Mrs. Edith Nourse Rogers on the floor of Congress.

Victor Riesel: I think that there's a great possibility. I have said in two years of columns and in whatever platform I could get, that on the New York waterfront there are Communist agents and that they have worked with some elements of the mobsters on the New York waterfront, and as a matter of fact they still are.

. . .

Murray Davis (*New York Telegram and Sun*): Vic, changing it just a little bit, now you have mentioned your columns against the waterfront crowd. Acid used on you is not a weapon of the waterfront. You know that it's a garment center weapon more than a waterfront weapon. . . . You haven't particularly addressed your columns toward the garment area, have you?

Riesel: Yes, we have.

Davis: Not recently?

Riesel: Well, on the Monday before I was hit in the early hours of that Thursday morning, April 5, I had a piece in which I very specifically talked of rackets in the garment area and the use of acid.

. . .

Abe Raskin (*New York Times*): Do you feel, Vic, there is the potentiality for a real uprising with labor itself? Do you feel the new united labor movement through its Ethical Practices Committee is going to make a real dent in this problem?

Riesel: I don't think that they're going to make a dent, Abe. This is no criticism of Al Hayes, its chairman. They don't have the power. . . . If you moved in on any one of the great unions that were corrupt or had corruption in it, they could just pull out.

. . .

Spivak: Vic, I want to get to that. Why do you think that Congress has ducked this investigation? Why do you think they haven't had an all-out investigation with a watchdog committee that kept it going once they have exposed this thing?

Riesel: First, I'd like to say, Larry, there ought to be a watchdog committee. We have a committee on internal security which goes after the commies; why not a committee on this kind of corruption? Is there less a danger in this underworld second government to the rank and people, to the public, to the man on the street? If this can happen to me, does anybody think it couldn't happen to anybody else? Why not another committee, standing committee?

While there is always reason to be cautious in making causal claims with respect to a specific historical event, there is good reason to believe that this is one of the episodes of *Meet the Press* that was as much a cause of social change as it was a reflection of it: more a stage for performance of meaning than a window into elite consciousness. On June 6, just three days after the episode, a *New York Times* story revealed that President Eisenhower had decided to begin an investigation into racketeering in the union movement. The reporter claimed that Eisenhower was inspired to this action by his Sunday-night viewing of Riesel's performance on *Meet the Press*. As Riesel himself explained, "I wasn't important as a man, but I was important as a symbol. . . . In hitting me, the underworld was thumbing its nose at the community and the forces of law and order."[7] This was a crucial political opportunity for labor's enemies. Not only were they blessed with a Republican administration that had been elected on an anticorruption agenda as much as on any other but they now had a trigger event that could be exploited to rein in the union power that had been rising since President Roosevelt had passed supportive legislation in 1935.

Fostering democratic practices within the unions and limiting their power to abuse their privileges soon became a central feature of the labor conversation. For every effort made by a heroic proponent of a deeper conception of social democracy like Walter Reuther, a single dramatic episode with a villain like Lee Pressman of the Mine Workers or Dave Beck of the Teamsters, leading figures in the "Reds and rackets" narratives, respectively,[8] could undo decades of foundation building. Essential as it is to have a good hero in a civil drama, it is more important to have a good villain, and the peg on which to hang a villain is a well-marketed atrocity. By failing to provide a broader ethical case for the union movement, thereby allowing associations to be made between labor and the underworld, unions were losing the battle of civil positioning. They were allowing themselves to become defined as undemocratic and tyrannical.

Despite Riesel's ultimate intention to promote the responsible use of union power, the underworld that he had helped expose became a guiding metaphor for unionism that ultimately helped undo the movement in the private sector.[9] To convey his alarm about the Riesel performance, President Eisenhower contacted George Meany of the AFL-CIO and conveyed his concerns about the problem of labor racketeering. Meany's response was, perhaps unsurprisingly, supportive, but Meany was worried that the goal of rooting out corrupting elements from existing unions could be used by the well-mobilized enemies of labor in both parties to weaken the union movement in general.[10] Labor leaders recognized the problems of corruption and the influence of organized crime just as they recognized their vulnerability to the stigmatizing effects of their Communist associations, but the events to follow played out in the national conversation in a way that largely confirmed Meany's fears that the taint of criminal corruption would drag down labor's image and its clout.

Just as "McCarthyism" would become an epithet with which civil libertarians could bludgeon their opponents for decades to come, "gangsterism," the union underworld imagery, and the broader sense of self-serving corruption that came with the picture of "big labor" would make it easier for labor's opponents to ensure an "exceptional" (from an international comparative perspective) role for unions as institutions and collective bargaining as a mechanism in the American political economy. Unions would in no way disappear from the economic and political scene, but their influence in the private sector peaked in the Eisenhower era.

The tensions between the supposedly middle-of-the-road Eisenhower administration and the working public were occasionally pronounced, as when Secretary of Defense (and former CEO of General Motors) Charles Wilson compared unemployed workers to "kennel dogs," which he contrasted with "bird dogs" who would go out and "hunt for food rather than sit on their fannies and yell."[11] The flavor of class politics and the language of social rights were developed and available for public deployment in this period in ways that would later seem appropriate only for marginalized figures like Ralph Nader. Here is an example from Reuther's appearance on October 17, 1954, in response to the firestorm over Wilson's comments.

Ruth Montgomery (*New York Daily News*): As Mr. Brooks pointed out, you were the first one this week to make capital of Mr. Wilson's remark about kennel dogs. I have here a copy of the transcript of the record when you testified before the Senate Labor Committee last January, in which you said: "If you really want to stir the animals up and have more problems, that is the shortest way to do it." Well now, who were you referring to as animals?

Walter Reuther: Well, you know, I brought the whole copy along. And I tell you frankly, I appreciate the commercial you're giving my testimony, and I would say to anyone listening in that if you'll write my office, we'll send you a copy of the whole transcript, and you'll see what I said was quite different than what Mr. Wilson said. I said, "If you permitted collective bargaining to revert to the law of the jungle and the spirit of the jungle, then instead of trying to minimize differences and getting people to settle issues based upon fairness and justice and human decency, you would be stirring up the animals and stirring up man's basic animal instincts. I wasn't referring to laborers. I was referring to labor leaders, to industrial leaders, to everybody. And under the old system in Ford, when Mr. Bennett and his gang were in control, we had collective bargaining by the law of the jungle and we didn't settle things on the basis of fairness.

Montgomery: You said you didn't mean labor with that crack. You even repeated that crack. Another time you said you're going to have an election campaign to see who can stir up the animals the most. Well, it would just be the laborers who were voting.

Reuther: I recommend you read the whole transcript and find out. Exactly what I said is that you can't have collective bargaining based upon the law of the jungle. It ought to be settled based upon economic facts and not economic power. In every case, both labor and management must conduct collective bargaining in the knowledge that they have a joint responsibility and that the interests of the whole community come ahead of the interest of either labor or management.

Picking up on this line of questioning, Larry Spivak provided one of the most fascinating exchanges on economic theory as it related to union goals in *Meet the Press* history.

Larry Spivak: Where do all of those profits go eventually? Don't they go into increased employment, larger plants, into taxes? Or does a man die and take them with him?

Reuther: Fortunately, they don't. Mr. Humphrey, who is the secretary of the treasury—

Spivak: You're not answering my questions. You go off on political speeches.

Reuther: I'm trying to tell you what happens.

Spivak: I want to know what happens to all these profits that General Motors makes, Wilson makes. Doesn't the government eventually get them? Don't they go into increased plant expansion, and don't they come to you in one form or another?

Reuther: That's the theory. The theory is if you give greater and greater concentration in the hands of the owners of industry, ultimately that will trickle down into the economy.

Spivak: Isn't that our system? Isn't that what we know as our system of free enterprise, and isn't that the way this country has grown great, through what you
called the trickle system?

Reuther: That was the theory before the crash of 1929. The theory was if you give
people on top greater and greater incentive, they will find investment opportunities to get that money into circulation, new plants, new factories, and
that will create employment and that prosperity will seep down.

Spivak: Hasn't it?

Reuther: No. That's why we got in trouble in '29. That's why we're getting in trouble
now. The basic problem today is the serious imbalance between the ability to
create wealth and the lack of adequate purchasing power in the hands of the
people.

Raymond Brandt (*St. Louis Post-Dispatch*): Are you satisfied with Mr. Wilson's
explanation, or do you think he should be retired from private life?

Reuther: I have accepted his apology, and I think we ought to quit talking about
dogs and talk about people. People in America are important.

The penetration of the narrative of the rising threat of union power en-
dured after the Riesel blinding incident. When the Republican secretary
of labor James Mitchell appeared on the show on September 2, 1956, one
can see evidence of the reactive (if not reactionary) forces mobilizing. Secretary Mitchell was no fire-breathing union buster. He had been described by
Time magazine just years before as a "quiet, practical, genial Irish Catholic
with deep-set blue eyes, a massive, laugh-crinkled face, huge shoulders and
bristling hair,"[12] and he had an interest in labor-management relations that
made him a favorite among labor leaders. In fact, Mitchell was known to
many union leaders as the best labor secretary they could expect under the
leadership of the Republican Party, whose main actions on this score in
Congress had been to limit the Wagner Act of 1935, which had spurred
union growth to previously unthinkable levels, with their own bill, the
Taft-Hartley Act of 1947.[13] But by today's standards, Mitchell backed a fairly robust program of institutional supports for a social rights agenda, one
that would have placed him somewhere to the left of Jimmy Carter twenty
years later. In his first appearance on *Meet the Press* on April 17, 1954, he
demonstrated his conciliatory views and support for guaranteed income.

Larry Spivak: Do you favor a guaranteed annual wage as an objective, as a general
objective?

James Mitchell: I believe that the workers of this country are entitled to some rea-
    sonable degree of assurance of stability of employment, and that will take
    many forms in terms of the industry concerned. . . . For instance, you've had
    a guaranteed annual wage in the packing industry for some years.

To a class warrior like the radical Harry Bridges, who had managed to
survive the Red purges of the McCarthy era, Mitchell must have been
easy to dismiss as a "good cop" who was simply being used to balance
the outright enemies of labor like Senator Barry Goldwater of Arizona. But for most labor leaders of the time, Mitchell was not a union
man but a man you could work with. Not only was he reasonable and
imminently civil but he had a style of leadership that seemed perfect
for the times.

Mitchell had a difficult job ahead of him to smooth over relations
between the Republican administration and the labor movement. Style
(this is, the techniques of self-presentation) was king in this era, and this
comes through clearly on television. While the crude, macho, and clubby
antics characteristic of the urban machines and labor organizations were
once well accepted in the public sphere, America was coming to see itself
as a middle-class society. Walter Reuther could rise in this setting, but
those older, chest-beating, table-pounding politicians were easy to portray as déclassé, almost un-American. When Eisenhower came to power,
a wag joked that the New Dealers had been replaced by the car dealers.
He might have said instead that the golf club of the suburban elite had
replaced the political club of the urban machine.[14]

As with most Eisenhower officials, when Secretary Mitchell appeared
on *Meet the Press* in September 1956 to discuss the role that labor unions
would play in the upcoming presidential election, he came with a strategy
that was as much about how he presented himself as what he presented.
Central to his message was a calm and reassuring tone intended to assure
the viewer that all was well; the adults were in charge. The populist barbs
that energized crowds in the Roosevelt-Truman years didn't sting him.
In his responses to tough questions, he appeared to find it quite easy to
return to the Republican rhetorical high ground.

William Hines (*Washington Star*): Mr. Secretary, your party rightly or wrongly has
    gained a pretty wide reputation in this country of being the party of big busi-
    ness. With that in mind, I wonder how you propose to go about getting the
    labor vote this November.

James Mitchell: . . . Mr. Hines, when you look at the degree of employment, the high degree of employment in this country, the high wages, the degree of job security, the welfare benefits, the high prosperity which most men and women of this country are enjoying at this time, I can't see how the label that you have stated some people place on the party is a correct one.

Hines: Well, you spoke of full employment, and earlier this year you had some pretty severe unemployment in Detroit, at which time I believe one of the White House aides, Governor Pyle of Arizona, made a remark that the right to suffer is one of the joys of a free society. Is this the kind of technique that you're going to use to woo the labor union members?

Mitchell: Well, of course, Mr. Hines, I might tell you, I have some figures here which will be public on Tuesday, which will show that as of August of this year there were sixty-six million, eight hundred thousand workers employed in this country, the highest in our history, and the highest level of employment in our history.

Fifty years earlier, in an era of Republican dominance, President McKinley was known for his philosophy of "the full dinner pail," an image that implied that what workers wanted was not participation in the administration of the economy but rather a prosperous economy that enabled the consumer lifestyle that America was increasingly becoming known for. Mitchell also bragged about the prosperity of the era—the low inflation, the high rates of employment and wages—and warned labor not to become too closely associated with a political party or too attached to the symbolic value of a particular piece of legislation.

Roscoe Drummond (*New York Herald Tribune*): I'd like to raise an aspect of the Taft-Hartley law. . . . What reason have we to suspect that either party will live up to its new commitments on this subject?

Mitchell: Well, I would hope, Mr. Drummond, that at some point, and I hope it isn't too far distant, that we can take the Taft-Hartley law out of the political context that it's in and get an objective look at it so that the Taft-Hartley law could be overhauled as promised by the Republican platform. . . . The Taft-Hartley law is one law which affects labor; there are many more which have to do with safety, with union health and welfare funds, with many things that the workers of the country are concerned with.

Mitchell's quiet and confident representation of the heroic President Eisenhower suggested that stability and growth were what the worker wanted, not a union movement that got its hands dirty in politics and industrial policy. From the perspective of the political scene of 1956, the Republicans had only yesterday been painted as the party of Depression, complete with arresting imagery of Hoovervilles and bread lines. Mitchell was on air to help reclaim the mantle of competent economic manager for the modern Republican Party that Eisenhower would build.[15] This civil challenge to the more forward-looking members of the labor movement like Walter Reuther could not have been more apparent, however soft the sell, but the soft sell itself was substantive in this era. These soothing appeals were effective even if they did not satisfy all of the critics. In a striking letter written in response to the program, R. L. Masters of Torrance, California, complained that Mitchell was not pushed by the questioners in his response to a question about the states' rights provision of the widely vilified Taft-Hartley Act. He wrote: "He should have been asked and reminded that if the law needed repeal at the state level then why in the hell don't you favor nullification at the Federal level. . . . Is there no place one can turn to get information that isn't tainted with Republicanism? Precious Lord, take our hand and lead us on."[16]

The looming challenge for the Democrats came not from the likes of Republican Secretary Mitchell but rather from their southern Democratic allies, who were among the staunchest opponents of labor initiatives like the union shop and minimum wages. Among these southern adversaries was the Democratic senator from the anti-union state of Arkansas, John McClellan, who had inherited Joseph McCarthy's position as chair of the Permanent Subcommittee on Investigations when the Democrats took over the Senate in 1954. His *Meet the Press* appearance on March 31, 1957, as chairman of the newly established Select Committee on Improper Activities in Labor and Management, coincided with the dramatic, high-profile committee investigations into the activities of union leaders, which served as the greatest public relations disaster for the union movement of the postwar period. The immediate issue at hand was the testimony of embattled Teamster's president Dave Beck, who, as a result of the hearings, was removed from office and sentenced to jail. The larger implication of the McClellan hearings was that they dramatized the widespread corruption of the labor movement and thus enabled a shift against labor and the class-struggle model in the Democratic Party. The most notable convert to McClellan's cause was his assistant, the future attorney general of the United States, Robert F. Kennedy.[17]

As should be clear, Larry Spivak was no friend of Leftists and unions, but in the current political climate Spivak felt obliged to seek some balance between the two sides.

Larry Spivak: Senator, the Senate created your Select Committee to investigate both labor and management. Thus far most of your hearings have been on labor. Do you plan similar hearings on management?

John McClellan: Yes, there will be similar hearings on management. . . .

Spivak: Why did you start on labor when the directive was for both labor and management?

McClellan: Our interest in it started when we discovered labor racketeering in the procurement field.

And the connection to the Riesel affair was clear enough.

Jack Bell (Associated Press): In your New York investigation, will you subpoena the notorious Johnny Dio, who is under indictment in the acid blinding of columnist Victor Riesel?

McClellan: I think the public can reasonably expect his appearance before the committee.

As is often the case, we learn more about the national mood in such public fora from the questions asked than from the answers given by the guest. As a case in point, we can turn to the questions asked of McClellan by May Craig. In her interaction with Senator McClellan, Craig quickly pivoted from questioning to promoting the anti-union line, providing McClellan with many opportunities to promote his agenda.

May Craig: Senator, no matter what you find out at the hearings, all you can do is turn evidence over to the courts and then recommend legislation?

McClellan: That is correct. That is the only affirmative action the committee can take.

Craig: What kind of legislation? Could you end the tax exemption, where they have been making money?

McClellan: I would think it worthy of Congress's consideration. . . .

Craig: Could you subject them to antitrust legislation the way corporations are now?

McClellan: I am confident the Congress could do it.

Craig: Now, the root part of the evil is the union shop, where a man must belong in order to earn his living, and that is giving power to the officials who may not wish to take care of the welfare of them. Would you be favorable to taking the union shop out of Taft-Hartley?

McClellan: I have supported this in my state, a state right-to-work law. . . . These hearings may reveal circumstances and conditions to make it imperative that we have a federal right-to-work law. I prefer to leave it to the states, but I do think this: The power of compulsion of a union shop or closed shop takes away the liberty of the individual worker. We speak so much of civil rights. I think one of the highest civil rights any citizen has, or any person has, is the right to pursue happiness, the right to pursue a livelihood of his choosing without paying tribute if he does not choose to do so to any higher authority.

Craig: Is there any other large field of legislation you can think of?

McClellan: Oh, yes. I think the hearings have already indicated that we must enact some legislation. . . . There should be federal legislation to ensure the democratic processes in unions, next to the security of their funds, so they cannot be dissipated or misappropriated or stolen or diverted to any other purposes than union purposes.

What is most fascinating about the McClellan performance is the way it demonstrates how boldly the discourses of liberty and repression were employed at a critical moment in history. Not only did Craig provide the signal keyword "evil" as a starting point for the exchange but in his response, with a single and, from the reaction of the panel, uncontested sentence, the senator manages to undermine the attacks on white supremacy mounting in the school integration standoff in Little Rock ("we hear so much about civil rights") and condemn the institutional supports that have been put in place to limit the abuses of concentrated economic power ("the right to pursue a livelihood of his choosing without paying tribute if he does not choose to do so to any higher authority"), while validating a conception of the liberal tradition that fits quite nicely into the story line drawn from the founding documents ("the right to pursue happiness"). This is quite a virtuoso performance, which, to union leaders like Meany and Reuther, must have sounded like a wish list of union-busting demands. On May 31, 1959, responding to a congressional committee that had proposed federal legislation in response to McClellan's findings, John L. Lewis provided a characteristic response.

Ned Brooks (moderator): If we were to eliminate all federal regulation, isn't it likely that the states might move in with legislation more repressive than what you have now?

John L. Lewis: That would depend, of course, upon the rapacity of the corporations and the large employers of our country, as to whether or not their policies would superinduce such a demand.

If there is a general lesson to take from the McClellan appearance on *Meet the Press* in March 1957, it was that it served as a demonstration of how Victor Riesel's tragic experience had been translated into practical action. Remember his dramatic calls for a congressional committee. Much has been written about the McClellan committee and its effects on labor leadership and the movement more generally, and rightfully so,[18] but by shifting the literary genre of the national conversation from descriptive to tragic, the events set in motion by Riesel in June 1956 had created a political opportunity for anti-union forces that cleared the stage for the transformative public shaming of labor leaders. This, in turn, tainted their image for decades. In 1958 the next Congress overrode moderate attempts to contain labor racketeering promoted by John F. Kennedy in favor of the restrictive Labor Management Reporting and Disclosure Act favored by Republicans. It then proved difficult for union representatives to avoid being painted with uncivil representations as crooked and selfish labor bosses. The old laissez-faire line that unions were at best opposed to economic solutions, if not the key part of any problem that the country was facing, was settling into the conventional wisdom. Labor was on its way to becoming just another special interest in the public mind, a term once reserved for business organizations.[19] Labor was the problem, and a problem like this demanded an iconic enemy image, an Al Capone for labor. And they found him.

The Pack Is After Hoffa

I don't join the mob every time it hollers "stop thief" and pursues a man down the road and turns pack on him. . . . The pack is after Hoffa, and they haven't got him yet.

—John L. Lewis, May 31, 1959

What Joseph McCarthy would come to represent in the domain of civil liberties, Jimmy Hoffa would represent in the realm of labor racketeering, and ironically, it would be from McCarthy's former post in the Senate that much of the public relations damage to Jimmy Hoffa would be done. Hoffa became the perfect emblem of what Seymour Martin Lipset called "working class authoritarianism."[20] He was a fast-rising dark star in the International Brotherhood of Teamsters who had been pivotal in securing the election of its president, Dave Beck, at the time of the Riesel attack, and who had been singled out as among the most intimidating and possibly corrupt of the union leaders in the nation. The suspicion of corruption was the result of both Hoffa's personal style and his professional habits. He dealt only in cash, leaving no trace of his dealings; advocated centralized power in the union (the Teamsters had recently moved its headquarters from Detroit to Washington, D.C., and vested decision-making power in a national convention); and was known for his associations with recognized gangsters and toughs whom he was reluctant to remove from positions of power in the union even when they were exposed for wrongdoing. But whatever else Hoffa was, he was a power in the Teamsters union that was growing steadily.

In the mid-1950s, the name Hoffa was on its way to iconic status, a one-word signifier much like Gandhi or Hitler that pointed toward an idea that could be invoked by the name. The Hoffa style (he himself had a tendency to refer to himself in the third person) was a tough and defensive approach that reveled in the vitiated grandeur of the simple possession of power and the fear that this inspired in others. Unlike Walter Reuther, Jimmy Hoffa would provide no democratic cover in public for his power grabs; he simply accepted justification of union power as axiomatic. What made Hoffa such a household name was his ability to secure favorable contracts for his rank and file and the power that came with his success.

While he was clearly tolerant of criminality in his ranks, a fair assessment of Hoffa would probably vindicate the man of many of the symbolic associations that were later attached to him. Jimmy Hoffa was less a criminal and more a calculating and tough-minded political realist. Certainly though, Hoffa was willfully complicit in his symbolic transformation from a successful leader of a movement for social justice into an icon of incivility, this at a time that required of him heroic rear-guard campaigns to reframe the labor movement. Labor was fast being positioned as an uncivil force with no ethical sense of its duty to the public. Leaders like Jimmy Hoffa were too confident in the rightness of their cause to successfully position their institutions in civil discourse. This complicated figure made sense to himself if not to others. He knew why his power politics was consistent with higher moral claims, but in public he presented the very picture of a corrupt and power-hungry union boss. This put him at odds with leaders of both parties, most notably the Kennedy brothers, Jack and Robert, and it was the Kennedys who would undo Jimmy Hoffa and therefore the Kennedys who would transform the labor conversation in America for the next half century.[21]

In a moment in which decisions were being made about the moral character of labor as an institution,[22] Hoffa was a man too consumed with himself to recognize that his brilliance and determination were not what that moment required of him. The period from the Riesel affair to the election of John Kennedy to the presidency represents a political opportunity in which competing framings of the union movement were broadly in play. On the labor question, it was a period of high drama and intense ideology. By allowing his opponents to draw moral boundaries around not only himself but also his organizing tactics, personal style, and basic philosophy, Hoffa became the profane symbol that helped labor's opponents rein in most of the projects to which he had dedicated his life.[23]

The Teamsters was a well-established organization in the 1950s and had successfully navigated the transition from horse-drawn to motorized transportation under the leadership of longtime president Daniel Joseph Tobin. Tobin had guided the union through tense and occasionally violent jurisdictional struggles that had left their mark on the character of the organization. When he was forced out of leadership in 1952, he was replaced by Dave Beck, a leader of the western faction of the union.

The way these Teamsters had been imagined in public can be seen in how they performed on television when given an opportunity. Early in his tenure as Teamster president on March 7, 1954, Beck appeared on *Meet the Press*. At this point, the conversation about union corruption and the complicity of union leadership was already fast developing. What Dave Beck did in his appearance on this national stage did little to assuage the public's concerns. Beck was a large, bald, smiling man who had a tendency to shout his answers to convey a sense of deeply held conviction. In his *Meet the Press* debut, he did much of this in response to his very professional questioners, who in both their demeanor and their questions worked to portray Beck as a perfect representative of the ineffectual if not corrupt leadership of unions.

If we adopt the sociologist Philip Smith's take on how these contests emerge, the Beck interview can be thought of as a genre struggle between himself and the questioners. As Smith describes this dynamic, a genre struggle is a public performance in which each side attempts to impose a definition of the situation that is compatible with a certain kind of interpretation of what is going on. To discourage a demand for serious action, one side might attempt to downplay the drama of the case, while the other might highlight the tragic and profound implications in every subtle feature of the evolving context. Such was the case with this interview with the soon-to-be-embattled Teamsters president. Beck repeatedly tried to portray the situation in prosaic and legalistic terms (albeit with much emotion and shouting that seemed to work against his purposes), and his interlocutors countered with an interpretation compatible with the genre of tragic decline. For Beck, his should be seen as a story of low-grade heroism with himself as the lead. For those who pursued him it was little short of a television trial.

If Beck had a difficult time framing the problem of Teamsters corruption in low dramatic form, by the time that revelations from the McClellan committee had helped remove him from office and place him in prison, the challenge was far more difficult for those who followed him. When it became clear that his likely successor was to be Jimmy Hoffa, the public outrage was palpable. This was the same Hoffa who was referred to in a question to Beck from Riesel himself on that 1954 appearance (prior to the assault on Riesel), asking if it were true that Jimmy Hoffa was "the brains behind this shakedown and power grab" and was engaged "in a wicked conspiracy to extort." Despite a vigorous and expensive public relations campaign by Beck to shore his image, these portrayals of corrupt goons and thugs running the ever more powerful unions, ongoing crisis, corruption, and uncivil realpolitik proved to be pervasive in this period.

It is difficult to overstate how important it was to establish the moral basis of union power and to anchor it in democratic theory, particularly in such a heady environment. Labor was a fragile institution that was, in its contemporary form, an explicit product of New Deal political strategy.[24] The crisis invoked a contest for civil power that most union leaders were simply unable to match given their temperament and training. The Teamsters had been associated with the national labor association, the American Federation of Labor from its origins, but

AFL-CIO president George Meany had threatened to expel the Teamsters in 1957 if Hoffa were elected its president. A challenger to Hoffa tried his hand to forestall this result and appeared on *Meet the Press* on September 22, 1957.

Ned Brooks (moderator): Organized labor is moving into its greatest crisis since the merger in its drive to clean its own house of corruption. Considerable attention is on the Teamsters union. A few days ago, labor's own Ethical Practices Committee issued a report saying the union is dominated by corrupt influence. It issued what amounts to a warning that if Vice President James Hoffa is elevated to the presidency, the union will be expelled from the AFL-CIO. . . . The man regarded as the principal challenger to Mr. Hoffa is Mr. Tom J. Haggerty of Chicago, who is our guest today.

In his questions, Larry Spivak stuck to a prosecutorial line, the main point of which was to demonstrate that Haggerty himself had not done enough to oppose corruption in the Teamsters union and that little would change if he were elected. The same is characteristic of the questions of other reporters like Ernest K. Lindley and Clark Mollenhoff, who later wrote a devastating book about Hoffa.

Clark Mollenhoff (Cowles Publications): Mr. Haggerty, there seems to be just a little reluctance on your part to specifically condemn Mr. Hoffa's remarks. I wonder if there is any fear on your part of what Mr. Hoffa might do to you, or what some of his friends might do to you, if you fail in your chance to become president.

Tom Haggerty: Mr. Mollenhoff, I come from the back-of-the-yards area in the city of Chicago. We don't believe in pushing people, but we are not easily pushed ourselves. I think fear is what created a Hitler, a Mussolini, and a Stalin. I think 99.9 percent of the Teamsters' members aren't in the category that would be interested in accepting fear.

In short, Haggerty, who lost that election decidedly, could only respond by validating the premise of Mollenhoff's concerns about the repressive potential of an America under the thumb of Hoffa. On the next episode on September 29, Secretary James Mitchell was peppered with questions about why he had done so little to clean up the mess with the unions. The press wanted to know when, if ever, the government will take "moral leadership in the labor movement."

Marquis Childs (*St. Louis Post-Dispatch*): I just want to get this straight. If it had
    not been for the McClellan committee, neither you nor anyone else would
    have known anything about this frightful abuse that has been exposed.

James Mitchell: The McClellan committee, with its powers of subpoena, is per-
    forming a function that a congressional committee should perform, yes.

In this civil forum, a tragic and almost apocalyptic genre was winning the
contest to define the labor problem, much as May Craig had noted. It was
as if the great confrontation between the Soviet Union and the United
States were playing out in the allegorical form of the conflict between the
government and the Teamsters. Had not the real source of this existential anxiety rocketed onto the national stage with the launch of *Sputnik*
the Friday after Secretary Mitchell defended the actions that he and the
government had taken against Hoffa and the Teamsters, there may have
been an appetite to further explore the tragic implications of the rise of a
man like Hoffa to such a position of power. Instead, *Meet the Press* began
its long love affair with the details of missile technology and the space
program.

But the union story did not go away after 1957. When given the
chance to make his moral case for union power in an appearance on May
31, 1959, John L. Lewis did little better than the Teamsters' leadership
class had done. He located the source of abusive and polluting power in
the repressive forces of the rapacious corporations, but he could not make
a case for moral leadership that grounded his own position in democratic
principles. In fact, he demonstrated a kind of contempt for such considerations altogether. In this, Lewis's interrogator was again the inimitable
May Craig.

May Craig: Did you attend any of the hearings of the McClellan committee?

John L. Lewis: Which committee?

Craig: The McClellan committee.

Lewis: As I search my memory, I will have to answer in the negative; I have not.

Craig: Did you read any of the testimony?

Lewis: Whatever the newspapers chronicled.

Craig: Weren't you shocked and horrified at the arson and the dynamite and the
    killing and the coercion and the sweetheart contracts revealed there?

Lewis: No more than I was shocked yesterday or the day before.

Craig: About what?

Lewis: When I found that a government agency in Denver for fourteen years had had two hundred employees of some division of the Department of the Interior on its payroll.

Craig: But as a labor leader, you are responsible for the general morals of labor but not for government, sir.

Lewis: As a leader of labor and one of its spokesmen, I am not responsible for the morals of any part of our population.

Craig: Don't you think the time—

Lewis: We're getting into the area where now the moral code is involved and the question of sin, wholesale and in the individual sense.

Craig: Sir, you brought in the government, and I am saying as a labor leader you should be concerned with morals of the general labor movement, if you expect to have public sympathy—which I find is declining for labor unions, and I am a labor union member.

Smelling blood in the water, the questioners ensured that the rest of the Lewis interview went badly for him. Among other things, he would find himself defensively supporting his sarcastic comments about Jimmy Hoffa, such as, "I occupied the proud position that Jimmy Hoffa occupies today." In one revealing exchange, Clark Mollenhoff confronted Lewis about the anticivil emotion of fear just as he had with Thomas Haggerty two years before.

Clark Mollenhoff: I am wondering whether—are you afraid to criticize Jimmy Hoffa? You have been very forthright in criticizing other union officials around the country—Walter Reuther, Meany—you'll say anything you want to, but you never say anything—are you afraid of Jimmy Hoffa?

Lewis: I am neither afraid of Hoffa nor you.

Mollenhoff: I am not in this.

Lewis: Yes, you are in it. You are injecting yourself in it.

Not until almost four years later did the arch villain in this tragedy, Jimmy Hoffa, appear on the program on July 9, 1961 (he had appeared on *Face the Nation* in 1959). In the interim, much had transpired. Two Kennedy brothers had made appearances in which they debated the issue of union power in general, and Hoffa's power in particular, with frank and disturbing directness.

When John Kennedy appeared on the first show to air after the 1958 midterm elections, he was celebrated first and foremost for his stand in the Senate against union corruption. Kennedy had sponsored a fairly moderate anticorruption bill for unions known as the Kennedy-Ives bill. The producers of *Meet the Press* presented this as the very reason for the historic victory he achieved in his Senate bid of 1958. In the introduction to his appearance on November 9, 1958, the announcers credited Kennedy's victory to his role in this corruption drama.

> Ned Brooks (moderator): Our guest is Senator John F. Kennedy, Democrat of Massachusetts. Last week while the Democrats were strengthening their hold on Congress, Senator Kennedy was rolling up a landslide of his own. . . . Both Democrats and Republicans now agree that his three-to-one victory has placed him more solidly in the front rank for the presidential race of 1960. In the new Congress Senator Kennedy will be in the forefront of the battle for legislation to correct abuses in labor unions. He was the coauthor of the Kennedy-Ives bill, which failed to become law at the last session but which did become a major issue in the campaign. He is a member of the special committee investigating labor racketeering.

If Kennedy is now remembered for his famous call to Martin Luther King and his stand on civil rights, for promoting Medicare, or for demonstrating mettle in the Cuban missile crisis, in 1958 he was known for his efforts to rein in labor racketeering and union corruption. There were larger political issues at stake. In the 1960 campaign, Kennedy engaged in the subtle repositioning of the Democratic Party on civil rights to demonstrate to blacks that he was with them and to southern whites that he was no radical like Hubert Humphrey. His position on union corruption was equally subtle. In his on-air performance, Kennedy's responses to questions of union abuses revealed all the poise of a soon-to-be-elected president. He cautioned that business, like labor, was occasionally granted too much power, took the Republican Party to task for campaigning against honest and democratically minded union leaders, and made a powerful case for working on behalf of the common good.

> Ned Brooks (moderator): In view of those election results, do you think there is any chance of getting a labor reform bill which has not been approved in advance by the leaders of organized labor?

John Kennedy: The Kennedy-Ives bill was not approved in advance. In fact, it was
   opposed for some time by members of labor. They supported it in the end
   because, I think, they thought it was in the public interest, and I believe they
   are going to support it again. I must say that I think it has been unfortunate
   that the Republicans waged their campaign this time against Walter Reuther,
   who according to our investigation of the Kohler strike, runs an honest
   union, instead of Mr. Hoffa, whom I didn't hear mentioned at all by any Republican candidates, who was surrounded by racketeers and crooks and who
   himself shouldn't hold the position of responsibility that he does.

Ever savvy and aware of the power of positioning oneself in the mainstream of the public interest, Kennedy recognized that the discursive
currents that then carried the racketeering conversation could also quite
easily destroy the labor movement and the Democratic Party if they were
not handled deftly. In a demonstration of what lay behind the Kennedy
charm, he played his cards as the proper guardian of civil society in moral
balance. This is best demonstrated in his response to *Newsweek*'s Ernest K.
Lindley, who challenged Kennedy directly on the issue of excessive union
power: "Do you reject completely the allegation that unions, or some of
them, are too strong?" His response humanized union membership (who
are also voters, of course) and served to deescalate the discussion, without
providing much room for union leaders to assert their civic credentials.
"When I think of a union, I don't always think of a labor boss sitting
behind a table, although I have seen a lot of labor bosses as a member of
the McClellan committee for the last two years, just as I have seen a lot
of management people who are irresponsible." In essence, the members of
unions are good, but the bosses are another matter.[25]

   Later, Robert Kennedy, who was the chief counsel to Senator McClellan throughout the consequential hearings, was asked during a July 26,
1959, interview about the "frightening power" that he has attributed to
the unions and the institutional nature of the problem to be confronted.
He answered, "I think that Mr. Hoffa or Mr. Beck or any of these other
individuals are not important, nor is my relationship with them, that they
just represent something that is very bad and evil." The introduction to
the episode says it all.

Ned Brooks (moderator): Welcome once again to *Meet the Press*. The Senate investigation of racketeering in labor and management is now approaching its
   climax. After two and a half years of intensive effort the inquiry has resolved

itself into a drive for labor reform legislation. It promises to be the leading issue before Congress in the days ahead. One of the principal figures in laying the groundwork for labor reform is the chief counsel of Senator McClellan's committee, Mr. Robert Kennedy, who is our guest today. Mr. Kennedy's interrogation of President Jimmy Hoffa of the Teamsters union has been one of the dramatic highlights of the investigation, a clash of strong personalities.

In managing the crisis brought on by the developing story of powerful unions run by what Riesel called the "underworld second government," the Kennedys showed the future of the stance taken by the Democratic Party. A professional (if not a patrician) style of political governance would become the norm, driving the old, tough-guy, machine-boss type out of the cast of characters who would be celebrated in the party's future. While it was clear that much change was in store for workers' organizations, it was not yet clear what this would mean for the future of workers.

When it finally came time for Hoffa himself to appear on *Meet the Press*, the images of labor as an antidemocratic and uncivil force were all present in Hoffa's performance, roughly in this order of emphasis: excessive power, ethical irresponsibility, lack of professional judgment, Machiavellian realism, irascibility, and hubris.[26] Jimmy Hoffa had been a newsmaker for more than a decade in 1961, and what he revealed on *Meet the Press* was typical of the media image that he had developed to that point. But what his performance revealed about how labor leaders were viewed and the extent to which the power of unions was feared leaves the first Jimmy Hoffa interview with few equals in the archive.

First impressions always linger, and the *Meet the Press* introduction often suggests much about where the figure being interviewed was positioned in the current state of the national conversation. Hoffa was introduced as having been granted "new powers" and a "salary increase," as being one of "labor's most controversial figures" and one who rose to power "by a rougher and more complex course than most labor leaders." The lead question was given to Larry Spivak, whose mode of cutting to the emotional chase had always been the key feature of the *Meet the Press* brand. Spivak's gift was his ability to indulge hyperbole within the reasonable parameters of the suspension of disbelief. He asked what Hoffa's conception of his responsibility to the public was, given that he had "just been elected to the most powerful union in the world." Whether the Teamsters really were the most powerful union in the world or not, the case could certainly be made that they were, and moreover, this line played to the vanity of the guest in a way that lured the victim into Spivak's trap. Note also that the evocative language—"most powerful in the world"—brings with it the emotional priming that is perfectly suited for a dramatic confrontation.

Larry Spivak: Mr. Hoffa, at the McClellan hearings, in answer to a question you said, "I recognize my responsibility to the public." You have just been elected to the most powerful union in the world and have been given some increased powers. Will you tell our audience your conception of your responsibility to the public?

Jimmy Hoffa: My responsibility, Mr. Spivak, is to organize the unorganized workers of America, to negotiate contracts with a minimum of lost man-hours, to recognize my responsibility for betterment of the aged, for pensions, welfare, and for the protection of those individuals who belong to our unions. . . .

Spivak: That is largely an explanation of your responsibility to your own Teamsters. What about your responsibility of your great power to the public itself? Do you see no special responsibility that you have because you are president of this powerful union?

Hoffa: The responsibility of power is no different in the union than it is in our courts, legislature, or big business. . . .

Spivak: Mr. Hoffa, would you say there is anything in your past record which would give the American people the assurance that you will exercise this vast power you now have in their best interests? You haven't forgotten that there has been a McClellan hearing, and a great many charges have been brought out against you. . . . These are all charges that the public themselves feel are harmful in their interests.

Hoffa: I am not responsible for information that the press, radio, television, or misguided senators would place in the record for the consumption of the American public. . . . Anybody who believes that Hoffa has violated the law has a right to take Hoffa into court under an indictment. . . . How many times must an American find himself innocent?

Hoffa, like many of the other labor leaders who had appeared on the show before him, could not resist evoking the feel of a courtroom in his answers. Indeed, it is almost as if they were always ready to go to trial. Sticking to this defensive line, Hoffa did little to connect with the audience in emotional terms. In stark contrast to the smooth civility of John Kennedy's performance nearly three years before, Hoffa failed to engender a clear conception of his moral purpose in running this "most powerful union in the world." Missing from any of his answers is what Durkheim wrote about as a sense of collective purpose—a rationale for situating his efforts with a broader plan for promoting the well-being of civil society in general. Throughout the Sunday interview, Hoffa was on the defense and clearly saw his role primarily as a defendant, and perhaps a victim of a conspiracy run by the president's brother, the attorney general. This was the substance of Spivak's trap; he knew that Hoffa would resist what was always demanded of guests on his program: to demonstrate how their work helped keep the world in moral order.[27] The trap being sprung, the rest of the remaining questioners treated Hoffa as a kind of caged animal at which they could safely poke at will.

Hoffa's responses were unconvincing. He claimed that he was not responsible for what is falsely reported in the press, radio, television, or by "misguided senators." He stood by "what actually happens" and "not on what you would like to believe but actually on what Hoffa does." His philosophy was to "live by the record, not by what you would have people believe with fancy words." When chastised for associating with "thugs and gangsters," he futilely attempted to reframe the conversation in terms of his pragmatic realism by suggesting that the reporters on the panel must also make such associations in the course of their work. When challenged on his legalistic retorts and seeming lack of ethical standards, he suggested that all institutions suffer from the problem of setting such ethical benchmarks. "I question whether or not any three men would be able to agree on what morality is," he retorted to a pointed question.

Max Lerner, who had recently written the influential book *America as a Civilization*, was particularly brutal on Hoffa.[28] Whereas Spivak's questions had the character of carefully laid traps, Lerner's were phrased as verbal assaults. He opened his line of questioning sardonically: "I guess I am one of these reporters whom you say associate with thugs" and averred that Hoffa was saying either that "there is no code of ethics" or that "each man is an ethical law unto himself." When Hoffa answered in his typically stoic and defensive style, Lerner was incredulous in his next question: "Seriously, Mr. Hoffa, [do you have any coherent position on] ethical standards that a large community agrees on which ought to furnish the basis for judging the behavior of trade union leaders like yourself?"

Here Lerner, a widely recognized authority, has named the civil problem of the labor movement in precise terms: labor had no coherent ethical standards that could legitimate its rising position in the moral order.[29] Whatever efforts later leaders like Leonard Woodcock, Lane Kirkland, John Sweeney, and even Jimmy Hoffa's son would try to do to repair the symbolic loss of moral authority that was represented by Lerner's attitude toward Jimmy Hoffa, the damage had been done.[30] The conversation had been set, and the story was clear. Under its current leadership, labor was an unruly and largely uncivil force in society that abused noble goals and objectives like improving the lot of the average working person and providing for the "decency and respect for the man who has a job," as Hoffa stated on his 1961 *Meet the Press* interview, by accumulating power in Washington with ultimately self-serving goals and misconceived theories of economic change. Perhaps the best summary of union politics in the era of its maturity can be found in Hoffa's return appearance on October 14, 1973, upon the decision of the Supreme Court not to review his appeal to return to office in the Teamsters union. Little had changed.

Larry Spivak: Mr. Hoffa, you have frequently been quoted as saying that you believe every man and particularly every politician can be bought. Do you really believe that?

Jimmy Hoffa: It isn't a question of being bought with money; it is being bought in various ways. I do believe that almost everybody in this world has a price based upon what he desires to have in the way of life, whether it is employment, financial security, whether or not it is a combination of both, you can hire them.

If we consider Jimmy Hoffa a political realist, with a faith in the mechanisms of democratic pluralism, his positions can be seen as principled and reasonable in the setting. But at this state of the conversation, described by John L. Lewis as one in which the mob had "turned pack on Hoffa" and labor leaders in general, Hoffa comes off as churlish. Although labor unions had been a stable part of the industrial scene for decades, the postwar period represented one of those moments when unions came of age and found their level in the institutional hierarchy of the American civil order. This level was not as high as its leaders had hoped. Unions were here to stay, but those who advocated for them from this point found it difficult to shake off the vitiating associations of criminality, selfishness, and corruption that were set in the public mind in this period.

These Vast Social Problems

Larry Spivak: What is your explanation then for the fact that two-thirds
of the elementary school pupils in New York City read below the
national norm or their grades, according to reports I have seen?

Albert Shanker [American Federation of Teachers]: . . . When we
measure reading scores, we are not measuring poor quality of
teaching. What we are measuring are problems from the rest
of society. We are measuring the problems of broken homes, of
poverty, the effect of discrimination, lack of health care. This, by
the way, is the other reason that teachers should be in the labor
movement, that you really can't solve educational problems within
schools alone. Teachers have to join with others to help to undo
some of these vast social problems which have this horrible impact
on the ability of some children to learn.

—September 1, 1974

Just as the final edits were being made to the uncivil Teamster boss narrative in the early 1970s, a new story of public-sector unionization was
being scripted. Even in an environment in which the legitimacy of union
power had been largely undermined, it is interesting that public-sector
unions have flourished in an era of private-sector union retrenchment.
Where private-sector union mobilization has been localized to unions like
the Service Employees International Union, the public-sector unions have
realized great success in their organization drives, and employees in those
jobs have done relatively well relative to their private-sector compatriots.
In the public sector, employers (that is, governments) have been less hostile
to the concept of a unionized workforce. Apart from the effort to ensure
that the Department of Homeland Security would be nonunion, it has
been less common for public employers to actively subvert unionization
efforts.

Perhaps the most salient example of the surge in support of the civil
virtues of public-sector unions was an appearance by Albert Shanker as
the new president of the American Federation of Teachers on September
1, 1974. Unsurprisingly, Shanker was confronted by the same kinds of
desecrating arguments about concentrated economic power in the union
that other union officials had been; there were questions about the power
of the union, the threat it represented to the public interest, and the moral
status of declaring a strike when children's educations were on the line

(Edwin Newman described him in the introduction as "one of the most powerful and controversial figures in public education"). Even though the questioners harried Shanker with the examples of past abuses, he managed his interrogation in a way that suggested that something new was emerging in the field of collective bargaining.

More than anything else, Shanker's performance had precisely that element that Jimmy Hoffa's lacked: professionalism. He had little trouble articulating a clear sense of how his pragmatic vision of the union movement fit into the ethical standards of the larger community. Shanker's civic spirit and the comfort he demonstrated in applying Jeffrey Alexander's binary codes of civil discourse to the teachers' union's struggle for economic justice were less susceptible to the older stereotypes than the traditional unions had been. He was rescripting unionism on the fly—every bit as professional as Secretary of Labor Mitchell had been two decades before in his attacks on labor sectarianism. One gets the sense that as this new kind of union movement rose, its power might be somewhat less frightening.

Abe Raskin (*New York Times*): Mr. Shanker, the AFL-CIO, of which you are a vice president, is about to organize a new public employees department. . . . Will this group be too powerful in its relation to the government?

Albert Shanker: No, I don't think so. . . .

Raskin: That would, of course, include the right to strike on a national basis. Wouldn't that be a great threat to the public welfare?

Shanker: I guess that would depend on who went on strike and for how long and what the consequences were. I believe very strongly that, like other democratic nations in this world, the United States should not, or state and local governments should not, have a blanket restriction on public employees' strikes. There is no other democratic nation in the world where teachers' strikes, for instance, are prohibited, and there is no reason why in this respect we should resemble Iron Curtain countries rather than democratic nations.

Another place to sample the flavor of the debate about the power and public-spiritedness of public-sector unions came in a special hour-long Labor Day episode with a variety of union leaders on August 31, 1975. There we see the persistence of the taint of anticivil union power in the line of questioning by Hobart Rowen of the *Washington Post* in an exchange with John Ryor of the National Education Association.

Hobart Rowen: As part of the growing power of the public unions sector—the unions in the public sector, the firemen, the policemen, the teachers, and so on—how do you respond to the charge that the plight of the cities today can be blamed in large part on the higher wage and pensions this group of unions has won and is winning at a time when the cities are hard hit by recession?

John Ryor: To begin with, I don't believe that is true. I don't believe that the teachers and the public employees in our major cities are the cause of the problem. It has always been a source of amazement to me that the victims are so often blamed for the situation.

The images and prejudices that apply well to truck drivers do not apply as well to teachers and nurses, but this did not restrict the use of that imagery in public debate. The legitimacy of a strike against the government was deeply contested, as was the very principle of fielding a union in an industry where the strike was inappropriate. Whether these public workers were victims was moot, but there would be more opportunities to blame them in the future as their power continued to expand.

Although public-sector unions had been flourishing in environments in which employers approached them as legitimate institutions, in the fall of 1981, things shifted at the federal level. When the Professional Air Traffic Controllers Organization (PATCO) became involved in a dispute with the Reagan administration over wages, hours, and working conditions, the stage was set for one of the more riveting civil dramas in union history. The producers of *Meet the Press* recognized the importance of the confrontation that was developing between the air traffic controllers and the Reagan administration and had scheduled an episode with William French Smith, then US attorney general, on the topic of the potential strike. What made this confrontation so interesting was that it was technically illegal for government employees to strike, and the tough-talking Reagan administration was showing quite a bit of pique in response to the threats the union was making.

When Smith appeared on *Meet the Press* on August 3, 1981, the tension had peaked between the union and the administration. He stated categorically that not only would a strike by the controllers be illegal but that those who went out on strike would be criminals. Although Smith's rhetoric was strident and his threats clear, the full dramatic potential of this confrontation was not obvious. In fact, the episode had more the character of administrative updating in low dramatic style than one of the most dramatic confrontations in American labor history. The largest portion of the interview was dedicated to questions about Reagan's immigration policy, not the PATCO strike that would be declared the following day. In retrospect, given Smith's confrontational language (and Reagan's similarly petulant press conference that same day), it is perhaps not surprising that President Reagan would take the unprecedented step of moving to decertify the union and fire the striking workers. But before the fact, it was almost impossible to imagine.

The symbolic associations of unions as threats to civil peace that were infiltrated by criminals and other corrupting influences had placed unions in a precarious position in the public imagination. Unlike the earlier era in which only union leaders were labeled as criminals, here the whole striking workforce fell into that anticivil category. The criminality of the striking PATCO workers was right at the center of debate. How far this had developed is clear in the August 23, 1981, interview with Secretary of Transportation Drew Lewis and Robert E. Poli of PATCO.

Bill Monroe (moderator): Mr. Secretary, you have called the controllers' long-range grievances probably legitimate. They have years of training, years invested in their jobs; they have families. If they should come along and say in the weeks ahead that "we made a mistake and we give up our strike; we'd just like to be back on the job," would you and President Reagan really treat them at that point as criminals toward whom no avenue of accommodation or forgiveness is possible?

Drew Lewis: First of all, we have not treated them as criminals. As you know, they could be subject to arrest; they could be subject to fines and also to prison sentences. Specifically, the president and I have both asked that this not be the case.

. . .

Monroe: Mr. Poli, your strike is now three weeks old. The airlines are running at about 75 percent of normal operations. The president says he won't tolerate an illegal strike, and the public is apparently behind the president in that. You seem to have lost the game or to be on the way to losing it. Do you see any way that PATCO can come out on top in this situation?

Robert Poli: I certainly do. I do not believe that all of those statistics are correct. . . . The truth of the matter is that it has hurt the aviation community, the public, very, very much. The unreasonableness that has been displayed, the attempts to break our union, the insensitive attitude toward what our issues were, the promises that we had received prior to going into negotiations, and the failure of the government to address our particular issues leaves us with only one position. . . . We believe that reasonableness will prevail, not only on the part of the government but by other people in this country, because we do see the polls changing in favor of the air traffic controller, once our story has been told.

Poli hoped for salvation that would not come. When Harry Truman moved to draft striking steelworkers into state service in 1952, he was portrayed as an overreaching tyrant who threatened the free-enterprise system. When President Reagan fired the air traffic controllers, he was simply seen as a tough negotiator—at least he didn't throw them in jail, as was his right. The days of union power and the egalitarian politics that had supported it had been fundamentally transformed. Reagan's actions and the inability of the labor movement to counter them with the civil power would have devastating consequences for the future and power of unions in America.

The mechanisms through which that influence played out demonstrate how important contingent interventions into the national conversation can be. After the Reagan intervention, private employers became tougher in their negotiations with their unions as well. It is not obvious why private employers suddenly felt emboldened to demand concessions from unions (which they did) given the president's show of force in this case, other than a sense that the rules had changed. In putting down the unions, Reagan fought for his liberal vision much like he would fight the Soviet Union and Salvadorian Leftists; he believed with John McClellan in "the liberty of the individual worker" who need not pay "tribute" to the bearers of the coercive and frightening power of the union.

To Change the Course of History

Scott Walker (governor of Wisconsin): In Wisconsin's history—little did I know how big it would be nationally—in Wisconsin's history I said, "This is our moment; this is our time to change the course of history."

—Scott Walker's reply during a prank phone call, February 23, 2011 (audiotape)

The midterm elections of 2010 were of critical importance for the union movement because, unknown to many voters who participated in them, they were an uncelebrated political target for that season's incoming Republican leadership. Barack Obama, not having made "the theory of the case" for the recession-fighting aspects of his healthcare bill, had left the unions to fend for themselves without political support in the sights of the fresh Republican recruits. In what must have been a surprise to most union leaders, unions and union power would return for a time to center stage of the national conversation.

The most shocking feature of the record on public unions specifically and labor unions in general is a pattern of near-complete silence on the topic—shocking because the topic was such a salient subject of discussion when the show was founded. In the period from late 2003 to early 2011 there is only one reference to collective bargaining in the *Meet the Press* transcripts, and this is in reference to a baseball strike. The primary references to labor unions are examples of constituency pressure and abuse of the same—"The labor unions raised $80 million for Barack Obama" (November 16, 2008); "Is government getting too big? Is spending too big? Are labor's too—are labor unions too powerful?" (November 8, 2009); and "I don't want anybody running for president telling the unions what they want to hear at the expense of the credibility of the United States" (June 22, 2008). Labor, collective bargaining, and class struggle on the whole had simply disappeared from the mainstream of the serious national conversation.

The absence of attention to the issue of bargaining power and the tendency to portray labor unions in anticivil terms help explain the dumbfounded response of the policy elite when the governor of Wisconsin initiated a plan to remove the traditional collective bargaining rights of public-sector workers in the very state where such social protections had first been implemented. Unable to recognize the source of perceived injustice that would direct thousands of grassroots activists into the civil drama of the Wisconsin labor crackdown, American opinion leaders could only compare the Wisconsin class struggle to the democratic liberation movements that people had been watching in the Arab world in places like Tunisia and Egypt, labeling Madison the "Tunisia of collective bargaining rights."[31] To many professionals, there was something almost ridiculous in the outcry of the largely white middle-class government workers who were roused to street protests on a scale not seen since the 1960s. Americans were still sensitive to the rhetoric of liberty as it applied in other parts of the world, but an unadorned rhetoric of equality had been effectively marginalized over decades of symbolic confrontation. Riots for democracy among people of color were intelligible, but irate midwesterners marching for economic justice for themselves seemed somehow out of place in the full shade of the eclipse of equality. In this light, it was perhaps the most surprising effect of the "Cheddar Revolution" in Madison that it had the capacity to bring the discussion of social rights back into national consciousness. Little wonder it was under the auspices of the "right to work" mentality that had been in steady play for decades.

One striking phase of this transformation occurred on February 20, 2011, when the topic broke through the *Meet the Press* threshold and the words "collective bargaining" were once again spoken on the NBC Sunday-morning show. Given the nature of the controversy, a guest on the roundtable, former governor of Michigan Jennifer Granholm, naturally gravitated toward the subject only to be abruptly cut off by David Gregory, who, using his well-calibrated D.C. political radar, knew instinctively that his banter had drifted too far into topics lacking currency and relevance. This produced a singular and unforgettable line in the history of the democratic class struggle: "I don't want to talk too much about collective bargaining and unions. OK." What was so special about this moment was not that Gregory was moved to silence a debate on collective bargaining (it had been mentioned ten times on the show by that time) but rather that his statement revealed something important about the conventional wisdom in Washington. It had been the informal line of *Meet the Press* for more than a decade not to talk too much about the industrial-era concept of collective bargaining. What Gregory revealed was not a bias (in the sense of a personal deviation from received best practice) but a fair judgment of what was worth talking about for how long.

Jennifer Granholm: If you want to have a discussion about collective bargaining, have that. But this is about deficits. And I can just tell you, as governor of Michigan over the past eight years, I cut more out of state government than—as a percentage, per capita—than any state in the country. Every single year we had to cut. . . . And I did it in partnership with the unions. Our unions gave over $700 million in concessions. I asked them to pay the new employees 20 percent toward their healthcare benefits. They don't even have a pension. They have 401(k)s. They have a defined contribution plan and not a defined benefit plan.

David Gregory: OK. I, I don't want to talk too much about collective bargaining and unions. OK.

Granholm: I'm just saying—

Gregory: I got it. Yeah. Ed.

Ed Gillespie (Republican strategist): All right. Well, let me end with this, which is
we're not talking about eliminating collective bargaining; what we're talking
about is limiting collective bargaining to wages, not the benefits package—

Gregory: Right, right.

Gillespie: —and having the union members vote themselves every year whether or
not they want to continue that.

Gregory: Let me, let me continue on this theme about who's kind of winning the,
the austerity conversation.

One week makes all the difference. By the time the February 28 program
rolled out, the massive protests in Wisconsin had become something that
no one in the nation could ignore. They were the talk of the town, as
was the governor's assault on the accepted practices of collective bargaining for public employees. A new narrative emerged to the effect that the
new governor of Wisconsin was masterminding an attempt to crush the
unions in Wisconsin in a reversal that he saw explicitly and self-consciously as modeled on the Reagan example in the 1981 PATCO strike. Walker
was promoting a bold programmatic agenda, but he was also engaged in
a massive civil positioning effort. He was creating facts on the ground.
Where no political debate existed, he created one over the laws guaran-
teeing public-sector collective bargaining. Framing the resulting political
phenomena in terms of the rhetoric of freedom, Walker hoped not only to
eliminate the unions from their positions of power but to change the conversation about the public-sector workforce, much like Reagan had done.
The mood was austerity following on the fiscal crises unfolding in Europe,
and the pathway to frugality and personal responsibility was through the
public unions.

A famous line from Karl Marx describes so many examples of civil
drama in public life: "History repeats itself, first as tragedy, second as
farce."[32] When Reagan crushed the air traffic controllers in a dramatic
move, it evoked pity from the *Meet the Press* moderator Bill Monroe.
This time Scott Walker, self-consciously emulating Reagan as a kind
of midwestern Louis Napoleon, found himself the butt of jokes as the
result of a crank phone call in which he admitted that his preemptive
strike on the public-sector unions was an attempt to change the course
of history much as Ronald Reagan had done in crushing the air traffic
controllers.

David Gregory: "Change the course of history." And this is where critics say, you know, this governor is really more of an ideologue than someone who wants to solve a serious problem. You're going farther than other Republicans who have taken on pension and healthcare costs to really go active—after collective bargaining. And by your own admission, you're saying, "Well, there's some areas where we just can't afford that level of austerity." But if you're serious about austerity, doesn't it have to be a situation where everybody gets affected?

Scott Walker: Well, in the end, the reason I made that comment, I do believe that this is our moment in Wisconsin's history. . . . We're broke. Like nearly every other state across the country, we're broke. And it's about time somebody stood up and told the truth in this state and said, "Here's our problem. Here's the solution," and acted on it. Because, if we don't, we fail to make a commitment to the future. Our children will face even more dire consequences than what we face today.

In the tradition of pointed *Meet the Press* questions, Gregory engaged in the drama of collective bargaining playing out before him by highlighting the strategic, even ideological, nature of Walker's actions.

Gregory: Governor, if you're really serious about the state being broke, you have a deal that you could take to get the contributions you need to solve the problem at hand. Why not separate that out from your views about collective bargaining?

Walker: But, but, David, my point is repeatedly, as a former local government official, I know that collective bargaining has a cost, and when I'm cutting out more [than] a billion dollars from aid to local governments in this next two-year budget, I need to do what no other governor's doing across the country. They're all cutting. All but a handful are cutting. The difference is where we want to be unique in Wisconsin is we have to give those local governments the tools.

. . .

Gregory: Governor, how does this end?

Walker: Well, I'm an optimist. I'm an eternal optimist.

The governor had reason to be optimistic. Walker's efforts to defang the public-sector unions of Wisconsin were largely successful, and he survived a recall effort. The stewards of private enterprise had secured one crucial piece in their larger project of narrative repair necessitated by the country's reaction to the Great Depression of the 1930s—they had positioned collective bargaining in opposition to democracy. The rhetorical fruits of the victory were juicy. Haley Barbour, chair of the Republican Governor's Association, had crowed on an October 31, 2010, episode, "Look, Democrats are running from Barack Obama on healthcare reform like scalded dogs."

Democrats were afraid to articulate ideas that had once been central to their cause. They could no longer animate their initiatives to counter the growing power of big business with alarming class villains drawn from the political storybook. In contrast, by stigmatizing the union boss as a reincarnated Jimmy Hoffa, the private enterprisers had added an unlikely and unwitting enemy of democratic civilization to the repertoire: the public schoolteacher. The irony was that over the course of the American Century, the main characters of the American political storybook had shifted. Where Progressives once told stories of capitalist fat cats and bloated bankers who abused their monopoly power to cheat the consumer, stick it to the borrower, crowd our the entrepreneur, and exploit the worker, the only symbolic bigwig available to public debate in the twenty-first century was the public schoolteacher and the unions that supported her. It took a lot of hard work to argue this eclipse of equality, but it was finally done.

At the height of the Great Recession brought on by the kind of casino capitalism that FDR was elected to constrain, the social rights agenda so crucial to the New Deal strategy had lost its authenticity and appeal. It no longer seemed like any question of democracy and human rights hung on the guarantee of collective bargaining rights, and no new institutions were being seriously proposed as a check on concentrated economic power in the workplace. A union supporter might imagine that she had been the real target of the giant wicked conspiracy, but that is a paranoid response. The transformation was accomplished in plain sight. Business had simply outmaneuvered and outargued labor in the public square. First they came for the Reds; then they came for the rackets, after which the private-enterprise agenda was safeguarded from any effective checks on its dominance.

In an environment so ripe for resistance, an economic progressive should have reason for hope. There may be reason to suspect that the widespread recognition of the problem of economic inequality dramatized by the Occupy Wall Street movement could trigger a new era of union growth and its accompanying social egalitarian agenda. Advocates for this approach look to the celebrated past with the hope that a new union movement could inject what Nelson Lichtenstein has called the vitalization of the democratic ethos that came with the union movement at its best.[33] But if that movement is still to come, it will face a political culture armed with the rich literary devices of a political storybook ready to dismiss it.

7

CONCLUSION
To Clarify American Opinion

Meet the Press is produced in cooperation with the editors of the
American Mercury, one of America's distinguished magazines of opinion.
Its purpose is to clarify American opinion on the major issues of the
day, to give America the opportunity to hear trained newspapermen
get the facts from those who have seen and studied them.

—Moderator Albert Warner, June 25, 1945

IN THIS BOOK I HAVE TRIED TO SHOW how the television program
Meet the Press is more than a rarefied form of entertainment or a mere platform for political public relations work, although it is both. *Meet the Press*
is a window with a view of the evolving landscape of central tendencies of
American political culture. It is a barometer of the conventional wisdom.
Beginning as an experimental radio program through which to publicize
the magazine of opinion *American Mercury*, *Meet the Press* has developed
into something that is perhaps unexpected. Over its nearly seventy-year
history, it has become the leading example of a now-established form
of mass democratic engagement, which along with its sister programs,
CBS's *Face the Nation*, *Fox News Sunday*, CNN's *State of the Union*, and
ABC's *This Week*, has opened a space within the national conversation for
a mediated but serious dialogue between an engaged mass public and the
political classes in Washington, D.C. In so doing, it has created a perfect
opportunity to study the evolution of elite opinion in the nation's capital.

Meet the Press has produced nearly seven decades of expertly crafted
focus groups and interviews with the best-positioned figures on the leading political subjects in American history, and it is hard to imagine a better
research design for this purpose. A touchstone of insider political culture,
it has become a kind of arbiter of the national conversation and a labora-
tory of legitimacy. And if it is nothing else, it is surely a singular record of

rhetorical history, meticulously preserved by the program's founder, Larry Spivak. It has much to teach us about who we are by taking us along a narrow journey along the path we have taken. The resulting story is not always pleasant or encouraging, but it is seldom dull.

Looking back over this rather daunting project, I realize it began with a jolt and a puzzle. The jolt was the death of Tim Russert, with whom I had spent so many Sunday mornings on my television screen that he felt like an old friend. The puzzle emerged soon after. I wondered why those with access to official public discourse in Washington reacted to the economic disaster of the Great Recession so differently than they had to the Great Depression seventy-five years before.

It is easy to be cynical about these things, but I was still somewhat surprised that there was so little respectable talk at that point about economic democracy, malefactors of great wealth, bargaining power in the workplace, contradictions of interest between capital and labor, and all of the other tropes and catchphrases that were so inseparable from my mediated memories of the New Deal. George W. Bush did feel alarmed enough to remark that he thought capitalism would survive, but to my eye, less than a handful of leaders of established opinion were willing to engage the old language of economic decline on the Democratic side.

The spirit of the puzzle was well represented by a frequent guest on *Meet the Press*, the influential columnist David Brooks, who described it in an appearance on July 11, 2010:

> David Brooks (*New York Times*): And to me the big picture is that if Harry Hopkins, the great liberal from FDR's administration, came back and said, "I'm going to create a perfect liberal moment. We're going to have a big financial crisis caused by Wall Street, sort of; we're going to have the biggest natural disaster in American history caused by an oil company; we're going to have a very talented Democratic president; we're going to give him some money to spend to create a lot of programs." And after all that, it's still not a liberal moment; it's a conservative moment. That makes me think liberalism isn't quite going to sell in this country at any moment. If it's not selling now, it'll never sell.

Liberalism used to sell like hotcakes to members of both parties. Something had changed since 1945, something of the first order of importance.[1] I was eager to find a way to demonstrate in a reliable and accurate way what that was. Although public opinion data suggested that Americans remained operational (policy) liberals even while they were ideological (symbolic) conservatives,[2] I suspected that the change had taken place on another level, not in the hearts of the people but in the minds of the leadership cadres of the American influential. I was inclined to favor the opinions of elites over the masses as evidence for my answer and the justifications for their actions provided in public debate as the data. Recognizing the obvious, I decided that *Meet the Press* would become my methodological vehicle in this analysis. Here is what I found.

The change in establishment reactions between the Great Depression and the Great Recession had much to do with how both Democrats and Republicans managed and deployed the American political storybook, in particular with respect to the two stylized narratives that had been joined in what we can think of as a master synthesis. What I call the master synthesis brought together the animating philosophies of two pivotal moments in modern American politics that I call the lessons of 1896 and 1932, respectively. In the realigning election of 1896, members of the Republican Party under William McKinley found a way to position its big-business program with the traditional values of small-business free markets and the virtue of personal freedom against the enemy-of-the-state bureaucrat. They consecrated this less-than-obvious, big business agenda with the label "private enterprise," and Americans of all persuasions paid homage to it. In the realigning election of 1932, the Democratic Party found a way to successfully position the populist and progressive social protection programs within the American rhetorical tradition by emphasizing the civil virtue of non-ascriptive equality against the abusive power of corporate bigwigs. They consecrated this approach with the label "social security," and Americans became similarly attached to it. By midcentury, these two ideas were joined in a master synthesis that defined both Democratic and Republican worldviews.

The practical significance of the consecration of these larger causes was that any person or party that systematically broke with either of them was guaranteed to be condemned with virulent and volatile opposition. Private enterprise was here to stay, but so, too, was social security (the idea, not just the popular program). On the left, this meant that both Communism and state-centered Socialism were officially no-nos. Any critique of concentrated economic power would have to respect the private-enterprise system or find itself branded as heretical. After 1896, private enterprise was a done deal, and Socialism wouldn't happen here. On the right, this meant that the nineteenth-century model of laissez-faire, laissez-passer economics would have to remain a thing of the past. A modern American economy was destined to remained one mixed between private and public sources of value creation. After 1932, domestic peace required that business respect the limited basket of social rights that Franklin Roosevelt had managed to fill for them with the more successful products of his "bold persistent experimentation" and at the same time that the people respect the corporation's capacity to fill the dinner pail.

This is the rhetorical mode through which the political classes forestalled political dysfunction in the form of class conflict. It worked for a long time, but certain powerful segments of the business community never really accepted it. After World War II, they set out to make the world safe for private enterprise, a project with both international (anticommunist) and intranational (antilabor) points of focus. From various centers of power and through various national champions, the Old Dealers successfully challenged the master synthesis in the court of public opinion and achieved remarkable success. Through the mechanisms of democratic competition and the cultivation of the political culture in directions consistent with their interests, the advocates of untrammeled private enterprise have successfully untaught the lesson of 1932 to successive cohorts of Americans. Suddenly, John Stuart Mill seems much more prescient than does John Maynard Keynes.

To paraphrase Eric Johnston, one of the leading architects of imagination in the era of the classless civil sphere, each of the truths we live by has a history.[3] This history of a classless America emerges in the *Meet the Press* record in the context of bloody tensions around race, culture, and eventually religion that could be exploited in a way that would fracture the midcentury master synthesis and return the American debate to its pre-Depression groove. The captains of global enterprise were less than bigots, but they were clever enough not to let the crises of the disruptive civil dramas of the 1960s go to waste, and this occasionally put them on the wrong side of the arc of history. They sought, with desperation, for a way to make the moral case for capitalism. In this effort, they could deploy their coercive powers, but they were clever enough to know that it was only through the invention of a new global solidarity on the American model that their visions could be realized. In their efforts they drew upon earlier examples of liberal innovation. In a major study of the role played by ideas in the development of industrial society, Reinhard Bendix described the process succinctly.

Wherever enterprises are set up, a few command and many obey. The few, however, have seldom been satisfied to command without a higher justification even when they abjured all interest in ideas, and the many have seldom been docile enough not to provoke such justifications.[4]

Through the patient efforts of cautious and artful opinion leaders like Ronald Reagan, Milton Friedman, Alan Greenspan, and Jack Kemp, the champions of resurgent neoliberalism in the 1970s were able to channel concerns about expansion in the scope of government from the social to the cultural dimension, thereby introducing paralyzing doubt in the persuadable public about the legitimacy of even minimal efforts toward social protection and economic security. They could exploit middle America's discomfort with the use of state power to eradicate cultural hegemony (the masculine, Anglo-American paradigm) to profane state efforts to increase economic opportunity and reduce economic disparities. In this way, the antidemocratic forces of intolerance (the racists, sexists, and homophobes) that were on display in the fight for racial justice and cultural rights were used to shift the ideological divide in partisan politics from class to culture. By channeling discomfort with cultural rights liberalism against previously acceptable social protection measures like Social Security and Medicare, liberals-now-known-as-conservatives could stymie and even roll back the social rights liberalism of the New Deal, all within the playbook of the individual rights liberalism of the nineteenth century.

For the corporate progressive and the classical liberal, this is winwin. When Republicans win, the welfare state is curtailed. When Democrats win, cultural diversity is expanded. For the traditional Democrat, the situation is rife with tension. On one front, their efforts to unseat bigotry have realized returns once impossible to imagine—the election of President Obama and the explosion of a gay rights agenda are apt expressions. But on the other, any efforts to aggressively curtail concentrated economic power come across as little more than nauseating displays of demagoguery.

This is a tension that has been with us for some time, as this example from the July 25, 1996, interview with the civil rights icon Andrew Young makes clear.

Andrew Young: You know, I think what I'm going to say is that America was on the way to dealing with its problems. We're doing well with the race problem. We're not doing well at all with the class problem. . . . We simply say the government—I simply say that we've got to take some responsibility for the least of these, God's children, in our society, and we're not going to be a great nation until we deal with the problems of poverty. Poverty is not black. Poverty is white. Poverty is largely female. Those are the big issues we have to address.

Tell a story in the halls of power about the abuse of power with a barbarian, bureaucrat, or a bigot as your villain and you will find a ready audience on one side or other of the aisle; but tell one about an abusive bigwig, and members of your audience will express little more than ambivalent concern, irrespective of their party affiliation; they have been ideologically inoculated. We have cut off Americans from their intuitive know-how in spotting abuses perpetrated by the private elite, what Aristotle called "the Few." All other societies appear susceptible to oligarchy, but America comes off as exceptional. We fear "the One" and "the Many" (anyone can demonize the Other), but our era of free-market capitalism now seems to us as the only one in history in which concentrated economic power poses no risks to the civil society. The result is protracted social conflict amid a confusion of categories. Americans know that something fundamental is wrong with their system of government, but they have no common language through which to bridge the gaps between and among them to develop an alternative.

Accordingly, American liberalism itself is stymied: one party fights for freedom, one party fights for tolerance, but no one fights for equality. One side demands the liberalization of markets and limits on government power in the economy. The other side demands respect for difference, cultural modernization, and active state support for a cosmopolitan ethic of diversity and inclusion. Each side signals its assent to the other by respecting the lines in the sand that they make clear the other must not cross. Republicans will brook no interference from government in the management of the free-enterprise system or taxes on its profits. They have successfully positioned these ideas within the rhetoric of freedom and the imagery of dependency and bureaucracy. Leading members of the Democratic coalition have become the modern defenders of inclusion. They will not tolerate any overt expressions of bigotry or any abuse of the power of cultural privilege to the disadvantage of members of vulnerable groups.

The rhetoric of tolerance and the uncivil image of the bigot have been their chosen routes to civil power. These two sides have found a modus operandi through which both the rhetoric of freedom and the rhetoric of tolerance can coexist insofar as the Right embraces inclusivity and the Left does not interfere with the right of management to manage. As a side effect, outrage about economic inequality is slotted to take on only symbolic expression. This modus operandi is the eclipse of equality, and you just lived through it.

But there are hints that the eclipse is ending. We may be on the cusp of an epochal pivot from the rhetoric of tolerance to that of equality. As things that can't go on forever don't, we begin to see hints in leadership rhetoric on both sides suggestive of a subtle rebalancing of priorities. Republicans, Democrats, and libertarians are all scrambling to occupy the abandoned high ground of egalitarian principles in a time of spiraling inequality. A Democrat is as solicitous of a fat cat as a member of the next coalition, and our corporate leaders generally fear the very mention of social rights for economic groups enough to torpedo their own ship, but the natural balance in these efforts is in the direction of the center-left frame. As Lord Acton's maxim counsels, "power tends to corrupt," and the balance of power between the job creator and her workers, consumers, and stakeholders has pushed the needle steadily in the direction of corporate corruption for a generation.

Survey data suggest that Democrats are more likely to be elected if they can find a way to articulate their social protection agenda to an ambivalent electorate, but if it turns out that past is prologue, we have nothing to expect in the near term but increasing polarization amid surging waves of frustration and unrest. Someone usually finds a way to capitalize on those conditions. The conflicts of the future may well play out in the confused and increasingly unrealistic ways that have been characteristic of the national conversation over the past four decades. But wherever this river flows, you can watch the wheels go round each Sunday on *Meet the Press.*

EPILOGUE
If It's Sunday, It's *Meet the Press*

As I was finishing this book in a coffee shop in the late summer of 2012, I happened to overhear a conversation between two hip women in their twenties about *Meet the Press* and the Sunday shows that spoke to my purpose in a way that only serendipitous events can. Their opening conversation began in this way:

First woman: What did you do this morning?

Second woman: I watched a bit of the Sunday shows. It's a guilty pleasure.

First woman: I'm not so sure that watching the Sunday-morning talk shows is a guilty pleasure; it's more of a civic responsibility.

Second woman: Well, yeah, but it hasn't been the same since Tim died.

First woman: I know; Tim Russert was the best questioner. He really cut to the heart of the story.

Second woman: I still love the morning shows though. I always loved *Meet the Press*. It's the best way keep up on what's really going on. It's just part of my ritual.

I don't know about you, but I wouldn't have been surprised to hear this kind of thing from a couple of middle-aged white guys schmoozing in some northern Virginia haunt where I wrote the book, but I didn't expect it from two urbane young women in Madison, Wisconsin. To me, this chance event speaks to a larger reality: *Meet the Press* is as relevant today as it was when it was first broadcast on the radio in June 1945, but in a different way. In those days, *Meet the Press* was a novel media crossover that made the jump from print to broadcast. Today it is the background against which newer media and formats trope and innovate. What those women I overheard recognized was that as stormy discourse proliferates, one requires a safe refuge in which to take one's bearings.[1] *Meet the Press* is that place for the Beltway influential and therefore for all of us who care about how they think and what they do.

It now seems somehow more exciting to turn to Twitter for the latest political news, yet the weekly rhythm of harried politicians answering pointed questions on Sunday morning helps us make political sense amid the noise of all those tweets. On Facebook we discover how our friends are lately rationalizing their existing convictions, but only on Sunday morning do we learn which of these clashing justifications has won the weekly battle. The *Daily Show* and *Saturday Night Live* are more likely to introduce clever new catchphrases and images to political culture, but on Sunday morning we see how these intuitive references meld with policy arguments as the coauthored narrative of our political drama unfolds. Among other things, C-Span provides steady, direct, and continuous access to official public debate, but lawmakers often speak there in cynical monologue to empty chambers for a detached media audience carrying little of the kind of heated and responsive dialogue we find on any typical Sunday morning. The opinion magazines and the op-ed pages of the leading national newspapers (along with the clearinghouse Web sites that distribute them) provide a sense of nuance and intellectual satisfaction, but on Sunday morning we discover how these deeper analyses can be defended by the political principals in the face of developing events. It is true that our twenty-four-hour public sphere has become more densely populated and structurally differentiated since 1945, but not one of the innovations just listed has replaced what we learn about ourselves on Sunday morning. *Meet the Press* is far from perfect, but it is where we go to get serious about politics.

Sometimes, the most important things are hidden in plain sight. From the standpoint of opinion research, *Meet the Press* is one of those things. Here we have a consistent and reliable record of the conversations that mattered each and every week dating back to the rise of the American global experiment in leadership, yet no one has systematically analyzed it. It is easy to become maudlin about these things, but Tim Russert was right to claim that the program archive is a national treasure; it is certainly a gold mine for the student of symbolic politics.

Much has changed in our moral politics since 1945, and we can find evidence in the *Meet the Press* archives. My summary of the change is the title for this book: "the eclipse of equality." It is hardly news to suggest that Americans have never thought wisely or well about matters of economic inequality, but in historical perspective we have become less likely to tell economic stories in which the lead villain is an economic bigwig abusing his competitive power in the marketplace than we were when *Meet the Press* first went on air.[2] If you are a Republican or a conservative, this is all for the better, but you will still have to recognize that it does represent a meaningful evolution in our rhetorical imaginary. Back in 1945, one could still find southern demagogues screaming fascist wherever they saw big businesses with market power. Today, policy elites are largely repulsed by insinuations that demonize the rich. That is meaningful change.

Consider this response from the African American mayor of Newark, Cory Booker, on May 20, 2012, in which he responded to an advertisement that President Obama aired attacking his opponent in the 2012 presidential race for his connections to a venture capital firm.

Cory Booker: But the last point I'll make is this kind of stuff is nauseating to me on both sides. It's nauseating to the American public. Enough is enough. Stop attacking private equity; stop attacking Jeremiah Wright. This stuff has got to stop because what it does is it undermines, to me, what this country should be focused on. It's a distraction from the real issues. It's either going to be a small campaign about this crap or it's going to be a big campaign, in my opinion, about the issues that the American public cares about.

What makes this example so striking is that Mayor Booker—a Democrat acting as a surrogate for a Democratic president—was nauseated by what he saw as demonizing attacks on unregulated finance capitalists where once Franklin Roosevelt had welcomed their hatred. No doubt misleading political attacks and diverting innuendos are nauseating for those in the know, but they are also the fare that feeds the moral imagination—the link between what the psychologist Jonathan Haidt calls "the emotional dog and its rational tail." It is in story-stuff that analytical arguments about theories of change and abstract principles become anchored in the literary intuitions of our political unconscious. Imagery and innuendo will always play a prominent role in politics, and we only become nauseated by those images that have crossed the line from fair to foul, from cooked to raw.[3] Where we draw that line on which issues is the vital matter.

It's these little moments that tell us so much about how far we have traveled. The ideological journey we have taken has been one in which something had to be given so that something else might be gained. Hindsight suggests that the American Left could fight its way toward cultural inclusion, ethnic tolerance, and celebration of group difference only by accepting institutional changes that led to spiraling economic inequality among individuals in all groups both at home and abroad. As a result of the consistent antigovernment focus of the forces arrayed against them, American liberals were consistently forced to choose between their two guiding principles and reliably chose diversity over equality, group rights over individual opportunities, bigots over bigwigs. Given the state of the world and the realities of political geography, few could blame them for it, but the result has been predictable; the institutions that once protected the competitively disadvantaged of every race, creed, and color from disruptive market forces have been whittled away with grudging public approval since the Kennedy administration.

Over the course of this transformation, *Meet the Press* has not only interviewed newsmakers but has also made news and continues to do so. Just two weeks prior to that interview with Mayor Booker, Vice President Joe Biden made history on the program in a conversation about the cutting-edge issue of the diversity wars, gay marriage.

David Gregory: I'm curious. You know, the president has said that his views on gay marriage, on same-sex marriage have evolved. But he's opposed to it. You're opposed to it. Have your views—evolved?

Joe Biden: Look—I just think—that—the good news is that as more and more Americans become to understand what this is all about is a simple proposition. Who do you love? Who do you love? And will you be loyal to the person you love? And that's what people are finding out is what—what all marriages, at their root, are about—whether they're marriages of lesbians or gay men or heterosexuals.

Gregory: Is that what you believe now? Are you—

Biden: That's what I believe.

Gregory: And you're comfortable with same-sex marriage now?

Biden: . . . I am absolutely comfortable with the fact that men marrying men, women marrying women, and heterosexual men and women marrying another are entitled to the same exact rights—all the civil rights, all the civil liberties. And quite frankly, I don't see much of a distinction beyond that.

That Sunday morning, David Gregory asked the question heard round the world, because Biden's answer and the response to it inspired President Obama to finally come out publicly with a statement that his views had changed on the subject of homosexuality. Joe Biden demonstrated in a setting to which influential people were paying attention that views on homosexuality had evolved, and it was time for one part of the political community to embrace an approach that vilified sexual bigotry and to haggle over it with the other side.

Little wonder that the issue that spoke to core convictions of the silent majority of the party's constituency was one that had almost nothing to do with economic inequality. In the opening days of the *Meet the Press* era, cultural rights for minorities were held in slight regard, but as we pass through the eclipse of equality, the only issues that prompt both outrage and policy response on the left have more to do with the recognition of group difference and less with structural legacies of economic disadvantage. As a group, African Americans were victims of both disrespect and systematic exploitation. In contrast, gay people, men of means in particular, are victims only of disrespect and its consequences.[4]

Obama's statement, and the policy shift it implied, was a watershed on the topic of sexuality and the American family, and few should be surprised that it all started on *Meet the Press*. *Meet the Press* is no longer the only game in town, but the genre of the Sunday-morning public affairs show that *Meet the Press* invented has no rival for what it does—test the boundaries of the conventional wisdom, otherwise known as the democratic consensus.

Let me repeat my suspicion that although I think the period after World War II can be described from a rhetorical perspective as an eclipse of equality, I don't think the situation can last. We have already seen murmurings for a rebalancing of values on the left as people struggle to remember what it felt like to be outraged by excessive occupational stratification. From a policy perspective, Occupy Wall Street was little more than a siren call, but the persuadable American can be roped to the mast for only so long. Locke argued in his *Letter Concerning Toleration* that oppression is a persistent inducement to "seditious commotions,"[5] and although from an impartial perspective one has to admit that American conservatives may prove right in their support of the ethical superiority of the laissez-faire doctrines of the nineteenth century, they are surely wrong to suppose that Americans will tolerate the perceived injustices that flow from them forever. Our political storybook is full enough of rich bigwigs and their misdeeds that someday soon, someone with enough power to act will be willing to explore it.

ACKNOWLEDGMENTS

WHENEVER A WRITER SETS OUT TO TACKLE A PROJECT as punishing as this one has been, he only does so knowing that many people are there to push him along and to pick up the pieces when they occasionally fail to fit together. These people come in many forms: family friends, colleagues, students, assistants, and service providers. I have relied upon the assistance of many people in all of these categories.

Let me begin by thanking my wife, Andrea Robles, who had the audacity and good sense to demand that I pursue a research project that in some way took advantage of my proximity to Washington, D.C.—even if it did mean that I would spend a few years commuting downtown when my office was conveniently located on the same side of the Virginia bridges as was the place I sleep. As any of you who have tackled a big project like this know, if your partner is not behind you, the project is on top of you; Andrea kept me on top of the project from beginning to end.

Along with Andrea, I thank my two daughters, Alessandra and Gabriela, who, in addition to being constant delights, were always as generous in yielding their Sunday morning Daddy time to *Meet the Press* as one could ever expect them to be. I thank my good friend Keenan Yoho for his passionate engagement with the ideas presented here as they developed. He is that irreplaceable intellectual companion who keeps the social scientist from losing touch with how those outside the Beltway think and feel, however jarring that may be. Thanks as well to my parents, Joan and Jim, who surrounded me with the interpretive materials through which to decode this perplexing democratic experiment: from my youth to the present day. There was never a time in my life when I wanted for books on social theory, politics, and modern life and a ready environment to discuss them. This also holds for the entire Simmons clan, a smart and hardy bunch, with special thanks to Jason and Kelly Simmons for tolerating my endless musings as this project developed.

Thanks as well to members of my new family for their support. I never knew what it was like to have brothers, but now I do in Javier and Ricardo Robles. Thanks as well to their supporting casts, Sorabel, Connie, Javiercito, Arianna, Katerina, and Derrick. I also appreciate how stabilizing it can be to have new parents as I do in Sergio Robles and Lili Sanchez-Ruiz; I think it's fair to say that without the selfless devotion of Lili in support of my little domestic platoon, there might have been no book.

Many colleagues have served me as guides on this journey. Foremost among these are Neil Gross, whose unmatched nose for social theory provided important clues toward a suitable frame for the project and whose consistent interest and advice at key moments made the difference; Byron Shafer, who cast his keen eye for American political culture over the proposal, helping me recognize both its promise and its faults; Rich Rubenstein, who more than anyone else served to keep my eye on the prize of writing a readable yet intellectually engaging book for a general audience; and Mark Goodale, who believed enough in the project to put some skin in the game. Thanks as well to Kevin Avruch, who, in addition to good advice, provided a venue for the early presentation of the research as it developed, and to the Point of View Committee for providing financial support. The dean of the School for Conflict Analysis and Resolution, Andrea Bartoli, has always been a big fan of my work, and I thank him for his steady encouragement and leadership as well as for promoting the project in various important ways.

I am also thankful to all of my other colleagues at George Mason University who provided me with valuable feedback on the project: Sara Cobb, Sandy Cheldelin, Leslie Dwyer, Thomas Flores, Susan Hirsch, Karina Korostelina, Terrence Lyons, Susan Allen Nan, Agnieszka Paczynska, Jamie Price, Dan Rothbart, Mara Schoeny, and Steven Vallas. Special thanks go to my research assistant Jana El Horr, who spent nearly as much time in the *Meet the Press* archives as I did in the ramifying early days of the project when I could have followed one path or another. As she well knows, without her assistance I would have written a very different book. I also want to thank my graduate research assistants who provided key technical assistance. R. J. Nickels and Hussein Yusuf were instrumental in guiding the sampling process, and Julie Minde read over the project in full and helped prepare the index. Thanks go to Sara Moore, a devout and attentive early editor, who pored over my prose with that invaluable sociologist's eye. As books have many different lives, I want to highlight the support of the incomparable Michael Shank, who was a great help in moving this conversation from the ivory tower to the realm of blood, toil, tears, and sweat.

The ideas developed here did not begin with this project. I would therefore like to thank those professors from my student days who helped me along toward what feels to me like clarity: William H. Sewell Sr., Bob Hauser, Erik Wright, Joel Rogers, Wolfgang Streeck, John Logan, Jonathan Zeitlin, Leann Tigges, Jeremy Freese, Pam Oliver, John Levi Martin, Gary Green, Jess Gilbert, Paula Voos, Robert B. Miller, and Werner De Bondt.

I want to give a special shout-out to the staff at the Library of Congress. This is an incredible bunch. The staff at the Motion Pictures and Television Reading Room were constant colleagues throughout. Thank you to Rosemary Hanes, Josie Walters-Johnston, and Zoran Sinobad for handling all those transcripts and teaching me to load 16mm film on a flatbed viewer. It almost made me feel like one of the film scholars around whom I worked. Just as helpful were those in the Recorded Sound Reference Center, Bryan Cornell, Karen Fishman, and Jan McKee, who were forced to digitize almost the whole of the *Meet the Press* collection just in time for my listening demand. I also appreciated the help with those fast-expiring passwords. I spent a good deal of time in the Manuscripts Division of the library as well and have nothing but awe and respect for their work.

It may be a little corny to thank your editor with profusion, but there can be no other in the business who operates as does Kate Wahl at Stanford University Press. Not only was she engaged in this idea early and often but she provided comments on drafts of the project from beginning to end. If ever an author was lucky in finding an editorial match, it is I.

I am grateful to a host of people who will not appear in these acknowledgments, but I would like to thank a number of reviewers of the project, including Gianpaolo Baiocchi, John Paul Lederach, Louis Kriesberg, and Lester Kurtz, along with three anonymous reviewers, whose feedback was at the same time bracing and inspiring.

I would also be remiss if I did not thank the members of the staff at the School for Conflict Analysis and Resolution (SCAR) who helped me with this project, among them Paul Snodgrass, Julie Shedd, Jay Moon, Cassie Ammen, and Jacquie Greif. What a great, dedicated bunch of world improvers they are. The same goes for the SCAR students who have listened to me and questioned my assumptions as they progressed.

A final thanks to all my friends, acquaintances, and interlocutors who haunt the coffee shops that served as my drafting office. Remember this: conviviality trumps writer's block. And thanks to Tom Zinnen and Kristen Velyvis for all those barbecues in the crunch.

Solon Simmons
Madison, Wisconsin
August 2012

NOTES

Chapter 1

1. All epigraphs are taken from transcript material from *Meet the Press*.

2. Ball and NBC News 1997, 3.

3. This langauge was part of the introductory material in the early days of the program.

4. C-SPAN 1991.

5. Goldman 2001, 85.

6. *Meet the Press* has long been a big newsmaker, but if your interest in it is related to the massive media effect you imagine it to have, you are missing what is most interesting about the program: an effect rather than a cause. Before anything else, *Meet the Press* is an indicator of the established mood and what it means to be taken seriously in big league American politics.

7. Gramsci 1971.

8. Most people are not aware that Chris Wallace, the well-known host of *Fox News Sunday*, was the moderator of *Meet the Press* before Tim Russert. His tenure was short but may be seen as a shift from the more liberal coverage that was characteristic of Kalb's era. No excerpts in the book draw on Wallace's questions, but he has become perhaps the dominant force on Sunday morning after Tim Russert's exit.

Chapter 2

1. Newcomb 1947.

2. Azar, Jureidini, and McLaurin 1978; Azar 1985, 1990.

3. One of the leading figures in decoding symbolic politics of the type I am speaking of here is George Lakoff. His work on authoritarianism and metaphors was pathbreaking and insightful but seems best subsumed in the more recent evolutionary interpretations of moral psychology like that of Jonathan Haidt. In the end, it's part of the family of brain interpretations. In the most convincing version of his model of moral foundations, which he describes in analogy to taste buds, these taste buds are conceived as modules that can be plugged into new biological systems and are hypothesized not to vary across individuals and cultures, although the "cuisines" offered by historical moral systems do vary a great deal. Evolutionary research suggests that at least five such taste buds exist

(a sixth liberty/oppression strikes me as a misspecification of the model): (1) care/harm, (2) sanctity/degradation, (3) fairness/cheating, (4) loyalty/betrayal, and (5) authority/subversion. Lakoff's strict father is a reinterpretation of the classic social science concept, the Authoritarian Personality, but is also directly related to Haidt's authority/subversion module. See Lakoff and Johnson 1980; Lakoff 2002, 2004; Haidt 2001, 2003, 2012; Adorno et al. 1950; Jay 1996.

4. De Waal 2009.

5. Petty, Cacioppo, and Schumann 1983; Petty and Cacioppo 1986, 1996.

6. Edelman 1964, 1975, 1985.

7. Wilson 1999.

8. Gould 1997.

9. Damasio 1994, 1999; Davidson et al. 2003; Westen 2007.

10. Marcus, Neuman, and Mackuen 2000.

11. Much of this debate and of twentieth-century social science is indebted, for good and ill, to Friedrich Nietzsche (2000). The ill is explored in Bloom 1987, but see also Badiou 2002.

12. Haidt 2012, 112.

13. It is useful to locate Habermas's ideas against the backdrop of the context in which they were developed. An important precursor idea to the public sphere was that of the "culture industry" promoted by Theodor Adorno and Max Horkheimer. See Horkheimer and Adorno 1989.

14. A theoretical discussion of how this space of opinion is organized can be found in Jacobs and Townsley 2011.

15. The literature on coded binaries in mythical thinking is both broad and deep, but among the classic treatments is that of Levi-Strauss. See Levi-Strauss 1968, 1989.

16. Alexander and Smith 1993; Alexander 1992, 2008, 2010.

17. We also find in Alexander how contingent are those links between analysis and imagery, between our final moral vocabularies and our policy preferences. This is in no way unique to Alexander's approach but is a key feature. It does mark this model as distinct from that proposed by the moral psychologists who presume a more direct link between objects and moral judgments than this mediated and socially constructed perspective suggests. The summary characterization of this approach to sociology is "the strong program." Alexander and Smith 2001.

18. Narrative works both on the level of conscious reason and on the level of moral intuition. It works on the level of conscious reasoning by supplying the conscious mind with abstract concepts—Alexander calls them codes, but we might think of these as principles that act as markers of civil virtues like security, freedom, equality, and tolerance—through which instrumental causes can be ennobled or defiled. And it works on the level of moral intuition by identifying these consecrated principles with our moral hardwiring (think here of Haidt's "taste buds of the righteous mind") through narrative techniques: association, imagery, and symbolism. Solidarity then emerges, or is constructed, in the space between analytical interpretation of the way the world works and intuitive identification of real events with archetypal associations. It emerges through coded narrative as

a product of consecrated causes. Our beliefs about just institutions are therefore deeply subjective and historically contingent, but they are based on objective and timeless intuitions about distinctive modes of abusing institutionalized power.

19. Alexander and Smith 2001; Smith 2005.

20. Alexander 2008, 231.

21. Jonathan Haidt has convincingly argued that in our private moral lives we can be described as riders on an elephant. The conscious and rational part of our soul has some influence on the unconscious and powerful elephant that drives our moral judgments, but this influence is sporadic, limited, and haphazard. This may be an appropriate image of moral life at the individual level, but at the aggregate level, the presence of strategic ideologues contesting for control of our animal intuitions suggests another image for public deliberation: a warhorse with two riders, each of whom is jockeying for the reins to drive the animal toward his desired goal and a horse that prefers each of the riders at different times and for different reasons. When one of the riders (liberals or conservatives) can get the reins, the warhorse can become a formidable weapon and respond to instruction with precision and ease.

22. I like to think of this as the next step in cultural theory. Clifford Geertz introduced the simile of culture as a text. Ann Swidler introduced the simile of culture as a tool kit, and Jeffrey Alexander introduced the idea of culture as a storybook. My contribution to this debate is to mix in Raymond Aron and treat culture as a storybook with four distinct genres. Geertz 1977; Swidler 1986; Alexander 2004; Aron 1955.

23. Locke 2010.

24. Weber and Turner 1991, 180. One of the things that is so useful about Weber's "power over" perspective is that it conforms to commonsense usages that are likely to produce powerful public narratives of abuses.

25. Weber and Turner 1991, 78.

26. Threats to civil peace are among the most potent of literary devices available to the politician, but so, too, are the canonical goals of civil activity. In the spirit of memorable alliterations, let me offer the following set to correspond to this typology: life, liberty, livelihood, and lifestyle.

27. It is interesting that Franklin Roosevelt understood this perspective quite clearly when he developed his philosophy of social security that blended concerns about equality with security in his second inaugural address ("Second Inaugural Address" 2012). He explicitly engaged in a process of novel vilification of institutional abuses.

> In fact, in these last four years, we have made the exercise of all power more democratic; for we have begun to bring private autocratic powers into their proper subordination to the public's government. The legend that they were invincible—above and beyond the processes of a democracy—has been shattered. They have been challenged and beaten. Our progress out of the depression is obvious. But that is not all that you and I mean by the new order of things. Our pledge was not merely to do a patchwork job with secondhand materials. By using the new materials of social justice we have undertaken to erect on the old foundations a more enduring structure for the better use of future generations.

28. Alexander 1992; Holt and Silverstein 1989; Silverstein and Holt 1989; Rubenstein 2010.

29. Note that Rockefeller stands out in this list, because in the United States we have no first-order class villains to speak of, whereas in other places this is not true. The only class villains or bigwigs that really play in America are the union bosses, not the capitalists.

30. The need for this theory of distinctive left perspectives came to me while reading Aron 1955. After World War II, in response to leftist enthusiasm in France, the sociologist Raymond Aron anticipated these distinctions when he suggested that the categories of Left and Right were distractingly composite. He saw that the anticapitalist Left at the beginning of the twentieth century had little in common with the antimonarchist Left in place at the beginning of the nineteenth. The Left was multiple, and the civil society it represented was multiple and could be differentiated by its choice of favored villain. Aron did not go far enough. If we follow the trail of this Weberian typology of power, we can see that there are not just two types of villains—one representing the abuse of concentrated economic power, and the other, the abuse of concentrated state authority—but four. The third represents abuses arising from majority cultural or ethnic status, and the fourth, the forces of disorder, criminality, and anticommunal energy itself. Thus, there are class and party villains, as Aron recognized, as well as status villains and enemies of the state, as Weber's ideas suggested. The distinction between the anticapitalist from the antimonarchist Left was the kernel that I needed to derive a more thorough typology of civil virtues. One might think of this as a theory of the "three Lefts" and the Right. The three Lefts correspond to the moral order that is opposed to the abusive forces of class, status, and party. The Right stands against disorder and many symbolic variants.

31. Marx 1967; Du Bois 1993; Locke 1980; Hobbes 1994.

32. Aristotle 1985.

33. Perhaps the best imagery in the history of political philosphy to describe the intersection of the abusive powers of the Few and the One, is that supplied by Mill 1978.

> To prevent the weaker members of the community from being preyed upon by innumerable vultures, it was needful that there should be an animal of prey stronger than the rest, commissioned to keep them down. But as the king of the vultures would be no less bent upon preying on the flock than any of the minor harpies, it was indispensable to be in a perpetual attitude of defence against his beak and claws. The aim, therefore, of patriots was to set limits to the power which the ruler should be suffered to exercise over the community

34. I should say again that the rhetorics are social constructions that provide us with contingent and subjective beliefs and convictions about which institutions and social policies are good and evil, but the virtues are universal and derive from lived abuses of power that recur always and everywhere. The cardinal virtues, security, freedom, equality, and tolerance, can be found in conflict narratives wherever and whenever one looks for them.

35. The entries of the storybook are similar to what the Russian folklorist Vladimir Propp (1968) described as the fabula: the raw story-stuff from which powerful, convincing, and living narratives (sjuzet) are derived. Narratives that lack compelling and well-

timed uses of imagery will fall flat and fail. This is where stories of economic equality and the common man have drifted over the decades since John F. Kennedy.

Chapter 3

1. Lippmann 1922, 3.

2. Scott 1987.

3. When former governor of New Hampshire John Sununu attacked President Obama in a campaign on a conference call on July 17, 2012, by saying, "I wish this president would learn how to be an American," he was referring to this approach to governing the economy rather than trying to characterize him as alien because of his race.

4. Trilling 1950; Hartz 1955; Ericson and Green 1999; Abbott 2005; Wilentz 2005.

5. Mill 1978; Hobhouse 1994.

6. This critical attitude of Larry Spivak toward Republican moral pollution of the Democratic Party on foreign policy in the postwar period can be seen in the following exchange with Herbert Brownell, national chairman of the Republican Committee, on December 14, 1945:

Larry Spivak: I have one question that I've wanted to ask all evening, and it's something that's bothered me when I read your speech out of Chicago, Mr. Brownell, and that is, you said, and I quote, "We shall insist that our international relations shall be conducted in conformity with the American constitutional system." And then you said "that there shall be no secret commitments that will cost millions of lives and billions of dollars." Are you suggesting that secret commitments of the Democratic Party cost millions of lives and billions of dollars?

Herbert Brownell: Well, we believe that, the brightest pages in American diplomacy were pages when the representatives of this country put everything on the table. Let the American people know about them.

. . .

Bill Slater (moderator): Well, have you good reason to believe that there are secret commitments today?

Brownell: They've been coming out piece by piece over the last eight months.

7. The anticommunist credentials of the program were quite clear. When Larry Spivak was attacked for a performance by the Red-baiting columnist Wexfield Pegler, Larry Spivak took it as a mark of pride. He says that "you haven't made it until you've been peglerized, and he can't pin the Communist label on me." Pegler's approach builds on a technique of promoting change that is well captured with the term "social drama." As I use the term throughout the book, I am indebted to Robin Wagner-Pacifici's (1986) interpretation.

8. *Meet the Press* was launched in 1945 as a television outlet for the arguments and stories developed for the magazine *American Mercury*. It is not far wrong to say that *Meet the Press* was a radio and then television version of H. L. Mencken's former magazine.

9. Mills 1956.

10. Perhaps one of the most important things to say about the human rights agenda is

also the most obvious; it grew directly out of the use of the Helsinki Accords by a prominent group of Russian intellectuals and dissidents that were associated with Andrei Sakharov, the Soviet dissident, nuclear physicist, and advocate of civil liberties. The greatest challenges to the use of a human rights perspective in international relations were directed at the problem they posed for US-Soviet relations. My argument is that the larger point is one that is often missed—human rights talk had a domestic meaning that was then translated into an international context. The point was to protect the rights of minorities to live secure lives, and this identitarian impulse in the program still has important effects.

11. As part of the pivot from class to culture in international affairs, the challenges of social identity necessarily came to the fore, as demonstrated by these comments Young made on July 18, 1976, just as Carter was developing his human rights agenda in the heat of the presidential campaign.

David Kraslow (Cox Newspapers): On one of your favorite subjects, American policy toward Africa, you have said Governor Carter, as a white southerner, is far more qualified to move in the direction of a creative African policy. Do you and Mr. Carter have the same definition of what that policy should be?

Andrew Young: I don't know that we have the same definition. We have talked about it on a couple of occasions, and I think we have the same sense of direction, basically growing out of our experience in the South. For one thing, most of the changes in the South were made by a coordination of political and economic activity. The other thing is that Governor Carter understands racism, and he understands that people can change. He has seen people change. He knows what is necessary to help them change.

12. The concept of group rights as compatible with liberal political theory has been usefully explored by Will Kymlicka in his *Multicultural Citizenship*. See Kymlicka 1996.

13. Lederach 2005.

14. Douglas 1852, 3.

15. It is interesting to note the wording Bill Monroe used in an April 20, 1980, interview and the tone of the question to get a sense of the suspicion about Ronald Reagan at this late date during the 1980 campaign: "Mr. Bush, Governor Reagan recently described the Vietnam War as a holy cause—as a noble cause. Would it be fair for a voter, particularly a young, draft-age voter, to conclude from that that a Reagan administration might be more inclined than a Carter administration to use American forces to try to stop the next similar Communist aggression in Asia?"

16. Carter's reflections on this era can serve as an indicator of how influential Andrew Young was on the Carter administration and what this turn to human rights meant to him: "I tried to speak with a clear voice and to let our influence be felt in regions where our country had long ignored the cries for an end to racial prejudice. When I chose Andrew Young and Don McHenry to speak for us as ambassadors to the United Nations, there was no doubt within the developing world that ours was an honest and sincere voice. We did not send a new message but repeated for others to hear the same beliefs that had helped to form and shape our own country. Throughout Africa and the rest of the Third World, there evolved a new confidence in what we had to say" (Carter 1995).

17. The Reagan Doctrine was a subject of debate in his presidency, and the dynamics I describe here were salient then. Consider this example from March 30, 1986, which Marvin Kalb introduced with the theme "the Reagan Doctrine, what is it?": "The Reagan administration has flexed its muscles in the Mediterranean and in Central America, in both cases in a very controlled way, though its official rhetoric suggested much more. And that has been characteristic of this administration from the very beginning, bold words mixed with cautious action, the exact opposite of Teddy Roosevelt's advice about speaking softly but carrying a big stick. And this recipe for a foreign policy has been dubbed the 'Reagan Doctrine,' producing both praise and some criticism."

18. Kennedy 1987.

19. Kirkpatrick (1979) was the author of the famous article in *Commentary* in which she distinguished between totalitarian governments and authoritarian governments. This made it possible to justify support for otherwise odious leaders who were active in support of the pro-business agenda of the United States, while cracking down on the enemies of American-style conceptions of property rights.

20. The role of Israel in American ideology is a fascinating topic in its own right, which demands a longer independent treatment. What might be ironic is that the most vocal defenders of Israel seem to throw their support to that country for what I have called here Johnstonian principles: respect for the sanctity of corporate property. But did the cause of Israel in particular and the Jewish people more generally inspire the multicultural agenda in the first place? The irony of this confluence of interpretations awaits investigation.

21. Morris 1999.

Chapter 4

1. Butler 2003.

2. Lasswell 2011.

3. Rothkopf 2009, 2012.

4. Blyth 2002.

5. Hofstadter 1955.

6. Gerring 1998. It is important to note that the embrace of laissez-faire by the Republican Party was a twentieth-century novelty. Party leaders had been supportive of the tariff for decades, only moving toward antigovernment rhetoric as corporations realized the full range of their global opportunities.

7. It is clear that Roosevelt knew that he was triangulating the class-struggle divide. His attacks on Illinois governor John Peter Altgeld as the most dangerous man in America are good illustrations of this: "Every true American, every man who thinks, and who if the occasion comes is ready to act, may do well to ponder upon the evil wrought by the lawlessness of the disorderly classes when once they are able to elect their own chiefs to power. If the Government generally got into the hands of men such as Altgeld, the Republic would go to pieces in a year" (Roosevelt 2001).

8. This is the subject of a classic social science debate (Sombart 1976; Lipset and Marks 2000).

9. Carmines and Stimson 1989; Dionne 1992; Edsall 1991.

10. Key 1984; Ladd 1978; Sundquist 1983; Fraser and Gerstle 1989.

11. Reagan 1964.

12. Perlstein 2008.

13. These linkages have been explored in a voluminous literature, for example, Kinder and Sears 1981.

14. Hofstadter 1989.

15. Lederach 2005, 146. "One way to understand cycles of violence and protracted conflict is to visualize them as a narrative broken. A people's story is marginalized or worse, destroyed by dominant culture, and by this act, meaning, identity, and a place in history are lost."

16. I owe this phrase to my colleagues at the *Washington Post*, but it was also the subject of an article in *Politico* (Smith 2007).

17. Douglas appeared twelve times on the show and was a central figure in American liberal politics through the 1950s and early 1960s.

18. When the Wallace full employment bill was amended in a Senate committee to the point that it no longer accomplished any of the objectives set out for it by its leading proponent, one thing it did achieve was to set up this new office of the Council of Economic Advisers. Ironically, this had the effect of giving academic economists (read bureaucrats) a much larger and more formal voice in the public sphere, while carrying over the taint of the Wallace agenda that opponents had successfully positioned as contrary to the principles of individual rights.

19. Blumenthal and Morone 2010.

20. It is important to note that although Humphrey was primarily known at this time for his muscular support for civil rights legislation, there is no attempt to link the Progressive policy he promotes in particularistic terms. Race and social legislation are separate ideas at this point in history.

21. Bell 2000.

22. It was unsurprising, then, that the political scientist Anthony Downs's promotion of the median voter theorem and an economic theory of elections was so popular during that period (Downs 1957). In the theory, the person in the middle of an ideological distribution is the deciding vote, whatever anyone else believes or wants. It is a mathematical demonstration of the disproportionate power that comes with positioning oneself as the fifty-first out of one hundred arrayed on a dimension.

23. Gerring 1998.

24. This kind of triangulation and history revision was common among Republican intellectuals of the time. A telling example is the performance of Undersecretary of Labor Arthur Larson on August 26, 1956:

Larry Spivak: One of the other fundamentals of the new republicanism—the government has a responsibility for the general welfare of the people. Didn't the Republicans fight that for many years, and wasn't it the New Deal that established that principle?

Arthur Larson: No, if you take the full span of the Republican Party, you'll find that the Republican Party established every single principle on which the New Deal was based in the first analysis.

Spivak: Well, are you telling me now that the Republicans did not fight Social Security? I don't think there was a Republican vote, as I remember it, for Social Security when it came up.

Larson: Oh no, that isn't true; there was widespread public support for Social Security.

Spivak: Among the Congress?

Larson: Oh yes, definitely. But as to my other point, the Republican Party has a long history and over the major part of its history it established such things as the first eight-hour law, the first law for protection of unions, first social insurance laws, first laws for protecting wages through federal contracts, and every basic principle of labor and social legislation was established in the first sixty years of the Republican Party.

25. The concept of democratic class struggle was introduced by Anderson and Davidson (1943) at the peak of Franklin Roosevelt's influence, as it became more widely accepted that democratic processes (as opposed to Socialist revolution) could be employed to promote social rights and economic equality.

26. The Kennedy tax cut became a key piece of partisan propaganda years later when Ronald Reagan and George W. Bush promoted their own. Heller remained a fan of the tax-cut stimulus idea but had a very different kind of emphasis than did these Republican supporters. The clearest example of this on *Meet the Press* can be found in the interview during the Ford administration.

27. For an argument describing this transition, see Hechter 2004.

28. Caro 2003.

29. For example, there was not a single episode dedicated to the passage of the act that established Medicare and Medicaid in 1965; there were only two sets of exchanges on the show in the lead-up that year on the subject, and these were buried in the middle portion of questioning.

30. From David McCullough's interview for *The American Experience*, "Lyndon Johnson."

31. Daniel Bell makes this concession in the 1988 edition of his *End of Ideology*.

32. This first reference on *Meet the Press* came on February 27, 1955, which was Senator Goldwater's first of ten appearances. In response to a question from Larry Spivak about regional focus, he replied:

Barry Goldwater: Larry, there's a great migration going on all over the country. We're finding we're picking up congressional seats down in the South. We had no place to go there but up. Out in the middle West where we have been strong all our lives, as a party we could go down, and that's what we have done. People have moved in there from other states. My own state of Arizona turned toward the Republican Party. It's still two and a half to one in favor of Democrats, but we've had a great migration from the great Republican states of the middle West and the East. That may be part of it, but I think frankly the Republican Party became apathetic and felt they were a majority party and could enjoy all the luxuries of fighting like a majority party among themselves.

33. These two authors had contributed the authoritative scripts for the coming eclipse of equality in their landmark books of 1944, *The Road to Serfdom* and *An American Dilemma*, respectively (Hayek 2007; Myrdal 1995). The two books define our era in the sense that they provide extended arguments isolating and orbiting the civil virtues of freedom and tolerance that play out in dysfunctional balance over the many decades that followed.

34. See Nash's (1976) work on the rise of the conservative intellectual movement.

35. Martin 2008.

36. In this argument, I break with the interpretation of John Gerring (1998) in *Party Ideologies*. Gerring was writing in the midst of the Clinton period of triangulation, but after the fact, it seems clear that he was grappling with the new problem of upgrading class politics to fit a middle-class frame.

37. To get a sense of what it meant to speak from that position, it is useful to look at the kind of story that the council's founder, Al From, presented in a retrospective tribute speech to President Clinton in 2005.

> Just as Franklin Roosevelt and the New Dealers—with new ideas to fit their times—modernized the Democratic Party for the Industrial Era, Bill Clinton and the New Democrats modernized their party for today. In the same Democratic tradition of innovation, the New Dealers brought America back from economic depression, and the New Democrats led an economic resurgence in the 1990s. By tempering the excesses of capitalism, Roosevelt saved capitalism. By modernizing Progressive governance, Clinton saved Progressive governance.

While this view from the rearview mirror may well be accurate, as we can see from the objective record of discursive struggle, the reasons for it probably have less to do with the centrist views that the Democratic Leadership Council championed and more to do with the uses to which Clinton put the centrist energies of the Democratic Party in formulating his postindustrial class politics. The key is to recognize that Clinton's best lines were often a direct repudiation of the Kennedy-era tendency to downplay economic villainy. Clinton fought as a heroic character in the dramatic struggle to extend the social rights secured in the New Deal to all of those who deserved to benefit from them. Al From may have been right to claim that the Clinton strategy modernized the party of the New Deal, but he didn't recognize that it worked because Clinton moved away from the party of the New Frontier back toward a retooled Fair Deal.

38. Porter (1990) himself acknowledged his debt to Joseph Schumpeter's *Theory of Economic Development*, which placed the entrepreneur at the heart of an economic process that was far different from that proposed by Adam Smith.

39. It is likely that the key to the Clinton innovation had less to do with Bill Clinton himself than it did with one of his key advisers, Robert Reich. In Reich's philosophy, the transformation of the economy did less to eliminate the older problems of vulnerability and insecurity that gave rise to the New Deal social compact than it did to shift the old

problems in new directions. White-collar workers were better off and more secure than were their blue-collar grandparents, but this had done little to alter the core logic of competitive capitalism. It was still quite possible for well-trained and disciplined workers to find themselves the victims of unresponsive corporate bureaucracies, poor industrial planning, and unregulated financial markets. In short, the new middle class was simply an upgrade of the old working class and faced many of the same problems that were once associated with the latter.

40. Reich's approach and influence can be contrasted with those of another more conventional Clinton adviser, Robert Rubin, in the June 26, 1994, episode of *Meet the Press*, which reveals the general focus of the Clinton triangulation between new and old Democratic economic policy.

Tim Russert: Hobart Rowen of the *Washington Post* says today, however, that we must attempt to restore confidence in the Clinton administration. The thinking on the street is that the Federal Reserve will raise interest rates next week unless . . . the dollar recovers this week. Is that fair?

Robert Rubin: You reference Bart Rowen's comment. I happened to also see it this morning. When I saw it, it occurred to me—I think the best comment on the confidence in the Clinton administration, particularly as it relates to economic matters, are people like Alan Greenspan, universally respected, who commented to the effect, as you've said, that the outlook in the fundamentals are better than they've been in many decades. And that's no accident. That is no accident. That, in large measure, is a function of the sea change that I just mentioned—the sea change in public policy in the economic area that has come into this—that has come forth with this president—deficit reduction, investment in education, training, technology—the areas that are critical to the future of this country.

41. This is, of course, the very language that conservatives adopted when the social security agenda was partially realized with Obama's Affordable Care Act. The first use of the "we're broke" line came on September 20, 2009, in the midst of debates about violent rhetoric and the public option. Senator Lindsay Graham and Representative John Boehner would both use it that day. Here is the exchange with Boehner.

David Gregory: That's fine. Do you think the president's a Socialist? Because that's what—

John Boehner: No.

Gregory: OK. But the head of the Republican Party is, is calling him that.

Boehner: Well, listen, I didn't call him that, and I'm not going to call him that. What's going on here is unsustainable. Our nation is broke. And, and at a time when we've got this serious economic problem, a near 10 percent unemployment, we ought to be looking to create jobs in America, not kill jobs in America. Their cap and trade proposal, all this spending, all of this debt, and now their healthcare plan will make it more difficult for employers to hire people, more difficult and more expensive to have employees, which means we're going to have less jobs in America. But Americans are scared. That's why they're speaking up, and that's why they're engaging in their government.

42. Reich's (1997) reflections from this time were captured in the book.

43. Another key part of the explanation must be that the leadership cadre of the Democratic Party of the time was locked into the New Democrat–Old Democrat line that missed the transformative power of the postindustrial class politics logic. In a telling interview with Gore's campaign manager William Daley, Russert reads off a list of centrist Democratic allies of Al Gore who disagree with his position on keeping the Social Security age at sixty-five. This phalanx of critics of the old Democratic line must have undermined Gore's capacity to pivot toward populism in any effective way.

44. This was a line from a dramatic moment of Al Gore's acceptance speech. The people-versus-the-powerful line has had an active life after the speech as well. It was assumed that since Gore had flirted with a populist line in his campaign, that his subsequent loss was a signal that populism didn't work. In fact, one will never know, because Gore's populism was always somewhat formulaic and better honored in the breach than in the observance. This may be the best example one can find of a story not being as important as the telling of it.

45. Given the subsequent history, it is difficult to ignore Ralph Nader's comments on this score as well from October 1, 2000: "Look at the cartoons. They illustrate that kind of character. You can't trust him. He's going around the country saying he's going to take on big oil, big HMOs, big drug companies, big corporate polluters. He's had eight years to convince us that we can't believe him on that, because he's surrendered to these interests, even when he's put in charge of the environmental portfolio by President Clinton."

46. Polanyi 1944.

47. To place this pivot in context, it is helpful to remember how the antiracist Jack Kemp managed the Hurricane Katrina disaster to push for free markets and less government as a solution to the acknowledged problem of racism.

Tim Russert: Let me turn to a domestic issue. The two of you have gone to the University of North Carolina and the University of Southern California to talk about poverty. Katrina: Jack Kemp, when you were in the Republican administration, you were seen as the outreach person to the African American community. Do you believe that the Bush administration response to Katrina has created an image problem with African Americans?

Jack Kemp: There's an image problem, no doubt about it. And government at every level failed the Katrina victims. And they are victims. This was a horrible—mismanaged at every level of government, and it uncovered not only a level of poverty that is unacceptable in the twenty-first-century America that we live in but a level of racism. I'm not accusing anybody, Republican or Democrat, of racism, but the generic attempt by government to handle this problem has led to, I think, a very big image problem for both political parties—and my party, which it should be thinking big time about what could be done. Abraham Lincoln had a Homesteading Act, Franklin Roosevelt had the FHA and GI Bill. We—I think the president has attempted to do the right thing. I think we need to go further. I think we need a total enterprise zone for the whole Gulf region. I think we need to bring Habitat for Humanity into this, and the president's talked about urban homesteading in the Gulf region.

We need a massive effort, dramatic effort, to build housing, schools, and create job opportunities for people in the Gulf Coast region.

48. Of course, the confrontation was also partially avoided because President Clinton took moves in 1996 to "end welfare as we know it," thereby handing the Republicans a key victory in their quest to liberate the American people from the economic security program of the master synthesis. But the costs of the program were relatively low and the target of the Republican revolution was always middle America, not the poor and minorities whom they often vilified as a strategy to move back toward a pre–New Deal conception of a free society, so this was not nearly enough to keep the ideological forces in check for long.

49. Berlin 1966.

Chapter 5

1. In an easily forgotten footnote of Tocqueville's landmark *Democracy in America*, he reveals what may be the source of the concern that he described as "the tyranny of the majority." As he described it, even in a formally open system dedicated to the preservation of basic civil and political rights, the majority can impose measures "however iniquitous and absurd" to which all must submit as well as they can. The footnote contains the following anecdote of a conversation with a Pennsylvanian that would be as apropos of 1965 as it was of 1835: "So, with you, Negroes do have the right to vote? Certainly. Then how was it that at the electoral college this morning I did not see a single one of them at the meeting? That is not the fault of the law said the American. It is true that Negroes have the right to be present at elections, but they voluntarily abstain from appearing. That is extraordinarily modest of them. Oh! It is not that they are reluctant to go there, but they are afraid they may be maltreated. With us it sometimes happens that the law lacks force when the majority does not support it " (Tocqueville 1988, 253).

2. In one telling example, the Humphrey-Hawkins Full Employment Act, which might have been used to initiate a New Deal–style public-sector jobs program in 1978, was marginalized in the discourse as an African American special-interest issue on President Carter's watch. Although Humphrey died in 1976, he triumphed in promoting a jobs program where Harry Truman had failed, even though race coding of the employment act carried the anticivil taint of busing and quotas for too many now-traumatized persuadable Americans and limited its effects.

3. The most sustained and blunt illustration of the decline of concerns about economic equality and its link to a new politics of personal morality is Walter Benn Michaels 2006.

4. There is no better indicator of this symbolic shift than the ubiquitous and brilliant bumper sticker for the Human Rights Campaign in support of rights for lesbian, gay, bisexual, transgender, and queer (LGBTQ) people. It is an equality sign that implies nothing about class struggle or economic inequality per se, i.e., in terms of some abstract indicator like the Gini coefficient.

5. In American politics, you know you have reached a high point of escalation when

the Nazi, Hitler, or Holocaust references increase in salience. This complex of iconic references has served as the master-villain genre of American politics since midcentury. The Nazi narrative remains so powerful that one has to be careful in ever injecting it into the national conversation, because it is something like the "double dog dare" of national debate. Once the Nazi sword is drawn, it has to draw blood, whether it is the blood of the target or the source of the attack. In America, friends don't call each other Hitler, and Ruth Marcus (2011), columnist for the *Washington Post*, has suggested that Holocaust imagery is avoided in almost all cases for just this reason.

6. For more on Eugene Talmadge and the politics of Georgia, see Dray 2003; Henderson and Roberts 1988; Anderson 1975, xiv, 237.

7. In his landmark book *Southern Politics*, V. O. Key (1984) explored the ways that the history of what he described as the black-belt along with local features of government like the county unit system helped to support Talmadgels extreme views.

8. For news accounts in 1946 and 2008, respectively, see Associated Press 1946, 2008.

9. Finley 2008.

10. It is intriguing to note that President Woodrow Wilson, a southerner, developed his creative approach to managing difference in global politics, ethnic self-determination, as a reaction to his experience of northern aggression. See Skowronek 2006.

11. As of January 2011 the Senate Web page describes the naming as follows: "In 1972 the Senate named the Old Senate Office Building after Senator Richard Brevard Russell, Jr., a Democrat from Georgia who had served from 1933 to 1971. Respected as a 'senator's senator,' Russell had chaired the Senate Armed Services Committee and the Appropriations Committee, and served as president pro tempore. A statue of Senator Russell stands in the Russell Building rotunda." http://www.senate.gov/pagelayout/visiting/d_three_sections_with_teasers/russel_senate_office_map_page.htm.

12. Given Senator Russell's influence over future president Lyndon Johnson, it may be no surprise that in his commencement address at Howard University in support of the Voting Rights Act of 1965, he made famous reference to a sports race: "You do not take a person who, for years, has been hobbled by chains and liberate him, bring him up to the starting line of a race, and then say, 'You are free to compete with all the others,' and still justly believe that you have been completely fair."

13. Jefferson's original lines were "sacred and undeniable rights," but live conversation often includes misquotes.

14. Marshall 1965.

15. It is quite clear that King saw his efforts in revolutionary terms and placed the civil rights movement in the tradition of social transformation of which the American Revolution was a key part. In a commencement address to Morehouse College on June 2, 1959, he said, "This world-shaking revolution which is engulfing our world is seen in the United States in the transition from a segregated to an integrated society. The social revolution which is taking place in this country is not an isolated, detached phenomenon" (Carson et al. 2005, 222). King also made this connection to the Boston Tea Party in his "Letter from Birmingham Jail."

16. Letter contained in Carson et al. 2005.

17. For more on politics of recognition, see Taylor and Gutmann 1994.

18. To get a feel for the era and the power of the revolutionary consciousness of the time, it is useful to turn to the opening monologue for the program given by NBC's reporter Frank McGee:

> There comes a time, there even comes a moment in the affairs of men when they sense that their lives are being altered forever—that an old order is dying and a new one is being born. That moment comes sooner for some, and for others it comes later; for some the moment arrives when a deed of new dimensions sets the hour apart; for others when familiar words are spoken more sharply. Later, but still suddenly it seems, men are saying things and doing things that they've never said or done before. And then we know we are experiencing a revolution. But we cannot say, though historians will try, when it began. We know that autumn does not begin with the turning of the leaves but earlier on some forgotten afternoon, when a shadow passed over the fields and it was no longer summer. So did this American revolution of '63 begin this year in Birmingham, or in 1955 in Montgomery? Or did it begin in 1954 with a Supreme Court decision, or in 1863 with a presidential proclamation? Some of its roots reach back to 1776 to an independence declaration or even the year 52 when the apostle Paul, preaching in Athens said, "God hath made of one blood all nations of men for to dwell on the face of the earth." Well, the truth is that the American Revolution of '63 began in all of those years, that those generations passed on to this one a restless vision that sometimes ebbs and sometimes flows, but moves forever toward freedom for all men.

19. See, for example, *Meet the Press* on July 29, 1962. James J. Kilpatrick had confronted William Anderson, the leader of the desegregation movement in Albany, Georgia, as follows:

James Kilpatrick: But don't you believe that your continued public protests and the showmanship and the dramatization and the martyrdom around them has helped to provoke some of this violence?
William Anderson: Of course, your question makes some suppositions that I may or may not agree with, and I cannot answer it directly.

20. This line of interpretation is broadly consistent with that of the historian Rick Perlstein (2008a, 2008b).

21. This is a good time to note that the most obvious character in this role, Malcolm X, never appeared on *Meet the Press*.

22. Jones 2009.

23. Graves 1967.

24. The first African American to appear on *Meet the Press*, Roy Wilkins had had to address concerns about Negro criminality back in 1956, but his incredulous responses suggested how ridiculous and frankly surprising this line of questioning was to him.

25. See Western 2006.

26. In Russell's imagination the problem with racial integration was one that might be labeled "the incorrigible incivility of the Negro." For Russell, blacks simply could never

attain the same level of civilization as the whites who "created their own opportunities" had done. Russell's greatest fear was miscegenation that would lead to a brown America, as Edwin R. Embree (1932) had discussed in a book of the time. The innately uncivil characteristics of blacks would for him degrade the virtues of the "good people of the South," as had the actions of men like Frederick Douglass's owner. Russell described them as "men here in the South that have sinned and sinned grievously against their civilization and against nature's god in that respect."

27. Stouffer et al. 1949; Merton 1968; Runciman 1966; Gurr 1971.

28. The intellectual villain is nothing novel, but the Democrats had only become associated with that imagery in the 1952 presidential campaign when the "egghead" epithet was applied to Adlai Stevenson. We see the concept developing in a fascinating way in an interview dated August 26, 1956, with Arthur Larson, a Republican idea man of the period.

Marquis Childs (*St. Louis Post-Dispatch*): Do you consider yourself an egghead, Mr. Larson, that is, a Republican egghead?

Arthur Larson: No, I don't know what the term means, but whatever it is, I don't consider myself.

Childs: It means intellectual; are you an intellectual at all?

Larson: I don't particularly like that word, no.

Childs: Why don't you?

Larson: Because my main job is to be undersecretary of labor and I have a very definite job to do in Washington, and that's what I'm here for.

Childs: I notice you're one of the leading forces in this new committee to recruit eggheads for Eisenhower, eggheads, intellectuals, artists, etc. How are you coming along?

Larson: I had a very small part. I was present at the organization meeting, but I understand that it's going very well indeed and a lot of people are subscribing and associating themselves with it.

Childs: How do you explain, Mr. Larson, the Republicans have had so few intellectuals and artists on their side?

Larson: I think they've had a lot more than anybody realized, but they didn't speak up, and I think this committee, Case Committee, arts and sciences for Eisenhower, is going to bring them out.

Childs: You're willing to let the eggheads stay on the Democratic side, are you?

Larson: No, I don't think so; I think the stimulus and challenge of this new Republicanism is going to bring a great many people of the type you call intellectuals into the fold.

29. Berlin 1966.

30. Alexander 2008.

31. Cited in Frady 2006.

32. Perhaps his low point came when he refused to apologize to Ward Connerly when asked on June 15, 1997, for calling him a "house slave."

33. As a point of intellectual history, "welfare" was once a very general term without

negative connotations, much like the term "utility." Over time, as political contests reshaped the language, welfare was linked to the programs of the New Deal and was then restricted to a single approach to social protection that provided aid to those who could not provide for themselves.

34. There is more than a little of the southern rebellious spirit that northern industrialists took on when they courted the white southerner. Looking over the strategies of the neoliberals in their assaults on the social rights agenda of the Democratic Party brings the famous military advice of T. J. "Stonewall" Jackson to mind: "Always mystify, mislead, and surprise the enemy, if possible; and when you strike and overcome him, never give up the pursuit as long as your men have strength to follow; for an army routed, if hotly pursued, becomes panic-stricken, and can then be destroyed by half their number. The other rule is, never fight against heavy odds, if by any possible maneuvering you can hurl your own force on only a part, and that the weakest part, of your enemy and crush it." Quoted in Tsouras 2005, 112.

35. Remnick 2010.

36. It should be noted that Obama's idea had drifted a long way from its use in Russell's time. Closer to Russell's meaning would have been the sentiment of a speech by former Georgia senator Benjamin Hill: "The whole African race, whether slaves or free, were not worth the American Union. One hour of the American Union has done more for human progress than all the governments formed by the African race in six thousand years. And the dear noble boys of the white race, North and South, who fell in the late war, fighting each other for the Negro, were worth more in civilization and happiness than the whole African race of the world" (quoted in Skowronek 2006, 390).

37. It is intriguing to compare the statement that Obama was compelled to make with an apologetic appearance of Eldridge Cleaver, a founder of the Black Panthers, that aired on August 29, 1976:

Eldridge Cleaver: I am sure that there are a lot of cynical people who immediately seek to find an interpretation of that sort when they see someone in the position that I am in. . . . Those who are looking for some hidden motivation or some secret deal or reason, they are welcome to look. I am willing to stand examination. . . . In my travels around the world, I took note of the fact that there are a lot of shortcomings in the form of governments that I have seen. . . . People in other countries . . . are really struggling to have the kind of democratic institutions that we have here.

38. Mayor Fenty's role in this drama of race and the rhetoric of liberty is an important one as well. In many ways Fenty mirrored the president as a symbol of potential racial reconciliation. The appointment of his chancellor of public schools, Michelle Rhee, was contentious and revived long-standing debates about the relative influence of structural and cultural factors in racial gaps in achievement. This helps explain his appearance that morning. The Rhee story played on an Asian anxiety: the sense that American failure to confront the "tangle of pathologies" that Moynihan described in his infamous report had exposed America to a more efficient Asian cultural model of education.

Chapter 6

1. Letter to Blair Moody of the *Detroit News*, Lawrence E. Spivak Papers, Box 199.

2. Although as late as December 4, 1955, Michael Quill was still facing questions about his past associations with Communists. This episode is more notable for its line of questioning on another less salient but no less important aspect of the democratic discourse about the unions, with Michael Quill's concerns about racism in the emerging AFL-CIO umbrella organization. These concerns are represented in a question by Victor Riesel:

Victor Riesel: Mr. Quill, what do you think will happen? You seem to be so terribly exorcised about what you call the three "Rs," race, racketeering, and raiding. What do you think will happen after the merger? Why don't you think they won't be able to handle races, racketeering, and raiding?

Michael Quill: Well, they haven't handled it up until now. You have racial discrimination in many locals throughout the United States against Negroes and other minority groups.

3. These reports and a discussion of their impact can be found in the recently reprinted reporting of Johnson, Schulberg, and Johnson 2005.

4. For an intriguing discussion about how television in this period transformed the perception of national issues, see Doherty 2003. Moreover, in this era of Republican resurgence, the last two presidential standard-bearers were famous for their anticorruption stands. Thomas Dewey was a prosecutor who had built a name in opposition to the threat of organized crime, and one of Eisenhower's main issues (insofar as he had them) in the 1952 election was rooting out the corruption of the Truman administration.

5. There are few better examples of what Jeffrey Alexander (2004, 2008) has called an authentic performance than this given by Riesel in defense of his own cause. The timely intervention into the debate about unions and corruption brought together the exact elements necessary to spur the nation to action. One can try to imagine how likely a McClellan committee would have been without the Riesel performance, but also consequently how much less humbled the union movement might have been without the McClellan committee. The fusion of background texts and the commonly recognized needs of the moment was profound in this case and was moving for a Washington audience willing to act on its fears.

6. Dorman 2000; Steinfels 1979.

7. Gelder 1995.

8. This imagery of Reds and rackets used here is derived from Kimeldorf's (1992) framing in *Reds or Rackets? The Making of Radical and Conservative Unions on the Waterfront*. Union democracy is an idea developed in Lipset, Trow, and Coleman 1956.

9. There is little question that there were widespread criminality and corruption in the union movement at this time, although it is not difficult to exaggerate the impact of actual corruption on the experience of the unions (see Fitch 2006). In all likelihood the politics of unions and unionism and the kinds of images and associations that attached to them were more influential than were the conditions on the ground.

10. "Eisenhower" 1956.

11. Quoted in Boyle 1998. This became part of the introductory material of Walter Reuther in the episode on October 17, 1954.

12. "National Affairs" 1953.

13. Of course, the issues of Taft-Hartley would act as a political football for decades. Among other things it was unpopular because it introduced what were seen as anti-union provisions such as restrictions on solidaristic actions like secondary boycott and enabling mechanisms like the closed shop. This last issue, the 14(b) clause, was, and to some extent remains, the most contested of the act.

14. One dramatic note in this period was the resignation of the only clear labor ally in the Eisenhower administration, Secretary of Labor Martin Durkin, making up the so-called nine millionaires and a plumber cabinet. Durkin resigned from the cabinet when it became clear that the president did not support key amendments to the Taft-Hartley Act that he had seemed to support in the 1952 presidential campaign. In an interview on September 13, 1953, George Meany described his reaction to the resignation as follows:

George Meany: President Eisenhower during his campaign last year pointed out there were certain things in Taft-Hartley that should be changed to make it more fair to labor. Now one of the things was the disenfranchisement of economic strikers by which an employer could put a union out of business using Taft-Hartley. President Eisenhower referred to that as a union-busting provision of the law. In his State of the Union, he set up an employer public and labor committee to try to find agreement under the law. Now the employers sabotaged that. And after two months of hearings in which the Democrats on the Senate committee were asking for an administration position, Mr. Eisenhower designated two cabinet officers to get an administration position working with secretaries from the White House, and of course it was that group that reached agreement on those amendments. Now when the agreement was repudiated, Mr. Durkin resigned.

15. Intriguingly enough, this aspect of Eisenhower's philosophy of government had been the subject of the previous week when Arthur Larson appeared to explain his book *New Republicanism*. One can clearly see that this new moderate philosophy is on the march in the fall of 1956 but also that the implications of this style of moderation for the national conversation about class and collective bargaining were anything but benign from labor's point of view. For many, the labor problem remained the "gravest problem facing the United States," and in a rare midterm election year in which the president's party largely maintained its position in the Congress and the opposition party's leadership was drawn disproportionately from right-to-work states, things were about to change. See Polsby 2004.

16. This letter can be found in the Lawrence E. Spivak Papers, Box 71.

17. To put the alliance between Kennedy and McClellan in context, note that Mc-Clellan was a major opponent of minimum-wage legislation as documented in Grossman 1978: "Southern Congressmen, in turn, challenged the Northern 'monopolists' who hypocritically 'loll on their tongues' words like 'slave labor' and 'sweat-shops' and support bills which sentence Southern industry to death. Some Southern employers told the De-

partment of Labor that they could not live with a 25-cent-an-hour minimum wage. They would have to fire all their people, they said. Adapting a biblical quotation, Representative John McClellan of Arkansas rhetorically asked, 'What profiteth the laborer of the South if he gain the enactment of a wage and hour law—40 cents per hour and 40 hours per week—if he then lose the opportunity to work?'" (quoted in Grossman 1978, 27–28).

18. This committee is often recognized as a kind of turning point in industrial relations in the country (see Baltakis 1999).

19. See Bimes 2002.

20. The intense debate about the concept began with an argument in Lipset 1960.

21. Hoffa was described by a sympathetic analyst of the era as follows: "Jimmy Hoffa is one of the country's best known and most powerful men. To understand his impact on society it is important to understand how his mind works. . . . He possesses a brilliant mind, but one which in many respects is non intellectual. He has built a well-deserved reputation for ruthlessness, but beneath the tough exterior is a genuine concern for others. . . . He views the world in terms of power relationships rather than in terms of what is right and wrong, yet he is motivated by a deeply instilled sense of morality" (James and James 1965, 48).

22. Goldman 1961; Kazin 1998.

23. In supplementary material reported about this interview in Ball and NBC News 1997, it becomes clear that Hoffa was unaware of the power of the forces of the civil sphere that Larry Spivak had mobilized against him. Reflecting on an interaction that he had with Hoffa after the interview, Spivak says, "It was obvious from everything that he said that he had accepted our invitation to be interviewed to make the point that he had done nothing illegal, and he was clearly nettled because we had indicated in our questioning that a leader of a great union had to be concerned with ethics and morality as much as legality."

24. An excellent discussion of how New Deal politicians promoted private-sector unionization as an explicit strategy can be found in Blyth 2002.

25. One might speculate about the reasons why the Kennedy brothers conspired in this symbolic deracination of the union movement. There is little question that it was politically expedient and founded in observable and outrageous facts, but one gets the sense that something more was at stake. The clubby, boisterous, crude, and corrupt organizational style of the union leaders was exactly what the Kennedys were not. The patrician Kennedy style was much closer to what a generation earlier would have been described as Progressive, and Progressive politics was largely inspired in opposition to the machine-style governance mechanisms that channeled working-class energies into stable and unresponsive leadership hierarchies that produced results at the cost of much that was unseemly (see Hofstadter 1955).

26. Really dramatic episodes of *Meet the Press* returned in the form of "Meet the Press Minute" in later episodes. These show directly how the conversations of the past can act as frames for current conversations. The Hoffa episode was used in this way twice in important periods many decades later.

27. Even where I have not adopted her language, I am indebted to Michele Lamont's (2002) interpretations of working-class worldviews in this chapter and elsewhere.

28. Lerner 1957.

29. Coming from Lerner, who had written in glowing terms about the possibility of the union movement throughout his career, this was devastating indeed.

30. This is not to say that union leaders throughout the 1960s, 1970s, and 1980s did not appear on the show to debate serious issues. There are important interviews on problems with unions in the auto, steel, and coal industries, but they are generally either of low dramatic value (suggesting that little in terms of fundamental ideology was being debated) or they play on the images and narratives of egoism and inefficiency that were cemented in these earlier debates. Aside from the symbolic episodes for Labor Day that were once common (no longer; in 2010 the Labor Day weekend episode only touched on issues such as these through the politics of the economy for the upcoming election), the other irony is that the baseball strike became one of the last noteworthy representations of union issues in the record. The image of wealthy and famous "bigwig" baseball players as bearers of the union tradition is perhaps fitting given the history of this conversation.

31. This evocative image was presented as a question in a *New York Times* article that was featured in the *Meet the Press* setup material (Cooper and Seelye 2011).

32. The actual quote was, "Hegel remarks somewhere that all great world-historic facts and personages appear, so to speak, twice. He forgot to add: the first time as tragedy, the second time as farce" (Andrews 1994, 409).

33. For a thorough history of the union movement in the twentieth century, see Lichtenstein 2003. Also of interest is the way that unions could take advantage of identity politics and the language of inclusion as described in Clawson 2003.

Chapter 7

1. Shafer 2003; Polsby 2004; McCarty, Poole, and Rosenthal 2006.

2. Free and Cantril 1968.

3. Johnston, 2010, 1.

4. Bendix 1956, 1.

Epilogue

1. This is a good time to point out one of the primary indirect findings of the project—the persistent marginalization of issues of gender on the program. Although women from Martha Rountree to May Craig to Gwen Ifill have been essential players from the first days of *Meet the Press*, women's issues as such have rarely been discussed. Gender has been central throughout this dramatic period of change from a politics of life chances to a politics of lifestyle (and perhaps as consequential in their silence as were considerations of race), but these discussions have largely passed under the radar of authoritative conversation. The clearest example that pertained to the theoretical perspective developed here was the episode dated August 26, 2012, in which a Republican candidate for the Missouri

Senate seat, Todd Akin, made himself an image of bigoted civil threat when he claimed that there were cases of "legitimate rape" and that women's bodies would not respond with a pregnancy in such circumstances. The most interesting aspect of the Akin affair is how it was framed here; in the introduction *Meet the Press* called it a distraction, and in the roundtable, the Republican media guru Mike Murphy dismissed it as trivia that the party needed to put behind them. Based on the content of the *Meet the Press* archive, that is the attitude of the Beltway influential about the very concept of gender as an issue in its own right. Women play a key role in our debates, but gender does not. This tendency may be changing. Although it might have something to do with current leadership, David Gregory has hosted more conversations about gender per se than did all of his predecessors combined. The era of women in the public sphere may be just ahead of us.

2. This is related to the sociological conversation sometimes referred to as the "death of class" debate (Brooks and Manza 1997; Clark and Lipset 1991, 2001; Hout, Brooks, and Manza 1995; Wright 1997; Pakulski and Waters 1996a, 1996b). My perspective differs from much that has been written on this debate in that I think that class has disappeared from public debate in elite discourse but not in the popular mind (Teixeira and Rogers 2000; Judis and Teixeira 2002; Shafer 1983). Factional approaches to economic issues are as common now in the public mind as they were when James Madison warned us of them, but convincing stories are less commonly circulated in the currents of the conventional wisdom.

3. It is no surprise that Booker invokes the imagery of nausea. This is one of our most powerful moral emotions, which seems to have co-opted our need to avoid spoiled food through group-selection mechanisms.

4. This is not to presuppose that there are no economic penalties for being gay, but the primary form of injustice visited upon people of alternative sexual orientation concerns classic considerations of social status and recognition. The best discussion of this can be found in Fraser and Honneth 2003; Fraser 2000; Michaels 2006.

5. Locke, 1956, 147.

REFERENCES

Abbott, Philip. 2005. "Still Louis Hartz After All These Years: A Defense of the Liberal Society Thesis." *Perspectives on Politics* 3 (1): 93–109. doi:10.1017/S1537592705050085.

Adorno, Theodor, Else Frenkel-Brunswik, Daniel J. Levinson, and R. Nevitt Sanford. 1950. *The Authoritarian Personality.* New York: Harper.

Alexander, Jeffrey C. 1992. "Citizen and Enemy as Symbolic Classification: On the Polarizing Discourse of Civil Society." In *Cultivating Differences: Symbolic Boundaries and the Making of Inequality,* edited by M. Fournier and Michèle Lamont, 289–308. Chicago: University of Chicago Press.

———. 2004. "Cultural Pragmatics: Social Performance Between Ritual and Strategy." *Sociological Theory* 22 (4): 527–573. doi:10.1111/j.0735-2751.2004.00233.

———. 2008. *The Civil Sphere.* New York: Oxford University Press.

———. 2010. *The Performance of Politics: Obama's Victory and the Democratic Struggle for Power.* New York: Oxford University Press.

Alexander, J. C., and P. Smith. 1993. "The Discourse of American Civil Society: A New Proposal for Cultural Studies." *Theory and Society* 22 (2): 151–207.

———. 2001. "The Strong Program in Cultural Theory: Elements of a Structural Hermeneutics." In *Handbook of Social Theory,* edited by J. Turner, 135–150. New York: Kluwer Academic Publishers.

Anderson, Dewey, and Percy E. Davidson. 1943. *Ballots and the Democratic Class Struggle.* Stanford: Stanford University Press.

Anderson, William. 1975. *The Wild Man from Sugar Creek: The Political Career of Eugene Talmadge.* Baton Rouge: Louisiana State University Press.

Andrews, Robert. 1993. *The Columbia Book of Quotations.* New York: Columbia University Press.

Aristotle. 1985. *The Politics.* Translated by Carnes Lord. Chicago: University of Chicago Press.

Aron, Raymond. 1955. *The Opium of the Intellectuals.* New Brunswick, NJ: Transaction Publishers.

Associated Press. 1946. "Church Appeals for Aid in Lynch Probe." *Daytona Beach Morning Journal.* Google News Archive Search, July 29. http://news.google.com/newspapers?id=zG8oAAAAIBAJ&sjid=rscEAAAAIBAJ&pg=1578,3886675&dq=lynching+-georgia+1946&hl=en.

———. 2008. "Ga. Authorities Probe 1946 Unsolved Lynchings." *USA Today,* July 2. http://www.usatoday.com/news/nation/2008-07-02-lynching-probe_N.htm.

Azar, Edward E. 1985. "Protracted International Conflicts: Ten Propositions." *International Interactions* 12 (1): 59–70.

———. 1990. *The Management of Protracted Social Conflict: Theory and Cases.* Sudbury, MA: Dartmouth Publishing.

Azar, Edward E., P. Jureidini, and R. McLaurin. 1978. "Protracted Social Conflict: Theory and Practice in the Middle East." *Journal of Palestine Studies* 8 (1): 41–60.

Badiou, Alain. 2002. *Ethics: An Essay on the Understanding of Evil.* Translated by Peter Hallward. London: Verso.

Ball, Rick, and NBC News. 1997. *Meet the Press: 50 Years of History in the Making.* New York: McGraw-Hill.

Baltakis, A. 1999. "On the Defensive: Walter Reuther's Testimony Before the McClellan Labor Rackets Committee." *Michigan Historical Review* 25 (2): 47–69.

Bell, Daniel. 2000. *The End of Ideology: On the Exhaustion of Political Ideas in the Fifties, with "The Resumption of History in the New Century."* 2nd ed. Cambridge, MA: Harvard University Press.

Bendix, Reinhard. 2001. *Work and Authority in Industry: Managerial Ideologies in the Course of Industrialization.* New Brunswick, NJ: Transaction Publishers.

Berlin, Isaiah. 1966. *Two Concepts of Liberty: An Inaugural Lecture Delivered Before the University of Oxford on 31 October 1958.* Oxford: Clarendon Press.

Bimes, Terri. 2002. "Ronald Reagan and the New Conservative Populism." *Institute of Government Studies.* University of California Berkeley Working Paper 2002-1.

Bloom, Allan. 1987. "How Nietzsche Conquered America." *Wilson Quarterly (1976–)* 11 (3): 80–93.

Blumenthal, David, and James Morone. 2010. *The Heart of Power: Health and Politics in the Oval Office, with a New Preface.* 2nd ed. Berkeley: University of California Press.

Blyth, Mark. 2002. *Great Transformations: Economic Ideas and Institutional Change in the Twentieth Century.* Cambridge: Cambridge University Press.

Boyle, Kevin. 1998. *The UAW and the Heyday of American Liberalism, 1945–1968.* Ithaca, NY: Cornell University Press.

Brooks, Clem, and Jeff Manza. 1997. "Social Cleavages and Political Alignments: U.S. Presidential Elections, 1960 to 1992." *American Journal of Sociology* 62 (6): 937–946.

Burton, J. 1991. "Conflict Resolution as a Political Philosophy." *Global Change, Peace & Security* 3 (1): 62–72.

Butler, Smedley D. 2003. *War Is a Racket: The Antiwar Classic by America's Most Decorated Soldier.* Port Townsend, WA: Feral House.

Carmines, Edward G., and James A. Stimson. 1989. *Issue Evolution: Race and the Transformation of American Politics.* Princeton: Princeton University Press.

Caro, Robert A. 2003. *The Years of Lyndon Johnson.* Vol. 3, *Master of the Senate.* New York: Vintage.

Carson, Clayborn, Tenisha Armstrong, Susan Carson, Adrienne Clay, and Kieran Taylor, eds. 2005. *The Papers of Martin Luther King, Jr.* Vol. 5, *Threshold of a New Decade.* Berkeley: University of California Press.

Carter, Jimmy. 1995. *Keeping Faith: Memoirs of a President*. Fayetteville: University of Arkansas Press.

Clark, Terry Nichols, and Seymour Martin Lipset. 1991. "Are Social Classes Dying?" *International Sociology* 6 (4): 397–410.

———. 2001. *The Breakdown of Class Politics: A Debate on Post-industrial Stratification*. Washington, DC: Woodrow Wilson Center Press.

Clawson, Dan. 2003. *The Next Upsurge: Labor and the New Social Movements*. Ithaca, NY: ILR Press.

Cooper, Michael, and Katharine Q. Seelye. 2011. "Wisconsin Leads Way as Workers Fight State Cuts." *New York Times*, February 18, sec. U.S./Politics.

C-SPAN. 1991. "Weekend Public Affairs Television Show Host." C-SPAN Video Library, June 23. http://c-spanvideo.org/program/ShowHo.

Damasio, Antonio. 1994. *Descartes' Error: Emotion, Reason, and the Human Brain*. New York: Bard.

———. 1999. *The Feeling of What Happens: Body and Emotion in the Making of Consciousness*. New York: Harcourt.

Davidson, R. J., J. Kabat-Zinn, J. Schumacher, M. Rosenkranz, D. Muller, S. F. Santorelli, F. Urbanowski, A. Harrington, K. Bonus, and J. F. Sheridan. 2003. "Alterations in Brain and Immune Function Produced by Mindfulness Meditation." *Psychosomatic Medicine* 65 (4): 564–570.

De Waal, F. 2009. *Primates and Philosophers: How Morality Evolved*. Princeton: Princeton University Press.

Dionne, E. J. 1992. *Why Americans Hate Politics*. New York: Simon and Schuster.

Doherty, Thomas Patrick. 2003. *Cold War, Cool Medium: Television, McCarthyism, and American Culture*. New York: Columbia University Press.

Dorman, Joseph. 2000. *Arguing the World: The New York Intellectuals in Their Own Words*. New York: Free Press.

Douglass, Frederick. 1852. *Oration Delivered in Corinthian Hall, Rochester*. http://hdl.handle.net/2027/inu.30000005087741.

Downs, Anthony. 1957. *An Economic Theory of Democracy*. New York: Harper.

Dray, Philip. 2003. *At the Hands of Persons Unknown: The Lynching of Black America*. New York: Random House.

Du Bois, W. E. B. 1993. *The Souls of Black Folk*. Unabridged ed. New York: Dover Publications.

Edelman, Murray. 1964. *Politics as Symbolic Action: Mass Arousal & Quiescence*. Institute for Research on Poverty Series. Chicago: Markham Publishing.

———. 1975. "Language, Myths and Rhetoric." *Society* 12 (5): 14–21.

———. 1985. "Political Language and Political Reality." *PS* 18 (1): 10–19.

Edsall, Thomas. 1991. *Chain Reaction*. New York: Norton.

"Eisenhower to Act on Union Rackets." 1956. *New York Times* (1923–Current File), June 6.

Embree, Edwin R. 1932. *Brown America: The Story of a New Race*. New York: Viking Press.

Ericson, D. F, and L. B Green. 1999. *The Liberal Tradition in American Politics: Reassessing the Legacy of American Liberalism*. New York: Routledge.

Finley, Keith M. 2008. *Delaying the Dream: Southern Senators and the Fight Against Civil Rights, 1938–1965*. Baton Rouge: Louisiana State University Press.

Fitch, Robert. 2006. *Solidarity for Sale: How Corruption Destroyed the Labor Movement and Undermined America's Promise*. Jackson, TN: PublicAffairs.

Frady, Marshall. 2006. *Jesse: The Life and Pilgrimage of Jesse Jackson*. New York: Simon and Schuster.

Fraser, Nancy. 2000. "Rethinking Recognition." *New Left Review* 3 (May–June): 107–120.

Fraser, Nancy, and Axel Honneth. 2003. *Redistribution or Recognition: A Political-Philosophical Exchange*. London: Verso.

Fraser, Steve, and Gary Gerstle. 1989. *The Rise and Fall of the New Deal Order, 1930–1980*. Princeton: Princeton University Press.

Free, Lloyd, and Hadley Cantril. 1968. *The Political Beliefs of Americans: A Study of Public Opinion*. New York: Simon and Schuster.

From, Al. 2005. "William Jefferson Clinton: 'New Democrat' from Hope." Hofstra Cultural Center. http://www.dlc.org/print5d93.html?contentid=253619.

Geertz, Clifford. 1977. *The Interpretation of Cultures*. New York: Basic Books.

Gelder, Lawrence Van. 1995. "Victor Riesel, 81, Columnist Blinded by Acid Attack, Dies." *New York Times*, January 5, sec. Obituaries. http://www.nytimes.com/1995/01/05/obituaries/victor-riesel-81-columnist-blinded-by-acid-attack-dies.html.

Gerring, John. 1998. *Party Ideologies in America 1828–1996*. Cambridge: Cambridge University Press.

Goldman, Eric F. 1961. *The Crucial Decade—and After: America, 1945–1960*. New York: Vintage.

——— 1997. *Rendezvous with Destiny: A History of Modern American Reform*. New York: Random House.

Gould, Stephen Jay. 1997. *Full House: The Spread of Excellence from Plato to Darwin*. New York: Three Rivers Press.

Gramsci, Antonio. 1971. *Selections from the Prison Notebooks*. Edited by Quintin Hoare and Geoffrey Nowell Smith. New York: International Publishers.

Graves, Frederick. 1967. "Racial Strife Making Milwaukee Infamous." *Jet Magazine*, September 21.

Grossman, Jonathan. 1978. "U.S. Department of Labor—History—Fair Labor Standards Act of 1938." Originally published in *Monthly Labor Review*, June. http://www.dol.gov/oasam/programs/history/flsa1938.htm.

Gurr, Ted R. 1971. *Why Men Rebel*. Princeton: Princeton University Press.

Haidt, Jonathan. 2001. "The Emotional Dog and Its Rational Tail: A Social Intuitionist Approach to Moral Judgment." *Psychological Review* 108 (4): 814–834.

———. 2003. "The Moral Emotions." In *Handbook of Affective Sciences*, edited by R. J. Davidson, K. R. Scherer, and H. H. Goldsmith, 852–870. Oxford: Oxford University Press.

————. 2012. *The Righteous Mind: Why Good People Are Divided by Politics and Religion*. New York: Pantheon.

Hartz, Louis. 1955. *The Liberal Tradition in America*. New York: Harvest.

Hayek, F. A. 2007. *The Road to Serfdom: Text and Documents—the Definitive Edition*. Edited by Bruce Caldwell. Chicago: University of Chicago Press.

Hechter, Michael. 2004. "From Class to Culture." *American Journal of Sociology* 110 (2): 400–445.

Henderson, Harold P., and Gary L. Roberts. 1988. *Georgia Governors in an Age of Change: From Ellis Arnall to George Busbee*. Athens: University of Georgia Press.

Hobbes, Thomas. 1994. *Leviathan: With Selected Variants from the Latin Edition of 1668*. Edited by Edwin Curley. Indianapolis, IN: Hackett Publishing.

Hobhouse, L. T. 1994. *Hobhouse: Liberalism and Other Writings*. Edited by James Meadowcroft. Cambridge: Cambridge University Press.

Hofstadter, Richard. 1955. *The Age of Reform from Bryan to F.D.R.* New York: Vintage Books.

————. 1989. *The American Political Tradition: And the Men Who Made It*. New York: Vintage.

Holt, R. R., and B. Silverstein. 1989. "On the Psychology of Enemy Images: Introduction and Overview." *Journal of Social Issues* 45 (2): 1–11. doi: 10.1111/j.1540-4560.1989 .tb01539.x.

Horkheimer, Max, and Theodor W. Adorno. 1989. *Dialectic of Enlightenment*. New York: Continuum.

Hout, Michael, Clem Brooks, and Jeff Manza. 1995. "The Democratic Class Struggle in the United States, 1948–1992." *American Sociological Review* 60 (6): 805–828.

Jacobs, Ronald N., and Eleanor Townsley. 2011. *The Space of Opinion: Media Intellectuals and the Public Sphere*. New York: Oxford University Press.

James, Ralph C., and Estelle Dinerstein James. 1965. *Hoffa and the Teamsters*. Princeton: D. Van Nostrand.

Jay, Martin. 1996. *The Dialectical Imagination: A History of the Frankfurt School and the Institute of Social Research, 1923–1950*. Berkeley: University of California Press.

Johnson, Malcolm, Budd Schulberg, and Haynes Johnson. 2005. *On the Waterfront: The Pulitzer Prize–Winning Articles That Inspired the Classic Film and Transformed the New York Harbor*. New York: Chamberlain Bros.

Johnston, Eric. 2010. *America Unlimited*. Whitefish, MT: Kessinger Publishing.

Jones, Patrick D. 2009. *The Selma of the North: Civil Rights Insurgency in Milwaukee*. Cambridge, MA: Harvard University Press.

Judis, John, and Ruy Teixeira. 2002. *The Emerging Democratic Majority*. New York: Scribner.

Kazin, Michael. 1998. *The Populist Persuasion: An American History*. Rev. ed. Ithaca, NY: Cornell University Press.

Kennedy, Paul. 1987. *The Rise and Fall of the Great Powers: Economic Change and Military Conflict from 1500 to 2000*. New York: Random House.

Key, V. O., Jr. 1984. *Southern Politics in State and Nation*. New ed. Knoxville: University of Tennessee Press.

Kimeldorf, Howard. 1992. *Reds or Rackets? The Making of Radical and Conservative Unions on the Waterfront*. Berkeley: University of California Press.

Kinder, Donald R., and David O. Sears. 1981. "Prejudice and Politics: Symbolic Racism Versus Racist Threats to the Good Life." *Journal of Personality and Social Psychology* 40 (3): 414–431.

King, Martin Luther, Jr. 1963. *Letter from Birmingham City Jail*. Philadelphia: American Friends Service Committee.

Kirkpatrick, Jeane. 1979. "Dictatorships & Double Standards." *Commentary* 68 (5): 34–45.

Kymlicka, Will. 1995. *Multicultural Citizenship: A Liberal Theory of Minority Rights*. New York: Oxford University Press.

Ladd, Everett Carll. 1978. *Transformations of the American Party Systems: Political Coalitions from the New Deal to the 1970's*. 2nd ed. New York: W. W. Norton.

Lakoff, George. 2002. *Moral Politics: How Liberals and Conservatives Think*. Chicago: University of Chicago Press.

———. 2004. *Don't Think of an Elephant! Know Your Values and Frame the Debate: The Essential Guide for Progressives*. White River Junction, VT: Chelsea Green.

Lakoff, George, and Mark Johnson. 1980. *Metaphors We Live By*. Chicago: University of Chicago Press.

Lamont, Michèle. 2002. *The Dignity of Working Men: Morality and the Boundaries of Race, Class, and Immigration*. Cambridge, MA: Harvard University Press.

Lasswell, Harold Dwight. 2011. *Politics: Who Gets What, When, How*. Whitefish, MT: Literary Licensing.

Lederach, John Paul. 2005. *The Moral Imagination: The Art and Soul of Building Peace*. Reprint. New York: Oxford University Press.

Lévi-Strauss, Claude. 1968. *The Savage Mind*. Chicago: University of Chicago Press.

———. 1983. *The Raw and the Cooked: Mythologiques, Volume 1*. Chicago: University of Chicago Press.

Lerner, Max. 1957. *America as a Civilization: Life and Thought in the United States Today*. New York: Simon and Schuster.

Lichtenstein, Nelson. 2003. *State of the Union: A Century of American Labor*. Princeton: Princeton University Press.

Lippmann, Walter. 1922. *Public Opinion*. New York: Free Press.

Lipset, Seymour Martin. 1960. *Political Man: The Social Bases of Politics*. Exp. ed. New York: Doubleday.

Lipset, Seymour Martin, and Gary Marks. 2000. *It Didn't Happen Here: Why Socialism Failed in the United States*. New York: W. W. Norton.

Lipset, Seymour Martin, Martin A. Trow, and James S. Coleman. 1956. *Union Democracy: The Internal Politics of the International Typographical Union*. New York: Columbia University Press.

Locke, John. 1956. *The Second Treatise of Government: And, A Letter Concerning Toleration*. North Chelmsford, MA: Courier Dover Publications.

Marcus, George E., W. Russell Neuman, and Michael Mackuen. 2000. *Affective Intelligence and Political Judgment*. Chicago: University of Chicago Press.

Marcus, Ruth. 2011. "Why Sarah Palin's 'Blood Libel' Was a Poor Choice of Words." *Washington Post*, January 12, PostPartisan edition. http://voices.washingtonpost.com/ postpartisan/2011/01/why_sarah_palins_blood_libel_w.html.

Marshall, T. H. 1965. *Class, Citizenship, and Social Development*. Garden City, NY: Anchor Books.

Martin, Isaac. 2008. *The Permanent Tax Revolt: How the Property Tax Transformed American Politics*. Stanford, CA: Stanford University Press.

Marx, Karl. 1967. *Capital*. Vol. 1, *A Critical Analysis of Capitalist Production*. New York: International Publishers.

McCarty, Nolan M., Keith T. Poole, and Howard Rosenthal. 2006. *Polarized America: The Dance of Ideology and Unequal Riches*. Cambridge, MA: MIT Press.

Merton, Robert K. 1968. *Social Theory and Social Structure*. New York: Free Press.

Michaels, Walter Benn. 2006. *The Trouble with Diversity: How We Learned to Love Identity and Ignore Inequality*. New York: Metropolitan Books.

Mill, John Stuart. 1978. *On Liberty*. Edited by Elizabeth Rapaport. Indianapolis, IN: Hackett Publishing.

Mills, C. Wright. 1956. *The Power Elite*. New York: Oxford University Press.

Morris, Edmund. 1999. *Dutch: A Memoir of Ronald Reagan*. New York: Random House.

Myrdal, Gunnar. 1995. *An American Dilemma*. Vol. 1, *The Negro Problem and Modern Democracy*. Black and African-American Studies. New ed. New Brunswick, NJ: Transaction Publishers.

Nash, George H. 1976. *The Conservative Intellectual Movement in America: Since 1945*. New York: Basic Books.

"National Affairs: James Paul Mitchell, Secretary of Labor." 1953. *Time*, October 19. http://www.time.com/time/magazine/article/0,9171,823045,00.html.

Newcomb, Theodore M. 1947. "Autistic Hostility and Social Reality." *Human Relations* 1:69-86. doi:10.1177/001872674700100105.

Nietzsche, Friedrich. 2000. *Basic Writings of Nietzsche*. New York: Random House Digital.

Pakulski, Jan, and Malcolm Waters. 1996a. *The Death of Class*. Thousand Oaks, CA: Sage Publications.

———. 1996b. "The Reshaping and Dissolution of Social Class in Advanced Society." *Theory and Society* 25 (5): 667–691.

Perlstein, Rick. 2008a. "The Meaning of Box 722." June 25. OurFuture.org. http://www .ourfuture.org/blog-entry/meaning-box-722.

———. 2008b. *Nixonland: The Rise of a President and the Fracturing of America*. New York: Scribner.

Petty, Richard E., and John T. Cacioppo. 1986. "The Elaboration Likelihood Model of Persuasion." *Advances in Experimental Social Psychology* 19 (1): 123–205.

———. 1996. *Attitudes and Persuasion: Classic and Contemporary Approaches*. Boulder, CO: Westview Press.

Petty, R. E., J. T. Cacioppo, and D. Schumann. 1983. "Central and Peripheral Routes to Advertising Effectiveness: The Moderating Role of Involvement." *Journal of Consumer Research* 10 (2): 135–146.

Polanyi, Karl. 1944. *The Great Transformation: The Political and Economic Origins of Our Time*. Boston: Beacon Press.

Polsby, Nelson W. 2004. *How Congress Evolves: Social Bases of Institutional Change*. Oxford: Oxford University Press.

Porter, Michael E. 1990. *The Competitive Advantage of Nations*. New York: Free Press.

Propp, V. 1968. *Morphology of the Folktale: Second Edition, Revised and Edited with Preface by Louis A. Wagner, Introduction by Alan Dundes*. Edited by Louis A. Wagner. Translated by Laurence Scott. 2nd ed. Austin: University of Texas Press.

Reagan, Ronald. 1964. "A Time for Choosing (The Speech—October 27, 1964)." http://www.reagan.utexas.edu/archives/reference/timechoosing.html.

Reich, Robert B. 1997. *Locked in the Cabinet*. New York: Knopf.

Remnick, David. 2010. *The Bridge: The Life and Rise of Barack Obama*. New York: Knopf.

Roosevelt, Theodore. 2001. *American Ideals: And Other Essays, Social and Political*. Colorado Springs, CO: Patrick Henry University Press.

Rothkopf, David. 2009. *Superclass: The Global Power Elite and the World They Are Making*. New York: Farrar, Straus and Giroux.

———. 2012. *Power, Inc.: The Epic Rivalry Between Big Business and Government—and the Reckoning That Lies Ahead*. New York: Farrar, Straus and Giroux.

Rubenstein, Richard E. 2010. *Reasons to Kill: Why Americans Choose War*. New York: Bloomsbury Press.

Runciman, W. G. 1966. *Relative Deprivation and Social Justice: A Study of Attitudes to Social Inequality in Twentieth-Century England*. London: Routledge and Kegan Paul.

Scott, James C. 1987. *Weapons of the Weak: Everyday Forms of Peasant Resistance*. New Haven, CT: Yale University Press.

"Second Inaugural Address of Franklin D. Roosevelt." 2012. *Inaugural Addresses of the Presidents of the United States: From George Washington 1789 to George Bush 1989*. http://avalon.law.yale.edu/20th_century/froos2.asp.

Shafer, Byron E. 1983. *Quiet Revolution: The Struggle for the Democratic Party and the Shaping of Post-reform Politics*. New York: Russell Sage Foundation.

———. 2003. *The Two Majorities & the Puzzle of Modern American Politics*. Lawrence: University Press of Kansas.

Silverstein, B., and R. R. Holt. 1989. "Research on Enemy Images: Present Status and Future Prospects." *Journal of Social Issues* 45 (2): 159–175.

Skowronek, Stephen. 2006. "The Reassociation of Ideas and Purposes: Racism, Liberalism, and the American Political Tradition." *American Political Science Review* 100 (3): 385–401.

Smith, Ben. 2007. "The Russert Primary." *Politico* (June 13). http://www.politico.com/blogs/bensmith/0607/The_Russert_Primary.html.

Smith, Philip. 2005. *Why War? The Cultural Logic of Iraq, the Gulf War, and Suez*. Chicago: University of Chicago Press.

Sombart, Werner. 1976. *Why Is There No Socialism in the United States?* White Plains, NY: M. E. Sharpe.

Spivak, Lawrence E. "Lawrence E. Spivak Papers." http://memory.loc.gov/service/mss/ eadxmlmss/eadpdfmss/2008/ms008103.pdf.

Steinfels, Peter. 1979. *The Neoconservatives.* New York: Simon and Schuster.

Stouffer, Samuel A., Edward A. Suchman, Leland C. DeVinney, Shirley A. Star, and Robin M. Williams. 1949. *The American Soldier.* Princeton: Princeton University Press.

Sundquist, James L. 1983. *Dynamics of the Party System.* Washington, DC: Brookings Institution.

Swidler, Ann. 1986. "Culture in Action: Symbols and Strategies." *American Sociological Review* 51 (2): 273–286.

Taylor, Charles, and Amy Gutmann. 1994. *Multiculturalism.* Princeton: Princeton University Press.

Teixeira, Ruy, and Joel Rogers. 2000. *America's Forgotten Majority: Why the White Working Class Still Matters.* New York: Basic Books.

Tocqueville, Alexis de. 1988. *Democracy in America.* Translated by George Lawrence. New York: Harper Perennial.

Trilling, Lionel. 1950. *The Liberal Imagination.* New York: Viking.

Tsouras, Peter G. 2005. *The Book of Military Quotations.* Minneapolis, MN: Zenith Imprint.

"Vice President Al Gore Accepts the Democratic Nomination for President." 2000. *PBS NewsHour.* Los Angeles: PBS. http://www.pbs.org/newshour/bb/politics/july-deco0/ gore-acceptance.html.

Wagner-Pacifici, Robin Erica. 1986. *The Moro Morality Play: Terrorism as Social Drama.* Chicago: University of Chicago Press.

Wallace, Henry Agard. 1945. *Sixty Million Jobs.* New York: Reynal and Hitchcock, Simon and Schuster.

Westen, Drew 2007. *The Political Brain: The Role of Emotion in Deciding the Fate of the Nation.* New York: Public Affairs.

Western, Bruce. 2006. *Punishment and Inequality in America.* New York: Russell Sage Foundation.

Wilentz, Sean. 2005. "Uses of the Liberal Tradition: Comments on 'Still Louis Hartz After All These Years.'" *Perspectives on Politics* 3 (1): 117–120. doi:10.1017/ S1537592705050103.

Wilson, E. O. 1999. *Consilience: The Unity of Knowledge.* New York: Vintage.

Wright, Erik Olin. 1997. *Class Counts: Comparative Studies in Class Analysis.* Cambridge: Cambridge University Press.

Wright, Richard. 1995. *The Color Curtain: A Report on the Bandung Conference.* Jackson: University Press of Mississippi.

INDEX